Analysis of the Early Bronze Age Graves in Tell Bi'a (Syria)

Ildikó Bősze

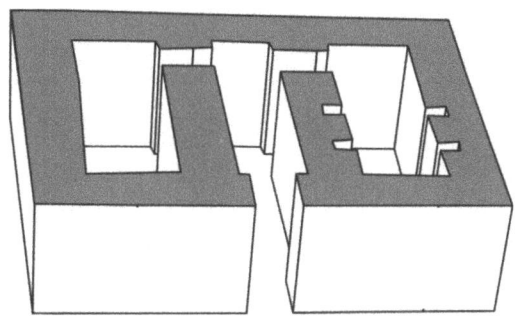

BAR International Series 1995
2009

Published in 2016 by
BAR Publishing, Oxford

BAR International Series 1995

Analysis of the Early Bronze Age Graves in Tell Bi'a (Syria)

ISBN 978 1 4073 0529 5

© I Bősze and the Publisher 2009

The author's moral rights under the 1988 UK Copyright,
Designs and Patents Act are hereby expressly asserted.

All rights reserved. No part of this work may be copied, reproduced, stored,
sold, distributed, scanned, saved in any form of digital format or transmitted
in any form digitally, without the written permission of the Publisher.

BAR Publishing is the trading name of British Archaeological Reports (Oxford) Ltd.
British Archaeological Reports was first incorporated in 1974 to publish the BAR
Series, International and British. In 1992 Hadrian Books Ltd became part of the BAR
group. This volume was originally published by Archaeopress in conjunction with
British Archaeological Reports (Oxford) Ltd / Hadrian Books Ltd, the Series principal
publisher, in 2009. This present volume is published by BAR Publishing, 2016.

Printed in England

BAR titles are available from:

          BAR Publishing
          122 Banbury Rd, Oxford, OX2 7BP, UK
EMAIL   info@barpublishing.com
PHONE +44 (0)1865 310431
FAX   +44 (0)1865 316916
          www.barpublishing.com

TO THE ANCESTORS

Acknowledgements

This study was handed in as my master thesis to the Johann-Wolfgang-Goethe University of Frankfurt/Main in 2002. It was compiled under the supervision of Prof. Jan-Waalke Meyer and Prof. Edgar Peltenburg.
Its inspiration goes back to a tutorial on "Early Bronze Age Mortuary Practices in the Near East" held by Prof. Edgar Peltenburg at the University of Frankfurt in the winter of 1999/2000.
I have profited enormously from Martin Devens', Ralph Hempelmann's, Matthias Jung's, Ursula Magen's and Thomas Richter's comments on my work.
I am grateful to Gwendolyn Alù, Martin Devens and Paul Larsen for proof-reading the manuscript.

Table of contents

Acknowledgements
Table of contents
List of Figures
List of Plates
Introduction ... 1

I	Overview	2
I.1	The theoretical basis	2
I.1.1	Theories and methods of chronological division	2
I.1.2	Rites of passage	2
I.1.3	The "dramatis personae" of funerary rites	3
I.1.4	Social structure and social organisation	3
I.1.5	Symbolism	4
I.1.6	Shortcomings in the archaeological data	4
I.2	Relative chronologies in archaeology	5
I.3	An historical outline	6
I.3.1	Tuttul in the Ebla archives	6
I.3.2	Tuttul in the royal inscriptions of Mesopotamia	8
I.3.3	Texts from Mari and Tell Bi'a	9
II	Analysis	10
II.1	The site and the excavations between 1980 and 1995	10
II.2	The site chronology	11
II.3	Description and typology of the burial evidence	12
II.3.1	Phase I	13
II.3.2	Phase II	14
II.3.3	Phase IIIa	14
II.3.4	Phase IIIb	15
II.4.	The demographic analysis	15
II.4.1	Phase I	15
II.4.2	Phase II	17
II.4.3	Phase IIIa	19
II.4.4	Phase IIIb	19
II.5	Detailed examination of the spatial organisation of the graves in cemetery U and on mound E	20
II.5.1	Phase I	20
II.5.2	Phase II	22
II.5.3	Phase IIIa	23
II.5.4	Phase IIIb	23
II.6	The grave goods	24
II.6.1	Phase I	24
II.6.2	Phase II	30
II.6.3	Phase IIIa	31
II.6.4	Phase IIIb	34
II.7	The marked pottery	34
II.7.1	Phase I	35
II.7.2	Phase II	36
II.7.3	Phase IIIa	36
III	Summary and conclusions	38
III.1	Summary of the analysis	38
III.1.1	Phase I	38
III.1.2	Phase II	40
III.1.3	Phase IIIa	40
III.1.4	Phase IIIb	41
III.2	Relations to the Syrian and Mesopotamian socio-cultural history	41
III.2.1	The chronological consequences: piecing together the archaeological and literary relative dating systems	41
III.2.2	Intramural above ground funerary monuments	43
III.2.3	The pottery marks	44
III.2.4	The Ebla texts: political organisation, burials and ancestor worship	44
Abbreviations		47

References		48
Catalogue		57
Plates		60

List of Figures

Fig. 1	Illustration of the theory of "*rites of passage*"	3
Fig. 2	Illustration of the theory of Hertz on the dramatic levels and the relationships between them during a funeral	3
Fig. 3	Illustration of Giddens's structuration-theory (according to Härke 1997)	4
Fig. 4	Individuals from Tuttul known from the Ebla texts	7
Fig. 5	Brief overview of the excavation areas at Tell Bi'a	10
Fig. 6	Typological scheme for *subterranean* burials (according to Carter – Parker 1995, Table 14.2)	12
Fig. 7	The dimensions of the mausolea	13
Fig. 8	The mortality rates in Tell Bi'a during phase I-IIIb	15
Fig. 9	The mortality rates in phase I	15
Fig. 10	Age and gender distribution of the burials in phase I	16
Fig. 11	Age and gender distribution in the mausolea	16
Fig. 12	The lengths of the *subterranean* graves during phase I	17
Fig. 13	Age and gender distribution in phase II	18
Fig. 14	The mortality rates in phase II	18
Fig. 15	Distribution of burial types and age and gender representation in phase IIIa	18
Fig. 16	The mortality rates in phase IIIa	19
Fig. 17	The lengths of *subterranean* graves in phase IIIa	19
Fig. 18	Distribution of burial-types and age and gender in phase IIIb	20
Fig. 19	The heights of open mouth pots and jars in cemetery U during phase I	24
Fig. 20	The heights of the "luxury vessels" in cemetery U in phase I	25
Fig. 21	Distribution of vessels in cemetery U in phase I	26
Fig. 22	The heights of WT/F in phase I	28
Fig. 23	The heights of the "luxury vessels" in the mausolea	28
Fig. 24	Distribution of vessels in phase II	31
Fig. 25	The heights of "luxury vessels" in phase II	31
Fig. 26	Distribution of vessels in phase IIIa	32
Fig. 27	The heights of "luxury vessels" in phase IIIa	32
Fig. 28	Distribution of vessels in phase IIIb	34
Fig. 29	Relationships between the mausolea and the grave-groups in cemetery U as perceived from the pottery marks	36
Fig. 30	Distribution of pottery marks in cemetery U in phase II	36
Fig. 31	Diagram of the conical clan system (according to Breuer 1990, 59 Fig. 4 with reference to Friedman 1979, 258)	40
Fig. 32	The duration of cemetery U	41
Fig. 33	Working hypotheses for the comparison of archaeological and historical data of the Akkadian Period	42

List of Plates

Plate 1	Situation of localities mentioned in the text
Plate 2	Relative chronological correlation of sites along the Middle and Upper Euphrates (according to Hempelmann 2005 with modification of Tell Bi'a.)
Plate 3	Relative chronology of Mesopotamian dynasties from the Akkadian period to the reign of Hammurabi of Babylon (synchronism from the Akkad to UrIII dynasties according to Dittmann 1994, 98 Tab. 7, synchronism from the UrIII dynasty to the reign of Hammurabi according to Gasche *et alia* 1998, Supplement Table)
Plate 4	Plan of Tell Bi'a (according to Strommenger – Kohlmeyer 1998, Pl. 6 and Pl. 136)
Plate 5	Harris-matrix of mound E
Plate 6	The mausolea and their inventories (after Strommenger – Kohlmeyer 1998, Pl. 56–98)
Plate 7	Burials in cemetery U during phase I (after Strommenger – Kohlmeyer 1998, App. 3)
Plate 8	Burials in cemetery U during phase II (after Strommenger – Kohlmeyer 1998, App. 3)
Plate 9	Burials in cemetery U during phase IIIa (after Strommenger – Kohlmeyer 1998, App. 3)
Plate 10	Burials in cemetery U during phases I to IIIa (after Strommenger – Kohlmeyer 1998, App. 3)
Plate 11	Orientation of graves

	1. Phase I
	2. Phase II
	3. Phase IIIa
Plate 12	1. Isometric reconstruction of the mausolea before the erection of G6
	2. Isometric reconstruction of the mausolea at the end of phase I
Plate 13	Phase I – Drinking vessels (Tg) and different bowl types (S, N and Sa)
Plate 14	Phase I – Open mouth pots (WT) and jars (F)
Plate 15	Phase I – Jars (F), spouted pots (TT), cooking pots (KT), miniature vessels (M), stands (SR) and sieves (Si)
Plate 16	Phase I – "Luxury vessels" (Lu)
Plate 17	Phase I – Metal objects: pins (Na), daggers or spears (DL), axes (B) and rings (R)
Plate 18	Phase II – Drinking vessels (Tg) and different bowl types (S and Sa)
Plate 19	Phase II – Open mouth pots (WT) and jars (F)
Plate 20	Phase II – Spouted pots (TT), cooking pots (KT), globular pots (KuT), miniature vessels (M) and sieves (Si)
Plate 21	Phase II – "Luxury vessels" (Lu) and bottles with narrow necks (EF)
Plate 22	Phase II – Metal objects: pins (Na), daggers or spears (DL), axes (B) and rings (R)
Plate 23	Phase IIIa – Drinking vessels (Tg) and different bowl types (S and Sa)
Plate 24	Phase IIIa – Open mouth pots (WT), globular pots (KuT) and jars (F)
Plate 25	Phase IIIa – Jars (F) and cooking pots (KT)
Plate 26	Phase IIIa – "Luxury vessels" (Lu) and bottles with narrow necks (EF)
Plate 27	Phase IIIa – Miniature vessels (M), sieves (Si), stone vessels (StS), pins (Na), daggers or spears (DL), axes (B), sheets of metal or hooks (Bl) and rings (R)
Plate 28	Artefacts of phase IIIb
Plate 29	Distribution of pots and jars in the mausolea
Plate 30	Distribution of drinking vessels and bowls in the mausolea
Plate 31	Distribution of stands and all vessels in the mausolea
Plate 32	1. Burial 23/46:3 after Strommenger – Kohlmeyer 1998, Pl. 98
	2. Reconstruction of the equipment of a warrior
	3. Inlay figure from Mari after Strommenger – Hirmer 1962, Fig. 74
	4. A limestone carving from the "Presargonic" palace in Mari (room XLVI) after Orthmann 1985, Plate 95c
	5. Warrior from the "standard of Ur" after Strommenger – Hirmer 1962, colour plate XI
Plate 33	Pottery marks in phase I
Plate 34	Pottery marks in phase II (a) and IIIa (b) and the map of the intramural cemetery (c)
Plate 35	Comparison of selected types from Tuttul (A-G after Strommenger – Kohlmeyer 2000, H-J after Strommenger – Kohlmeyer 1998) and Ebla (A, G, I-J after Matthiae et al. 1995, D-F after Mazzoni 1982, B, C, H after Mazzoni1985)
Plate 36	Comparison of pottery marks in Tell Bi'a and at the Euphrates region
Plate 37	Correlation of the relative chronology of the kings of Akkad and the archaeological results (Hypotheses I/1.A-C and I/2.A-C)
Plate 38	Correlation of the relative chronology of the kings of Akkad and the archaeological results (Hypotheses II/1.A-C and II/2.A-C)

Introduction

This study is about Early Bronze Age burials excavated on the mound of Tell Bi'a and in an area about three hundred meters further north.

The interpretation of burials is one of archaeology's central concerns. Though the earliest excavations first of all aimed at the discovery of monumental remains, graves have continued to fascinate from the beginning. They were found in very different archaeological contexts: in cemeteries, in or under houses, palaces or temples. Graves with monumental architecture and ones with abundant and rich grave goods caused much sensation and inspired the imagination of both scholar and layman.

Graves remind us that death is universal, but there is great diversity in the ways people react to it. Numerous psychological studies are concerned with this reaction on an individual level, whereas this is almost completely beyond the possibilities of archaeological interpretation. However, we can study a society's response to death.

After more than 150 years of Near Eastern archaeology, a great number of graves from different periods are known, but the reports contain very diverse information. There are only few graves and cemeteries – most of which have been excavated during the last three decades – that provide detailed information concerning funerary architecture and the exact positions of the skeletons or the objects recovered inside and next to the graves. Anthropological examinations too are quite scarce. For this reason data concerning gender and age related topics or even those leading to the determination of the exact number of individuals inside one grave have hardly ever been recorded. Even recent reports often present incomplete data since they mostly concern rescue excavations or robbed graves.

By contrast, the excavations of Tell Bi'a brought to light well preserved graves in an extramural cemetery as well as stratified intramural burials. The burial evidence found in the twelve campaigns between 1980 and 1995 was already published in 1998 together with preliminary anthropological results. The detailed presentation of the material enables and justifies further analyses presented in this case study. It is possible to observe differences between groups of contemporary burials and changes through time within the patterns of the burial practices at this site alone by analysing it as part of the ritual expression of the community's changing structure.

Before discussing the material evidence in the first part of this paper, the theoretical basis as well as the methods used for inferring the structure of a living society from funerary remains will be clarified. This is followed by an overview of the chronological framework as well as a historical outline of the Syrian Bronze Age in accordance with the current state of epigraphic and archaeological research, and finally by a formulation of the questions raised in this study.

In the second, empirical part the actual analysis of the burial evidence at Tell Bi'a itself is presented. A résumé of the research carried out on the site is followed by a presentation the site's inner chronology as based on evidence from stratigraphy and seriation. A primarily architectural description of the burials and a discussion of their typology are then followed by an anthropological and demographic analysis pertaining to the proportions of age and gender. In a next step the spatial arrangement of the graves is examined. The final topic of this part concerns the interpretation of grave goods with regard to their practical and symbolic implications.

The third part is more interpretative. It begins with a summary of the characteristics of each period and develops in exposing which questions can eventually be answered on the basis of the material presented here. It is only after this summary that it is possible to portray the wider relations from the evidence of Tell Bi'a to the Syrian and Mesopotamian sociocultural history.

I. Overview

I.1 The theoretical basis

The question as to what statements can be made about the relationship between society and burial practices in general, has been addressed in the past by several ethnologists, sociologists, anthropologists as well as archaeologists. To give a full overview of this is not the intention in this study.[1] Instead we will concentrate on the main theories and methods applied in the following chapters.

As mentioned above, the burial evidence can be seen as part of the ritual expression of a changing structure of a community. In general the concepts formulated and used by the classical archaeologist Ian Morris in his analyses will be followed.[2] His studies were based upon the following principles:

"As archaeologists, we excavate burials. But a burial is only a part of a funeral, and a funeral only part of the social circumstances surrounding the biological fact of death. [...] Funerals in most societies are tripartite, *rite of passage* affairs, where roles and *social personae* are attached to all the initiands, and are given symbolic recognition. While society certainly does not react as a living entity to death, neither funerary process simply a way to legitimise inequalities. Instead, it has been suggested that funerals help to create an ideal *social structure* which constrains and gives meaning to action without determining it. At least in principle, the archaeologist can hope to be able to follow the *development of structures through time*, and to identify points of structural revolution. In practice, of course, much will depend on the particular forms of *symbolism* employed, and their susceptibility to observation and interpretation."[3]

I.1.1 Theories and methods of chronological division

Ever since the early beginnings of modern archaeology relative chronology has been a major topic of study. Today graves are often dated by means of seriation. In an early evolutionist view of the past, Christian Jürgensen Thomsen (1788-1865) used a rough but effective form of seriation to scientifically prove his established chronological series.[4] Thomsen discussed not only the development of artefacts through time, but also the changing of burial customs and other aspects of prehistoric life.[5] The method of seriation has of course as well as the methods of stratigraphy undergone substantial refinement since that time. In the mid-1970s the Harris-Matrix[6] was developed for the dating of stratified sites. Computer programs such as the Bonn Archaeological Statistics Package[7] (BASP) and ArchEd[8] were then engineered to make work much easier.

The excavation report of Tell Bi'a[9] contains a seriation table drawn up by means of the BASP thus providing a basis for comparing of the seriation results with the stratigraphical evidence which eventually will result in a periodisation of the site. This local sequence will enable us to shed more light on the symbolic and hopefully the social structures of each period and to compare them to each other.

I.1.2 Rites of passage

The so called French School founded by the sociologist Emile Durkheim[10] at the turn of the 19th century focused on the processes of how beliefs and ideas help integrate individuals into a community. One of Durkheim's students, Robert Hertz in 1907[11] dealt with funerary evidence regarding death as a social, as well as a biological transformation.[12]

Two years later, Arnold Van Gennep who, though not member of the French School but in close contact with it, published his work on ritual structures in human life.[13] He recognised that a certain group of rituals that occur at transitional points or periods in human life generally follow a tripartite pattern. He described a first phase of separation from the original status, followed by the so-called marginal state (the stage of transformation), and finally the integration into the new status (the stage of aggregation).

This pattern of rites which accompany transformations from one social state to another, e.g. birth, marriage, adoption, or death was labelled as a *rite of passage*. Applied to the present discussion, this would mean that funerary rites can be interpreted according to this pattern (Fig. 1).[14]

In recent years the theories of Hertz and van Gennep have been revised and used for interpretative purposes,[15] also in Near Eastern archaeology.[16] Nevertheless, it has been argued in a number of studies, whether or not this pattern may be applied universally to funerary customs.[17] In view of the fact that our modern Western attitudes to

---

[1] Much has been published about death and mortuary practices in antiquity. Generally, see the bibliographies in Harrah – Harrah 1976 or Herfort-Koch 1992.
[2] Morris 1987 and 1992.
[3] Morris 1987, 42-43.
[4] Trigger 1989, 78; Thomsen 1837 [1836] – 1848 (in English).
[5] See e.g. Thomsen 1837, 57-64.
[6] Harris 1975 and 1979.
[7] See the User's Manual and Herzog 1993.
[8] ArchEd Version 1.0 developed by I. Poucharev, St. Thome, C. Hundock, P. Mutzel (contact per email: arche@mpi-sb.mpg.de).
[9] Strommenger – Kohlmeyer 1998.
[10] Huntington – Metcalf 1979.
[11] Hertz 1960 [1907].
[12] See also Chapter I.1.3..
[13] van Gennep 1986 [1909].
[14] Morris 1987, fig. 10.
[15] E.g. Morris 1987, 29-43.
[16] See e.g. Nasrabadi 1999, 7-10 and Meyer 2000.
[17] E.g. Huntington – Metcalf 1979 and McManners 1981.

I. Overview

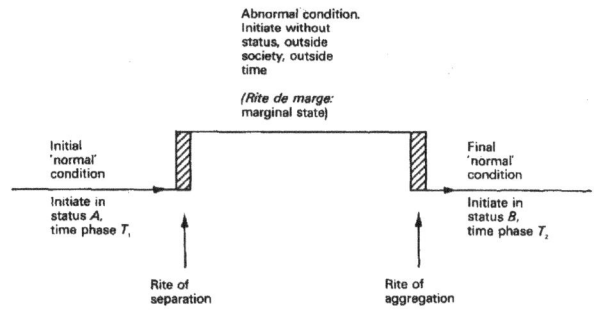

Fig. 1 Illustration of the theory of "rites of passage" (according to Morris 1987, 30 fig.10)

death are diverse,[18] the universal applicability of the concept has been challenged.

However, the only examples for a possible dissolution of this *rite of passage* pattern in funerary practices come from modern Western cultures, the reasons for their dissolution originating from the period of industrialisation.[19] This means that the pattern may all the same be adequate for the interpretation of pre-industrial mortuary practices.

I.1.3 The "*dramatis personae*" of funerary rites

Robert Hertz in his above mentioned work examined the transformational process which takes place during a funeral. He distinguishes between three participants on three dramatic levels: the corpse, the soul and the mourners. The relationships between these dramatic levels are expressed at different stages during the ritual (Fig. 2).[20]

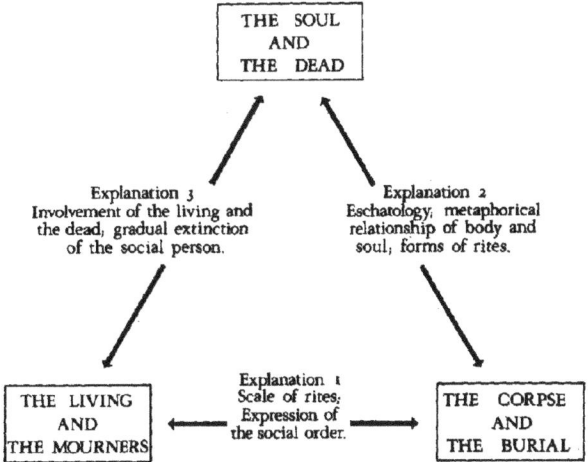

Fig. 2 Illustration of the theory of Hertz on the dramatic levels and the relationships between them during a funeral (according to Morris 1987, 31 fig. 11)

Nevertheless, the rites connecting the different dramatic levels can often be seen in more than one of these aspects. This means that we have to identify the dramatic levels and the participants before asking questions about the social consequences. Therefore it is quite likely that more than one explanation is possible for each of these symbolic[21] acts.

Arthur Saxe and Lewis Binford were the first to use Hertz's model for archaeological theory in the 1970s.[22] Their work represents the beginning of "New Archaeology". They concentrated mainly on rites from Hertz's first relationship (Fig. 2, Explanation 1). Binford was often criticised for oversimplification in explaining a wide variety of burial evidence in terms of social stratification alone.[23] However, this discussion opened the way for more complex and elaborate methods of interpreting burial remains by taking into account the dramatic levels too.

I.1.4 Social structure and social organisation

Even if we understand the sequence of events in ritual activities – in our case the mortuary ritual will be interpreted as a *rite of passage* – the question as to how we may infer social organisation from rituals still remains. First we must define what we mean by using the term "society".

In social anthropology society means a territorially defined political unit.[24] Societies consist of more than one group of interest, each group in the system identified by its "own, distinctive attributes such as linguistic usage, manners, styles of dress, food, housing, etc. The decoding of such systems of symbolic representation is the primary task of the social anthropologist."[25]

Morris points out that we have to distinguish between *social structure* and *social organisation*.

> "Organisation is taken to mean the empirical distribution of relationships in everyday experience, while structure is an ideal model, a mental template, of the relative placing of individuals within the world. This structure is created in the socialisation process, and in practice largely through rituals, such as the funeral. [...] The structure of society as enacted in ritual is not necessarily the same as the organisation of society in practical social action, and indeed can perhaps never be so. [...] If we are to interrogate burial evidence about ancient

---

[18] See e.g. Ariès 1974 or Huntington – Metcalf 1979, 184-211

[19] Morris 1987, 35: "It is clear, though that a fundamental change in attitudes occurred in the eighteenth century, both in Western Europe and in North America. It is here, I suggest that we will find the seeds of the dissolution of the rite of passage funeral." He referred to McManners 1981 and Stannard 1977.

[20] Huntington – Metcalf 1979, 66 Fig. 2. Hertz 1960 [1907] thought to prove his theory by using the example of secondary burials on Borneo. Huntington – Metcalf 1979, 13-17 were able to show the general validity of his theory.

[21] On symbolism in burial data see Chapter I.1.5..

[22] E.g. Binford 1971, 7.

[23] E.g. Hodder 1982, 140-146, O'Shea 1984, 5-8, 302.

[24] Leach 1986², 41. He continues in arguing that this political unit is "a segment of some larger political unit which might, in some slightly different context, also be described as 'a society'. The boundaries of such units are usually vague. They are determined by operational convenience rather than rational argument. But they are objective."

[25] Leach 1986², 43.

society, we must ask questions concerning social structure."[26]

Härke expresses a similar idea summarising the structuration-theory of Giddens[27] as follows (Fig. 3): "...society is not a given framework in which individuals play pre-ordained roles, but an interplay of rules (structuring principles) and actions (social practices), with ideology providing the legitimisation for the former. It follows that burial ritual is not mere passive reflection of society, but the result of actions which contribute to shaping society itself."[28]

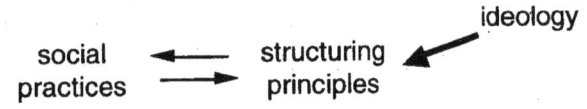

Fig. 3 Illustration of Giddens's structuration-theory (according to Härke 1997)

I.1.5 Symbolism

In order to achieve capability of decoding the symbolic structures mentioned above in connection with the burial ritual, we must first indicate where such symbolism might occur in the burial data. H. Härke identifies four spheres where symbolism may occur:

(1) location and landscape context
(2) grave form and monument
(3) grave goods
(4) decoration of artefacts in the grave[29]

In consequence, in attempting to decode these symbolic structures, we must always view our data in their context. In the following analysis the examination of these four spheres will occupy much of the discussion. The symbolic importance of the burial site (1) is evident because we are dealing with both *intra* as well as *extramural* burials. The great variety of grave forms (2) in the Syrian Upper and Middle Euphrates regions has been the subject of recent discussions.[30]

The aim is to find an explanation for the fact that different grave forms were used in Tell Bi'a at the same time and to identify the reasons for the changes in their use or construction.

The third attribute concerns the grave goods. Given that only a selection of artefacts was deposited inside the graves,[31] we will attempt to work out the reasons for this selection by induction. In this respect, the position of an object inside a grave can help us determine its function. Another aspect is the issue of sets, whether or not it is possible to identify certain patterns behind these selections. In a final step, it is also necessary to discuss the topic of "expensive", or imported grave goods and to assess how their occurrence in graves is interpreted.

J.-W. Meyer[32] proposes a method to classify grave goods from ancient Near Eastern burial contexts by considering ritual actions known from the epigraphic evidence. He distinguishes between "*Aufbahrungssitte*"(lying in state),[33] "*Beisetzungssitte*" (interment),[34] "*Trachtsitte*" (costume),[35] "*Beigabensitte*" (deposition of additional artefacts for cultic-religious reasons),[36] and "*Mitgaben*" (deposition of additional artefacts of social or personal significance).[37] These categories are considered in the examination of the archaeological remains. Any evidence suggesting activities on the burial site after the funeral and thus potentially indicative of ancestor worship is taken into account as well.

A final issue is the interpretation of decorated objects among the grave goods (4). The "function" of decoration, that is to say the question as to possible connotations of occurring symbols, will be raised. For the decoding of such symbolism we will focus on the evidence from the site itself. An assessment based on material from other sites as well as the epigraphic evidence then follows in a subsequent step.

I.1.6 Shortcomings in the archaeological data

Because it will never be possible to reconstruct the entire funerary ritual, we need to consider which data are available from the following four types of information on cult behaviour as suggested by Colin Renfrew.[38]

1. "Direct observation/participation in the rituals
2. Verbal testimony, oral or written, describing or explaining the rituals
3. Artistic representation of the rituals

---

[26] Morris 1987, 39 based on Pader 1982.
[27] Giddens 1979.
[28] Härke 1997a, 21.
[29] Härke 1997b, 193.
[30] See e.g. Carter – Parker 1995 and Meyer 1997, esp. 301-304.
[31] Härke 1997a, 22-23 calls it the "selective nature" of burial data.
[32] Meyer 2000.
[33] Meyer 2000, 23 means by "*Aufbahrungssitte*" all actions carried out between death and interment. It can include specific private or official presentations the corpse, positioning or rituals of purification and conservation. This phase ends with the funeral procession to the grave.
[34] Meyer 2000, 23 lists under the term "*Beisetzungssitte*" all actions connected with the interment, from the choice of the burial site (within or outside the city, house etc.) to the construction work at the inhumation site including the action of closing or filling of the tomb.
[35] According to Meyer 2000, 24 all artefacts directly associated to the corpse belong to the so called "*Trachtsitte*". They include garments, jewellery and sometimes weapons, though only on condition that they had belonged to the individual during his or her lifetime.
[36] With the term "*Beigabensitte*" Meyer 2000, 24 summarises such objects that had specially been manufactured for the funerary ritual, as well as common objects that receive additional cultic meanings during the ritual. Among them are artefacts with an apotropaic purpose or objects that might have been helpful on the way into the netherworld or afterlife. Therefore parts of the provisions as well as their containers also belong to this category.
[37] Meyer 2000, 24 includes to the category of "*Mitgaben*" additional objects referring to the dead person during his lifetime, specifying rank, social status, profession etc. They comprise jewellery or weapons that are not part of the costume, working tools, and emblems.
[38] Renfrew 1985, 12.

4. The material remains of rituals."[39]

In an archaeological context the first class is inaccessible. The second on the other hand, is available from the third millennium B.C. and later in the Near East, though the evidence from the first centuries of literacy it is particularly meagre[40] and difficult to work with. Nevertheless, the texts may give some clues as to the location, participants or objects used in the ceremonies. It is therefore possible to compare this information with the archaeological data. The problem of using written evidence, be it "synthetic"[41] or "one-off analysis",[42] to understand mortuary practices, has been discussed by Ian Morris in reference to the classical periods, and his methods may without doubt be applied to Near Eastern archaeology too.

The third class, artistic representation, is even less useful for the region and period under discussion. We can recognise so-called cultic or mythological representations as for example on seals, but we are far from clearly understanding them. In this respect libation or so-called banquet scenes may be depicted in different contexts, among others as funeral offerings or ritual meals, but we yet need to identify their implications with certainty.

The evidence of the final class, the material remains of ritual actions, too is far from being complete. The material remains have only survived in fractions, and the burial site was not necessarily the only place of the funerary ritual. Archaeologists have to cope with such doubts, but there are methods of crosschecking them.[43] In working with data from funerary contexts, Morris proposes five main aspects under which this data may be interpreted as cultural evidence: typology, time, context of deposition, space (burial arrangements compared to each other and to the settlement or landscape), and demography.[44] These aspects will be studied carefully in the second part of this study.

I.2 Relative chronologies in archaeology

During the last decades, extensive research has taken place in order to better understand Syria's past. As a result, the former approach based on a conception of the region as being a mere cultural province of Mesopotamian civilisation gradually changed to one which increasingly concentrated on its internal developments. The Syrian Bronze Age has recently been the subject of several individual studies[45] and conferences.[46] One of the central themes in recent discussions was to establish a well-defined chronological system more adapted to sites in the region.[47]

The Early Bronze Age (EBA) in the Southern Levant is traditionally – according to Albright's excavation in Tell Beit Mersim[48] – divided into four main periods numbered I to IV. This system was adopted in Northern Syria at Tell Mardīḫ for the Upper Euphrates, with a further subdivision of the fourth period into EBA IV A and IV B. This chronological system is widely used in archaeological publications, but without any accurate or uniform definition of its single periods.[49]

Most of these chronological systems are based on the comparison of ceramics; larger areas are divided into ceramic provinces by means of "characteristic or key-types and wares".[50] The immanent danger of such "archaeological constructs" has been recently discussed by S. Campbell.[51] As an alternative to construing such ceramic provinces, he proposed to optimise the chronological sequences of individual sites and to group them together in regional frameworks instead of fitting the evidence into an existing chronological scheme.

Such detailed chronological sequences of stratified settlements[52] and sometimes funerary assemblages[53] have already been generated by means of accurate statistical studies. As a starting point the correlation of settlement levels established by R. Hempelmann will be considered.[54] He compares sites of the upper Euphrates region with EBA III to MB I sequences from settlements in an area between Ebla in the southwest, Mari in the East and Lidar Höyük in the north (Plate 2).

His results can be compared with B. Einwag's analysis of the Middle Bronze Age (MBA) pottery at Tell Bi'a.[55]

---

[39] Morris 1992, 10.

[40] This is especially true for written sources of the 3rd millennium from Syria. Most of them are lists of offerings which are hardly comprehensible. See Xella 1988, 354-358.

[41] Morris 1992, 10-11 on the "synthetic method": "Often sources allude only to parts of rituals, and to create a fuller picture we have to stitch together texts spanning long periods of time. At best, we can describe 'the' ritual, but lose all chance of analysing how it changed through time or how different groups used it..."

[42] Morris 1992, 11: "The second method is the 'one-off' analysis of a single episode. The problem here is how to extrapolate from one event...to wider patterns of ritual actions."

[43] See e.g. O'Shea 1981; Morris 1987, 211-212 and 1992. The empirical methods used in these works can be applied to any archaeological period. Nasrabadi 1999 gives an example for an application in Near Eastern archaeology.

[44] Morris 1992, 24-29.

[45] For more references see e.g. Klengel 1992.

[46] See e.g. the reports on the conferences in 1998 in Barcelona (Del Olmo Lete – Montero Fenollós eds. 1999) and in Istanbul (Marro-Hauptmann eds. 2000).

[47] Many papers of the conferences mentioned above (note 46) debate this problem. See e.g. Porter 2000, Cooper 2000, Campbell 2000, Lebeau et al. 2000.

[48] Albright 1932 and 1933. Tell Beit Mersim is situated about 20 km south-west of Hebron (OxfEnc Band 1, 295). All other sites mentioned in the text are localised on Plate 1.

[49] For an overview of the different chronological systems for Syria see Einwag 1988, 39-42. For a further examination of these see Campbell 1999 and 2000.

[50] E.g. Rova 1997, Lebeau et al. 2001 and Pruß 2001.

[51] Campbell 1999.

[52] See e.g. Mazzoni 1985, Abay 1997, Einwag 1998 or most recently Hempelmann 2005 with further references.

[53] See e.g. Peltenburg 1999b; the importance of fixing the context of the assemblage before comparing it with other sites was the subject of Porter 2000.

[54] Hempelmann 2004 and 2005.

[55] Einwag 1998.

Further to the north, the longer chronological sequences of Samsat and Pirot Höyük have been compared with those of other Anatolian and Syrian sites by E. Abay.[56] Further south however, the chronology is based on that of Tell Harīrī/Mari, the key-site for connecting Syrian assemblages to pottery sequences in Southern Mesopotamian. Unfortunately, the pottery of this site has not been fully published yet. As for the north-East, the Workshop of the European Center for Upper Mesopotamian Studies has proposed a periodisation for the Syrian Ğazīra, especially the Hābur region.[57]

Fitting together this variety of regional chronological systems proves to be rather problematic. The discrepancies can be quite significant.[58] On one hand, they often ground on diverging ceramic type and ware terminologies[59] and on the other on dissimilar treatment of relative[60] or absolute[61] dating systems.

The above mentioned analyses by B. Einwag and R. Hempelmann seem to be an exception, insofar as their relative chronology systems largely seem to complement each other, and their period definitions seem to harmonize.

Given that this is a case study rather than squeezing the data into an existing scheme, an inner chronology of Tell Bi'a[62] will be developed as already recommended by S. Campbell. The question as to whether such an inner periodisation may help solving any of the above mentioned problems of chronology will be dealt with in the third part.

I.3   An historical outline

Two main source categories relate the ancient history of Syria, cuneiform texts and archaeological evidence. For Tell Bi'a we are lucky to have both. The following short overview of historical events in the Syrian Middle Euphrates region does not take into account the literary texts, because their historical accuracy is still under discussion.[63]

Absolute dates will be avoided because of the difficulties mentioned in the preceding chapter.

The relative chronology from the Akkadian to the Ur III dynasty has been reviewed under historical and archaeological aspects by R. Dittmann.[64] His convincing results shortened the time span that had elapsed between the end of the Akkad dynasty and the first king of the Ur III dynasty. This shortened chronology combined with the relative chronology of Ur III to the reign of Hammurabi presented by Gasche et al.,[65] furnishes a frame for the historical periods (Plate 3).

The ancient name of Tell Bi'a was Tuttul,[66] a well known city throughout the centuries. However, "Tuttul" belongs to a number of city-names that had a specific or very close correspondence in the East-Tigris region.[67] A third city with this name appears in a Late Assyrian list and described as being located on the Euphrates close to the modern city of Hīt; but this equation appears to be very problematic for the earlier texts.[68]

I.3.1   Tuttul in the Ebla archives

The earliest reports on Tuttul-on-the-Balīḫ originate from the Palace G archives of Tell Mardīḫ/Ebla.[69] The texts are dated *a priori* to the so-called Akkadian invasion into Northern Syria[70] and cover a time span of probably 40 years according to the yearly accounts.[71] The end of the Ebla archives is marked by the destruction of Palace G.[72]

There are relatively frequent references to Tuttul in the Ebla-archive.[73] Some texts state that high ranking people visited (DU.DU; kaskal; níg-kas$_4$; si-in *Du-du-lu*^{ki}) Tuttul,[74] as for instance even the "viziers of Ebla",

---

[56] Abay 1997, 342 Fig. 46 and 350 Fig. 47.

[57] Lebeau et al. 2000.

[58] See e.g. the different correlation of the graves from Tell Bi'a with other sites by Pruß 2001, 429 Fig.5 who synchronised Group 1-3 of the seriation = EBA IVA= EJ (Early Jezirah) IV and Group 4-7 = EBA IV B = EJ V= "postakkadian" (p.419, note 81) and by Hempelmann 2004, table 1 who synchronised Group 1-2 = EBA III = EDIII; Group 3= EBA IV A= Early Akkadian; Group 4-6 = EBA IV B = Late Akkadian; Group 7= EBA/MBA transitional = Ur III.

[59] See e.g. Pruß 2000 and 2001.

[60] Discussed more in detail in notes 49 and 58.

[61] The absolute chronology is also much discussed. See the symposium held at Schloß Haindorf 1996 and in Vienna 1998 – Bietak (ed.) 2000, especially the paper by Hunger 2000 – or the proposal by Gasche et al. 1998 and the ensuing discussion at the International Colloquium on Ancient Near Eastern Chronology (Ghent 7-9 July 2000), published in Akkadica 119-120 (Sept.-Dec. 2000). For an example of the range of suggested solutions compare the reign of Hammurabi of Babylon in Plate 3.

[62] The main stratigraphical data especially for the central mound E are available in Strommenger – Kohlmeyer 2000.

[63] See the different distributions in Liverani 1993. In his new edition on the Akkadian legends J. G. Westenholz (1997) announced a future volume with an evaluation of the texts including an investigation into their historical background.

[64] Dittmann 1994.

[65] Gasche et al. 1998, supplementary table.

[66] See the summary by Strommenger 1977 in MDOG 109 on the identification. New texts from Tell Bi'a published by M. Krebernik in MDOG 125, 51 and Krebernik 2001 confirm this identification.

[67] See Astour 1992, 12 especially note 47.

[68] Strommenger 1977 in MDOG 109, 13, but RGTC 1, 161-162.

[69] See a compilation of the texts in Archi 1990.

[70] Much has been published on the Akkadian presence in Northern Syria and its chronological connection to the Ebla texts; see Hempelmann 2004 and Archi 1996a. Sallaberger synchronised the end of the Ebla archives to the 30th year of Sargon. Another view advanced e.g. by Liverani 1993 dates it to the defeat by Narām-Sîn.

[71] Sallaberger 2004, 20 note 11 stating a personal communication by A. Archi as a rectification to Archi 1996a. 17 or 18 yearly metal accounts are dated to Ibrium and 17 to Ibbi-Zikir, 5 or 6 to their predecessor, Arennum.

[72] According to the archaeological comparison the destruction of Palace G in Ebla is roughly contemporary with the destruction of Palace B in Tell Bi'a or slightly later. Strommenger – Kohlmeyer 2000, 41 in addition demonstrate that the two palaces had been in use at the same time.

[73] The common spelling was *Du-du-lu*^{ki}. For the different spellings of the name of the city in the Ebla archive and the Sargonic text see Archi 1990, 197 note 4 and Krebernik 2001.

[74] Archi 1990, 201, texts 4, 8, 16, 17, 28, 33, 35, 38, 60.

Ibrium[75] and Ibbi-Zikir[76] and the en[77] (sovereign of Ebla). The probable reason for such visits was to make an offering (nídba) to Dagān[78] in his main temple (é ᵈBE *Du-du-lu*ᵏⁱ).[79] There were other important visitors at Tuttul such as the "ruler" (en) of Nagar[80] as well as his sons (dumu-nita-dumu-nita-*sù*) and other "rulers" (en-en) who took an oath (nam-ku₅) in the temple of the "Lord of Tuttul".[81]

The above texts suggest that the importance of Tuttul was based on its religious status in a region stretching from Ebla to distant cities as far as Nagar. Texts mentioning Tuttul with no reference to religion are less common.[82] Such texts often name individuals from different cities obtaining goods from Tuttul or vice versa, people accepting deliveries from other cities. Thus, there were links between Tuttul and other important cities like Ḫa-lam,[83] Mari[84] and Kiš.[85] It is interesting to take a closer look at the mentioned individuals from Tuttul; their names and professions are listed in Fig. 4.

The names are Semitic, and their structure is similar to that of the names in Ebla.[86] The only professions mentioned are "messengers" (u₅ and maškim u₅) and "merchants" (ga-raš and maškim ga-raš) as well as a "pašeš[87]-priest of Aštar".

So we don't know whether it was an en (sovereign) or a lugal (governor or main official of the administration in Ebla)[88] who resided at Tuttul. The texts do not reveal anything about high ranking officials from Tuttul.[89] Besides, Tuttul is not mentioned in the letter by Enna-Dagān[90] who gives an account of military campaigns by four kings of Mari against the sovereigns of Ebla. Both circumstances led to the interpretation that Tuttul was not controlled by Ebla, but already under the rule of Mari.[91]

Name	Profession
`À-sum	u₅
Áš-da-ma-NI	maškim ga-raš
Ba-ba	
En-na-Da-gan	
Ga-rí-ù	maškim u₅
Ib-gi-tum	maškim ga-raš
I-da-ì	pa₄-šeš ᵈAš-dar
Iš-dub-Il/ì	maškim ga-raš
Iš-la-ì	maškim ga-raš
Iš-ma-ì	u₅
Ku-wa-ma-NI-lum	
Mi-na-lum	
Si-ti-Ma-lik	
Šu-a-ḫa	
Šu-NI	maškim u₅
Wa-ba-rúm	ga-raš

Fig. 4 Individuals from Tuttul[92] known from the Ebla texts

The partially published, text fragment TM.75.G.1771 may modify this view: [...] šub *si-in* UNKEN-ak-*sù* lú ì-na-sum SA.ZAₓᵏⁱ in *Du-du-lu*ᵏⁱ in níg-kas₄ *Ma-rí*ᵏⁱ⁹³/ [...] "melted for the manufacture which the SA.ZAₓᵏⁱ in Tuttul gave for the provision of the journey to Mari".[94] This would mean that a SA.ZAₓᵏⁱ, a special term used to denote the "palace" or "administrative centre" in Ebla or otherwise a "toponym near by the city of Ebla",[95] also existed in Tuttul.

Furthermore, this suggests that Tuttul was a centre of a local economic entity,[96] possibly owing to of its influence

---

[75] Archi 1990, text 33.

[76] Archi 1990, text 4, 35, 38.

[77] The visit is mentioned in two texts: Archi 1990, Text 4 and 60.

[78] For Dagān in the texts of the 3rd mill. B.C. see Pettinato – Waetzoldt 1985. Most of the Ebla texts which refer to the name of the city actually do so with the combination of "ᵈBE *Du-du-lu*ᵏⁱ" – "Lord of Tuttul", an epithet for Dagān. It needs to be emphasised that it is not sure whether the offerings to the "Lord of Tuttul" always took place in Tuttul given that the god could have had temples in different cities. Archi 1990, 201 believes that some of the cult actions took place in Ebla itself.

[79] Archi 1990, 201.

[80] Commonly identified with Tell Brak in N-Syria. For further references, see also Matthews – Eidem 1993 and Sallaberger 1996.

[81] TM.75.G.2463 obv. V 17-VI 14. The text is partially published in Archi 1998, 5: 20 ma-na kù-bar₆ níg-ba en *Na-gàr*ᵏⁱ 7 ma-na kù-bar₆ níg-ba dumu-nita-dumu-nita-*sù* 5 ma-na kù-bar₆ níg-ba en-en *áš-ti* en *Na-gàr*ᵏⁱ DU.DU nam-ku₅ é ᵈBE *Du-du-lu*ᵏⁱ 10 gín kù-bar₆ *Ḫu-ra-NE Na-gàr*ᵏⁱ in *Du-du-lu*ᵏⁱ.

[82] See the comparison with Emar and Mari by Archi 1990, 198.

[83] Archi 1990, Text 42 (=TM.75.G.2375 v. II 14-18: 1+1 túg lú u₅ *Du-du-lu*ᵏⁱ in *Ḫa*-LAMᵏⁱ/ 1+1 garment which (is for) the messenger of Tuttul in Ḫalamᵏⁱ). Ḫalamᵏⁱ is identified with Ḫalab/Aleppo, see Archi – Piacentini – Pomponio 1993, 260.

[84] Archi 1990 and Archi – Piacentini – Pomponio 1993, 203-204.

[85] Archi 1990, Text 39 (=TM.75.G.2277 v. VI 5-10: 1+1+1 túg *Iš-du-bù* Kišᵏⁱ in *Du-du-lu*ᵏⁱ šu-ba₄-ti/1+1+1 garment received Išdubu from Kiš in Tuttul).

[86] Archi 1990, 202. He also remarks that the name of Ištup-Il is more like the names given in Mari and Kiš.

[87] Pomponio – Xella 1997, 64 A.II translate pa₄-šeš as "le préposé à l'onction". They obviously inferred from the Akkadian *pašīšu(m)* (see e.g. AHW II, 845 and Hirsch 1963, 41 Sargon inscription B6/47). In the Old Babylonian period the *pašīšu(m)*-priest was first of all responsible for bloodless offerings and for the "Totenopfer" (= offering to the dead). In a ritual in Mari he carried out a libation together with the *šangû*-priest. Renger 1969, 143-172 gives an overview of further duties of this priest. It is worth mentioning that the Akkadian word *pašīšu(m)* was written with the sumerogramm ᵍᵘ⁻ᵈᵘgudu₄ (see e.g. Renger 1969, 144) and not pa₄-šeš. ī

[88] For the meanings of "en" and "lugal" in the Ebla texts see Archi 1987

[89] Archi 1990, 199-200.

[90] TM.75.G.2367, first published and studied by Pettinato 1980 and revised by Edzard 1981.

[91] See Archi 1990, 197 and Meyer 1996, 156. For the opposite see Astour 1988, 145-146.

[92] According to Archi 1990, 202 appendix 1 and Archi – Piacentini – Pomponio 1993, 202-204

[93] Archi 1990, 204 text 24; accentuated by the author.

[94] Obv. V 1-9. Special thanks to Dr. Th. Richter, Frankfurt am Main (Germany) for this translation. The present translation and interpretation are very different from that of Archi 1990, 201.

[95] For the different translations see RGTC 12/1, 281-282.

[96] This would also correspond with the observation that Tell Bi'a at the end of the Early Bronze Age belonged to a "ceramic province"

in cultic affairs. Because the Ebla texts have remained mute as to the political organisation of Tuttul, there unfortunately seems to be no better option left than simply to wait for the long expected discovery of contemporary the archives at Tell Bi'a itself.

I.3.2 Tuttul in the royal inscriptions of Mesopotamia

Mesopotamian sources referring to Tuttul originate from the royal inscriptions of Sargon and Narām-Sîn in the Akkadian period, and Šū-Sîn in the Ur III period.

According to the re-interpretation by S. Franke,[97] Sargon's[98] inscription C2 refers to his foreign and commercial politics. In the first part (1-16) "Sargon, the king of Kiš"[99] relates to a military action (mentioning about 34 victorious fights and the razing of city-walls) which enabled "ships from Meluḫḫa,[100] Magan[101] and Tilmun[102] to anchor at the quay of Akkad".[103] In other words, his expansionist politics made it possible for Akkad to take part in the international sea-trade.

After repeating his name and title, Sargon goes on in the second part (17-35) about his politics in the north and West. It thus seems that he was able to enlarge his sphere of influence and political connections without military operations.[104] Following his description, he "Sargon, the king, bowed down to the god Dagān in Tuttul. He (the god Dagān) gave to him (Sargon) the Upper Land: Mari, Iarmuti and Ebla as far the Cedar Forest and the Silver Mountains."[105] Here again the text stresses the cultic significance of Tuttul in this region, this time conjunction with the god Dagān.

The third part (36-44) treats the effects of his successful politics bringing welfare described with the words "5400 men daily eat in the presence of Sargon..."[106]

The original text, as well as the copied inscriptions by his successors Rīmuš and Maništūsu, refer to booty and trading-goods coming in by the sea-route, but not from the northwestern region.[107] It is evident that they refer to interior politics in this latter region and to expansionist ones only in the south and East.[108]

Narām-Sîn, the successor of Maništūsu, began his reign with interior conflicts as indicated by the inscription C1.[109] Kiš and Uruk became independent kingdoms.[110] This and other inscriptions like C2, C3, C5[111] reveal his expansionist ambitions which continued toward the southeast, but initially included military campaigns against western and northern regions. It is indeed interesting to note that Narām-Sîn C5 declares that "...for all time since the creation of mankind, no king whosoever had destroyed Armānum and Ebla..."[112] but that he had done so.[113]

In two original inscriptions[114] he carries the title of "the conqueror of Armānum and Ebla (and Elam)" thus confirming the statement of the previous text. The texts also mention other regions in Syria and South-Anatolia like MAR.TU, the Cedar Forest, Subartu and the Upper Sea.

The city of Tuttul is not mentioned in this military context.[115] However, it appears in a different context in N-S 1, where the inhabitants (of his city Akkad) beseech 9 different gods, among whom Dagān in Tuttul,[116] to install Narām-Sîn as a tutelary god. Here again the religious significance of Dagān and Tuttul is thus highlighted.

After the reign of Narām-Sîn, the Akkadian influence in Syria became weaker, and one inscription by Šarkališarrī mentions a battle against Amurru at Bašar.[117] From the reigns of his successors there are no inscriptions about activities in the Syrian Euphrates region.

---

different to that of Ebla and Mari (Rova 1996, 37 and Hempelmann 2004 and 2005). As for the economic relations see the two normed vessel types identified in Halawa "Größengruppe 2 and 4b". For the distribution of those vessels see Hempelmann 2004, figs. 12 and 13.

[97] Franke 1995, 113-115.

[98] The Akkadian royal inscriptions are numbered Gelb – Kienast 1990. Sargon C2 is preserved in two copies from Nippur, one being bilingual (Sumerian and Akkadian), the other Akkadian: Gelb – Kienast 1990, 163-167. There are minor discrepancies, and it seems that they were copied from two different objects: a base and a statue.

[99] For the development of Sargon's titles from "šar akkade.KI" to "lugal Kiš" see Franke 1995, 94-102. This would mean that inscription C2 belongs to the later part of his reign.

[100] The northern region on the Persian Gulf and Arabian Sea as far as India according to RGTC 1, 121.

[101] The southern region on the Persian Gulf as far as Oman according to RGTC 1, 113-114.

[102] Probably Bahrain and the neighbouring mainland.

[103] Gelb – Kienast 1990, 166.

[104] In the texts Sargon C1 and C4 which are dated earlier than Sargon C2 and which mention the king of Mari, references to military actions against Syrian cities too are missing. See Franke 1995, 114-115. For a different interpretation with further references see Klengel 1992, 31-38.

[105] Translation by Frayne 1993, 28-29. For the localisation of the sites see RGTC 1.

[106] Translation by Frayne 1993, 31.

[107] See e.g. the original Inscription of Rīmuš 1 and 2, Maništūsu 1 in Gelb – Kienast 1990, 66-69, 75-78, 191-225.

[108] See Franke 1995, 129-158.

[109] Gelb – Kienast 1990, 226-243.

[110] Jacobsen 1978-1979; a different opinion on the independence of Kiš in Franke 1995, 160-161.

[111] Gelb – Kienast 1990, 244-264.

[112] Gelb – Kienast 1990, Narām-Sîn 1-10; Translation Frayne 1993, 132.

[113] Gelb – Kienast 1990, N-S. C5 7-19.

[114] Narām-Sîn 11and B7.

[115] There is a fragmentary text from Nippur mentioning Tu-tu-[x^{KI}] and Ur-k[i-x^{KI}] who rose in revolt against the king (of Akkade). Gelb – Kienast 1990: 284, Fragment C5 21-29. Michalowski 1986, 9 already suggested that the two broken names could be identified with Tuttul and Uršu (or Urkiš - note by the present author) of the western region. He proposed a date to the reign of Narām-Sîn (Michalowski 1986, 4). According to Gelb - Kienast 1990, 284 though, this date is unsure. Frayne 1993, 140-141 too, associates it with Narām-Sîn, but proposes to read Tu-tu-[uš-šè.KI].

[116] Narām-Sîn 1, 32-33 in Gelb – Kienast 1990, 82.

[117] Year-name of Šarkališarrī see Frayne 1993, 183. The place ba-ša-ar.KUR has been identified with Ğabal al-Bišri, see RGTC 1, 26.

In later periods, Mesopotamian sources portray Syria as an important trading partner. This is especially the case for the inscriptions by Gudea of Lagaš.[118] No information about Tuttul is available from this period.

From the period of the 3rd dynasty of Ur, a badly damaged inscription by Šū-Sîn mentions Tuttul in connection with Ebla, Mari, Urkiš, Mukiš and other cities in Syria.[119] The main text states a war that took place after a dynastic marriage of Šū-Sîn's daughter with a person (surely a sovereign) of Simanum. All of Northern Syria seems to have been involved in this war including the people of Amurru, a population speaking a Western Semitic language, whose political significance was increasing during that period.[120] In this inscription Šū-Sîn declared himself the victor.[121] There are also numerous economic and administrative texts from the Ur III period describing trade with the Syrian region.[122]

I.3.3 Texts from Mari and Tell Bi'a

From the time following the Ur III period only few fixed dates are available that outline the history of Syria if not that of Tuttul. This was the time of the *šakkanakku* in Mari, who apparently were in control of the Euphrates.[123] This is also the period described as the establishment of Amorite political rule in Syria.[124] References to Tuttul reappear in large numbers again, for the most part in the Mari archive[125] and at Tell Bi'a.[126]

They describe a campaign of Yaḫdun-Līm against some rulers of the Euphrates valley, among them Baḫlukū-Līm,[127] king of Tuttul and the land of the Amnaneans[128] (*šar Tuttul^{ki} u māt Amnāni*).[129] Those rulers were at the same time in charge of cities as well as tribal chiefs.[130] In some texts Yaḫdun-Līm is qualified as king of Mari, Tuttul[131] and the Hanneans.[132]

The supremacy of the kings of Mari over Tuttul continued until Šamšī-Adad broadened his kingdom in Upper Mesopotamia. He installed his son, Yasmaḫ-Adad in the office of king of Mari. Tuttul belonged to his dominions where he also had a palace in which he sometimes received his father.[133] Assyrian authority over Mari soon ended after the death of Šamšī-Adad (I) when Zimrī-Līm ascended to the throne of Mari. His rule over Tuttul has also been confirmed by a number year names from Tell Bi'a.[134]

The city is finally mentioned in the prologue of the Codex Hammurabi[135] together with Mari, therefore validating Hammurabi's claim over this region. But the flow of epigraphic evidence about Tuttul then drops to a minimum after his military campaign in Syria.

---

[118] See e.g. Gudea Statue B V 28- VI 20 6n imported raw materials, Steible 1991, 162-167.

[119] Frayne 1997, 295-301 especially Text 2 and Kärki 1986, 131, Šū-Sîn 20b, r. I'5-I'9,

[120] For more on the Amorites in the period of the third dynasty of Ur and later see Klengel 1992, 33-80.

[121] Kärki 1986, 131, Šū-Sîn 20b, IV 21-27.

[122] See Pettinato 1972.

[123] Durand 1985, 147-172.

[124] Klengel 1992, 39-80 (Chapter II.1.).

[125] See E. Strommenger in MDOG 109, 11 note 10 with a list of Mari texts and Klengel 1992, 46-47.

[126] Krebernik in MDOG 122, 123, 125 and 126.

[127] His name appears in some texts from Tell Bi'a. See Kohlmeyer – Strommenger in MDOG 127 (1995), 50 see M. Krebernik.

[128] Klengel 1992, 50; TUAT II/4 (1988) 501-504.

[129] Dossin 1955, 14, Col III 5-7.

[130] More on the tribes from the time of the Mari-archive in Anbar 1991 with further bibliography.

[131] The presence of Yaḫdun-Līm in Tell Bi'a is also documented by some tablets found on the site. See Strommenger-Kohlmeyer in MDOG 127 (1995), 50 see M. Krebernik.

[132] Klengel 1992, 50.

[133] Einwag 1998, 50 note 131.

[134] Strommenger-Kohlmeyer in MDOG 127 (1995), 50 see M. Krebernik.

[135] Strommenger in MDOG 109 (1977), 13 cf. Col. IV 13.

Areas	EBA characteristic features	burial	MBA characteristic features	burial	Later characteristic features	burial
B	houses	+			Roman/Byz. graves	+
C	city-wall, Houses,	+	city-wall, houses, *Anten-Tempel*		Roman graves	+
E	mausolea, Palace B, "Pfeilergebäude", graveyard, silo	+	Palace A, cuneiform tablets	+	LB Houses and graves; Roman graveyard, Byzant. monastery	+
F		?	big, communal building (temple of Dagæn?)			
H	city-wall?	+				
K	city-wall		city-wall	?		?
M	city-wall	+	city-wall	+		
U	graveyard	+			graves	+
V	graveyard	+				

Fig. 5 Brief overview of the excavation areas at Tell Bi'a

II. Analysis

II.1 The site and the excavations between 1980 and 1995

Tell Bi'a is located close to the modern city of Raqqa (Syria) near the confluence of Balīḫ and Euphrates (Plate 1).[136] The tell has an irregular shape, though more or less resembling to a triangle. Its total length measures approximately 850 m, its maximum width about 650 m (Plate 4). With its surface covering 36 ha, it is among the eight largest sites in the Big Bend Area of the Euphrates.[137]

On the tell there are nineteen elevations or mounds which were labelled with the letters "A" to "T" by the excavators. Eva Strommenger led the excavations in twelve campaigns from 1980 to 1995. To examine the structure of the tell, several of the mounds were surveyed (Plate 4 and Fig. 5). Two more areas, "U" and "V, were excavated in the plain near the tell.[138]

Preliminary reports were published in MDOG 113-127. The excavators expect the final report to cover ten volumes limited to the description of features and finds, keeping evaluation to a minimum, thus providing solid groundwork for further analysis and interpretation.[139]

The first volume of the final report treats the burials.[140] It is a compilation of all pre-Roman graves and tombs (more than 220 single and multiple burials) found within Tell Bi'a.

The *intramural* burials are referred to by the north and East co-ordinates within the ten meter grid plan of the site followed by a grave number for each quadrant (N co-ordinate/E co-ordinate: number). The numbering has no stratigraphical connotation, but merely follows the order of excavation. The burials in the mausolea (*G = Grabbau*) are identified by the number of the building and the room (*R*). The *extramural* burials are recognised by the area (U or V) and a grave-number. A catalogue of the burials belonging to the EBA is found in the appendix of this paper.

The stratigraphy and architecture in the central mound E[141] and the areas, B, C, F, K and M[142] have already been published. The final publications and preliminary reports[143] already allow for a brief overview of the main excavated features (Fig. 5).

The settlement of Tell Bi'a was a large city distinguished by the presence of city-walls during the EBA and MBA and great communal buildings like palaces and temples. This generally fits in well with the picture received from the written sources.[144]

The largest MBA occupation ended with signs of physical force in Palace A.[145]

After the MBA, only a limited area concentrating around the central parts of the tell was occupied. It is not yet clear whether or not there was a hiatus between the MBA and LBA settlement.

After the Bronze Age the tell remained unoccupied until

---

[136] According to Strommenger 1977, 5 the present-day distance from the site to the Euphrates is 2,5 km and 3 km to the Balīḫ.
[137] McClellan 2000, 413 Fig.1. The other cities are Tell Aḥmar measuring about 50? ha, Tell Halawa A and B 17 ha, Tell Selenkahiye 15-20 ha, Tell Banat 30 ha, Tell Sweyhat 30 ha, Karkemiš 42 ha and Tell Hadīdī 56 ha. In comparison Tell Mardīḫ/Ebla is about 60 ha large (Matthiae 1997, 180).
[138] It is quite plausible that the graves from both areas located over several hundred meters away from each other, once were part of a large necropolis.
[139] Strommenger – Kohlmeyer 1998, 5.
[140] Strommenger – Kohlmeyer 1998. The data used for this analysis is taken from this book unless otherwise noted.
[141] Strommenger – Kohlmeyer 2000, Miglus – Strommenger 2007.
[142] Miglus – Strommenger 2002.
[143] See MDOG 113-127.
[144] See Chapter I.3..
[145] Miglus – Strommenger 2007, 11.

the Roman Period. Some graveyards and thin settlement layers have survived from this period. In the Late Roman/Early Byzantine Period settlement activity increased. A very early Byzantine Monastery was built on central mound "E". Apart from some Islamic Period graves the tell reveals no traces of human activity after this period.

II.2   The site chronology

The first step in the analysis of the mortuary practices at Tell Bi´a is to assign the burial evidence to shorter time-spans while taking into account changes in the settlement structure.[146] The excavators published a seriation,[147] including graves and tombs from stratified layers in different areas as well as graves from the unstratified cemetery. They divided the graves into eleven seriation groups. An examination was carried out to prove whether the seriation results fit into the known stratigraphical evidence.[148]

This examination confirmed to begin with the pertinence of the seriation groups 1-7 to finer chronological division. Seriation groups 8-11 contained considerably less artefacts. Their chronological significance is therefore consequently lower.[149] All the graves from seriation groups 8-11 belong to MBA LBA contexts, their accurate subdivision is therefore not of any interest for the present study.

As previously mentioned in Chapter II.1, the stratigraphical evidence of mound E is already available for the EBA. As a result it becomes worthwhile to take a closer look at those graves as well as other structures from that area. Mound E is the highest elevation at Tell Bi´a and it was excavated most intensively during the twelve campaigns. Sixty-three burial features were found in the central part above and below Palace A. The published data are already sufficient to create a roughly sketched outline of a Harris-matrix connecting the funerary evidence with the main architectural features in this area (Plate 5).

The oldest level in this mound associated with funerary evidence revealed six mausolea (*Grabbauten*).[150] Below the mausolea in quadrants 23/46 and 23/47 and below G2R3, some architectural remains were recorded. Because the excavated surface in this low-lying level is rather limited, the interpretation of the structures' function is relatively unsure. Given that no burial remains were found here, the level is omitted in the periodisation.[151]

However, it is important to note that in these older buildings, a greater proportion of some pottery types was found that do not appear later on: e.g. drinking vessels with slightly inturned walls and with rims, that are either bevelled on the inside, unpronounced, or simply thickened.[152] Such drinking vessels were not used exclusively in public buildings, but also appear in contemporary domestic contexts in sounding 21/62 West.[153]

The burials in the mausolea all belong to the seriation groups 1 and 2. The oldest graves in cemetery U belong to the same seriation groups. The mentioned drinking vessel types are characteristic of a period just prior to the construction of the mausolea. They are also missing from the oldest burials in cemetery U, thus giving a *terminus post quem* for the beginning of the cemetery.

Palace B was built (it is a *terminus ante quem* for the seriation groups 1-2[154]) on top of the mausolea, at about the same time as the *"Pfeilergebäude"* (pillar-building of Bauphase 1).[155] No graves are associated with this phase on mound E.

After Palace B had burnt down (*terminus post quem* for the graves above the Palace), the *"Pfeilergebäude"* still remained in use (Bauphase 2-4).[156] Some badly preserved architectural features and graves of seriation groups 4-7 were found above the ruins of Palace B. After the *"Pfeilergebäude"* was abandoned, some debris layers accumulated on top of its walls.[157] The graves of seriation group 7 were recovered from these layers.[158] Only few architectural remains, a silo and some installations, are known from this time.[159]

In the next period Palace A was erected and came into use. The ceramic assemblage from the foundation trench was examined by B. Einwag.[160] It includes shapes typical of the late EBA, but some new ones distinctive of the MBA were discovered as well.[161] The earliest occupation phase of Palace A is characterised by a MBA ceramic assemblage.[162] This provides the *terminus ante quem* for the layers below Palace A. The latest occupation phase of Palace A (*"Jüngere Umnutzung"*,[163] in the matrix on Plate 5 this phase is referred to as: Palace AL) contained

---

[146] See Chapter I.1.1..
[147] Strommenger – Kohlmeyer 1998, 121-129, app. 4.
[148] Strommenger – Kohlmeyer 1998, 128-129.
[149] Strommenger – Kohlmeyer 1998, 129.
[150] Strommenger – Kohlmeyer 2000, 5-8 and Pl. 3 and 4.
[151] The pottery types from the official buildings are related to the vessels from the mausolea above them. Therefore, the older layers may be viewed as an older sub-phase of Phase I. This periodisation is of course preliminary, further excavation might change the subdivision or its numbering.
[152] E.g. Strommenger – Kohlmeyer 2000, Pl. 5/38-49, Pl. 6/24, 26-36.
[153] Strommenger – Kohlmeyer 2000, 89 and 93/Figs. 2, 3 and 5. Some sub-types are characteristic only for levels 15 and 16 and for the public buildings below the mausolea, thus revealing their contemporariness. In Strommenger–Kohlmeyer 2000, 93/ Fig.3 18% of all rims display the shapes mentioned above.
[154] Some C[14]-samples were taken from this palace. MDOG 125, 61-68 by J. Görsdorf and Görsdorf 2000.
[155] Strommenger – Kohlmeyer 2000, 42.
[156] Strommenger – Kohlmeyer 2000, 43-52.
[157] Strommenger – Kohlmeyer 2000, App. 9.
[158] Strommenger – Kohlmeyer 2000, 52.
[159] Strommenger – Kohlmeyer 2000, 53-64.
[160] Einwag 1998, *Keramikkomplex* 2.
[161] Einwag 1998, 81.
[162] Einwag 1998, *Keramikkomplex* 3.
[163] Einwag 1998, 51 Fig. 15.

Fig. 6 Typological scheme for subterranean burials (according to Carter – Parker 1995, Table 14.2)

some graves. These graves, as well as the ones from the layers on top of Palace A, belong to seriation groups 8-11.

Owing to the stratigraphical evidence described above, it is possible to establish a periodisation of Tell Bi'a for a time-span earlier than the MBA Palace A:

- *Phase I* (young)[164] is equivalent with the time of the mausolea in mound E and the beginning of the cemeteries U and V. The connected seriation groups are groups 1 and 2.
- *Phase II* corresponds with the building and occupation of Palace B and the founding of the *"Pfeilergebäude"*. The graves of seriation group 3 can be associated to this phase.[165] Cemetery U and depression H contain burials from this phase.
- *Phase III* is equivalent with the later occupation of the *"Pfeilergebäude"* (Bauphase 2-4) and the time interval prior to the building of Palace A. The burials associated to this phase belong to seriation groups 4-7. During the excavation it was mostly impossible to establish from which debris layers the graves were dug. However, the superposition of the graves of seriation group 7 and the *"Pfeilergebäude"* (Plate 5), and the fact that graveyard U ended with seriation group 6 supports the division of this phase into two chronological *sub-phases*.[166]
- *Phase IIIa* corresponds with the use of levels 2-4 of the *"Pfeilergebäude"* associated to the graves from seriation groups 4-6.
- *Phase IIIb* corresponds with the time span after the *"Pfeilergebäude"* was abandoned and the time before Palace A was built. Graves from seriation group 7 are associated with this phase. The first occupation phase of Palace A already belongs to the MBA. This phase also brings to a close the EBA

occupation at Tell Bi'a. B. Einwag's work has already demonstrated that the ceramic repertoire of this phase has a transitional character.[167]

II.3 Description and typology of the burial evidence[168]

E. Carter and A Parker presented a typology of burial forms established for the 3rd millennium Syro-Anatolian region.[169] Since their publication some new burial types have appeared that do not fit into their model. Their classification therefore needs to be amended.[170] The most evident attribute, and hence the most apparent level of symbolism,[171] is whether the burial was originally located above or below the ground.[172]

Above ground burials[173] can be subdivided by their architectural characteristics. *Subterranean* burials can be subdivided according to E. Carter and A. Parker (Fig. 6).[174] Only three *subterranean* types appear at Tell Bi'a: the simple *pit-grave* without stone covering (though occasionally a mud brick cover was recorded), the constructed, earth-cut *shaft tomb* with one or two side chambers, and the *pot-grave*, consisting of a simple ware pottery container.

It is also necessary to differentiate by location. At Tell Bi'a there are both, *intramural* as well as *extramural* burials.

Another distinctive feature is the functional period of a grave. There are graves with *single* as well as *multiple* (simultaneous) burials, and ones which served more than once. Sometimes it is difficult to distinguish between

---

[164] Further referred to only as Phase I. In this study neither the deep sounding 21/62 West (Strommenger – Kohlmeyer 2000, 70-103), nor the architectural remains below the mausolea are taken into account (see also notes 154 and 155), as neither of them produced burial remains. Future excavations will most probably change the labelling of the phases.

[165] The ceramic material from Palace B compares well with that from the graves of seriation group 3 (Strommenger – Kohlmeyer 2000, 41). Indirect evidence supports this finding as there are graves with seriation groups 1 and 2 below Palace B. Above Palace B are graves from seriation groups 4-7. This on its own already makes a chronological overlapping of Palace B and the graves of seriation group 3 likely.

[166] This working hypothesis will be revised in the following chapters.

[167] Einwag 1995, 75-81 and 147-149.

[168] The data of the burials are all based on Strommenger – Kohlmeyer 1998, if not marked otherwise. A reference to the publication is found in the catalogue.

[169] Carter – Parker 1995, 104-108, Table 14.2, 14.3.

[170] There are of course also types in this scheme which do not appear at Tell Bi'a.

[171] For more about the possible symbolic meanings see Chapter II.1.1.

[172] Structures that were probably dug half-way into the ground while their coverings were visible above the surface are also known from a number of Mesopotamian (see e.g. Eickhoff 1993 with a list of other sites) and probably North-Syrian (see Valdés 1999, 120-121) sites. This variant does not appear at Tell Bi'a, which is the reason why it was not included in the present typology.

[173] Monumental chamber tombs and monumental tumuli at Cooper 2006.

[174] For further definition of the single types see Carter – Parker 104-108.

	Number of chambers	Max. dimensions outside (m)	Chamber dimensions (m)			Entrance width (m)		
			R1	R2	R3	Entrance (G2)	From G2 to G1	From G2 to G3
G1	-	W:>7,2	-	-	-	-	-	-
G2	-	W: 6,3	-	-	W:~3,70	-	-	-
G3	3	10,8x8,4 90,72 m²	5,8x1,8 10,44 m²	5,8x1,5 8,7 m²	5,8x1,9 11,2 m²	1,1	1,05	0,85
G4	3	11,1x6,2 68,82 m²	3,5x 3,1 10,85 m²	3,5x 1,4 4,9 m²	3,5x1,7 5,95 m²	0,8	0,85	0,55
G5	1	6,0x3,8 22,8 m²		4,3x2,2 9,46 m²		original (West): 1,15 secondary (East): 1,3		
G6	3(?)	>10x8,2 more than 82 m²	6x2,8 16,8 m²	6x2 12 m²	6x?	1,4	1,6	-

Fig. 7 The dimensions of the mausolea

multiple and repeatedly used burials.

It is necessary to distinguish between *inhumations* and *cremations*. At Tell Bi'a all graves exclusively contained *inhumations*. The skeleton orientations are discussed together with the spatial analysis of the graves.

II.3.1 Phase I

Above ground as well as *subterranean* graves from this phase are known from central mound E (*intramural*) as well as from graveyards U and V (*extramural)*.

The *above ground* structures cleared on mound E are all *intramural*. Six such mausolea[175] have been partially or fully unearthed (Plate 6). Two main architectural types are discerned: tripartite[176] (G3 and G4 and G6 probably also G1, G2) and single chambered ones (G5).

The dimensions of the mausolea vary a lot as can be seen in Fig. 7.

The excavators recorded a preserved height of 2 m for G3 and 1,8 m for G4.

The buildings were of mud brick and without bedding trenches. G3 had a stone foundation below the mud bricks. The floors and both sides of the walls were covered in white plaster. The entrances as well as some of the interior door passages were framed with mud bricks.

The mausolea G3, G4 and G5 were completely excavated, the third room of G6 was eroded, while G1 and G2 were only partially cleared.

The mausolea were not built at the same time[177] but were all visible at the end of their existence. They all contained more than one inhumation. My suggestion is that the rooms of the mausolea were used and re-used for inhumations over a longer period of time. In other words, they were *multiply used* facilities.[178]

There is evidence to support this. For example, in *G2R3*, two floor levels were recorded. Otherwise, in *G6R2*, there were two inhumations: 23/46:3 and 23/46:2. 23/46:2 had been disturbed and changing its location toward the eastern wall of the room. By contrast burial 23/46:3 was lying undisturbed on the floor of R2, next to the southern wall and close to the entrance.[179] The different states of preservation of the skeletons indicate that the bodies had not been buried at the same time.

There were also thirty-one *extramural subterranean* burials belonging to *phase I*. Five were found by workmen in a sand pit. The grave goods were collected, but there is no hard information as to the burial forms.

The other graves are from graveyard U (Plate 7). Three graves are simple *pit-graves* and twenty-three are *shaft tombs,* generally consisting of one chamber, and in one case of two.[180] The shafts were normally sealed with mud brick.

During phase I only Grave U:15 was used twice. One skeleton was recorded lying in the chamber, the other was found in the shaft. Some *shaft tombs*[181] were used for burying people until phase III. They were thus used as *single* tombs as well as a *multiply used* tombs with a *secondary* burial. There are no signs of *multiple burials*.

The dimensions of the individual graves varied between 0,8 m and 2,8 m, for both shaft tombs and pit-graves. A discussion as to the possibilities of linking this discrepancy to age, sex, or status will follow in the next chapter.

---

[175] They are referred to as *"Grabbauten"* in the publications, here they have been given the abbreviation G. Strommenger – Kohlmeyer: 1998: 48-49; the outside walls were plastered and lacking any evidence hinting to the presence of foundation trenches.

[176] For possible interpretations of tripartite buildings in Mesopotamian in funerary context see Al-Khalesi 1977.

[177] According to Strommenger – Kohlmeyer 1998:48-49; the oldest buildings were G1 and G2. This is revealed by a later, walled-up south passage in G2. G 3 and G4 were built later, their floor levels being 0.7-0,8 m deeper than the highest surrounding pebble-street. To the south there were no buildings, only a large open area. Here G5 and finally G6 were built which caused the moving of the door of G5 from east to west.

[178] Also Strommenger in MDOG 126, 18.

[179] Strommenger – Kohlmeyer 1998: 73-76, Pl. 97 and 98. The exact location inside the room is not given.

[180] Burial U:43.

[181] Graves U:7, U:32, U:34 and U:43.

Digging a larger grave evidently required more work. However, it took much less effort to dig the largest grave than it took to build a mausoleum.

The building of a mausoleum calls for well organised collaboration within a limited time interval. This had to happen around the occurrence of death of the first person buried, possibly during the *rite de marge*.[182] If this was the case, then there were considerably more *dramatis personae*[183] involved during this second stage, than during a "normal" burial.

The construction of an unusual grave with a markedly significant involvement from the community singled out the deceased. It acted as a statement as to the social importance of the departed individual as well as that of his successors.

II.3.2 Phase II

No graves from this phase were excavated on mound E. The *intramural* graves within "depression H" bear no real stratigraphical evidence. They were discovered during the excavation of a clay-quarry to provide building material for the excavation house. Only the grave goods were collected by the workmen. No records were made as to the burials themselves.

Ten burials were discovered in cemetery U (Plate 8). All were *shaft-graves*, and most of them were *primary* burials. The only suspicion of the presence of a secondary burial occurred in the case of a recent corpse lowered into grave U:34.[184] Grave U:7 contained ceramics of phase II in its filling. Some pottery was also found in grave U:25, however it was not clearly associable with any of the three individuals buried there later. It is possible that the pottery belonged to a disturbed primary burial.

The lengths of the newly dug graves varied between 1,60 m and 2,50 m. This variance is smaller than in those of phase I, but the sample is too small for interpretation.

Above ground funerary structures are missing in this phase. A planned alteration of the settlement structure was probably the reason for this finding. The area located on top of the mausolea was carefully levelled out to form a terrace on top of which a palace was subsequently erected.[185] This modification of the settlement structure may represent an intended break with the foregoing tradition.[186] To what extent it too may have served as an act of legitimisation is discussed in the chapters below.

II.3.3 Phase IIIa

In total 54 graves, consisting of 26 shaft tombs and 21 pit-graves, are ascribed to this phase. The poor preservation of the remaining graves does not permit any closer determination. The grave lengths are independent of their locations. The lengths of *intramural* as well as *extramural* graves varied between 0,70 m and 2,80 m, similarly to the ones from phase I.

Intramural burials were found on mound B (6 graves), mound C (6 graves) and mound E (23 graves). The graves on mounds B and C were dug below or close to the houses. As for mound E, it is not certain whether the graves belonged to the few architectural remains or whether they were part of a new cemetery.[187]

Four graves were found in area M near the city-wall, of which three contained the skeletons of children, the fourth was only partially excavated. A pottery collection was recovered from depression H. It may have belonged to a grave near the city-wall, but no skeletal remains were found.

The area above the burned remains of palace B was again used for funerary purposes. All these graves were *subterranean*.

Seventeen *extramural* graves were found in cemetery U. The cemetery was no longer used after this phase.[188] Secondary burials occurred in a higher number than in earlier phases. As the cemetery continued to fill up, the number of secondary burials increased, and finally the cemetery had to be abandoned.

II.3.4 Phase IIIb

There are 26 *intramural* graves from this phase. Four were found on mound B, ten on mound C, eight on mound E, one on mound F, and two near the city-wall on mound K.

The pit-grave seems to have been the most common burial form (20). Only one shaft-grave[189] was found. At this time the first pot-grave appeared. In five cases the burial form is uncertain because they were either only

---

[182] See chapter I.1.2.

[183] I.e. those, who were involved in the preparation of the burial. This had no incidence on the number of people who took part in the interment.

[184] The second burial in U:34 was not seriated, because only one pot was associated with the skeleton. We are able to date the second burial by placing it between the date of the first and the third burial. The first burial in this grave belongs to seriation group 1 (Phase I). The younger burial belongs to seriation group 4 (Phase IIIa). The pot belongs to type WT/F 6 (see chapter II.6) and was not used after Phase II (Plate 19).

[185] Strommenger – Kohlmeyer 1998, 2000.

[186] See e.g. Strommenger – Kohlmeyer 2000, 13. They interpreted the mausolea as the burial sites of a dynasty of sovereigns of Tuttul. The intended discarding of this area would thus have stood as a symbol for a new group coming to power with no obligations to the previous one.

[187] Only a few architectural remains belong to phase IIIa west of the "*Pfeilergebäude*" (Strommenger – Kohlmeyer 2000, 28-29 and app. 6).

[188] Eight graves in graveyard U are not stratified and therefore not included in the seriation. There seems to have been a discrepancy between the stratigraphy and the seriation in U:32. The youngest burial seems to belong to seriation group 6, but the assemblage from layers below belongs to seriation group 7 (U:32äBK in Strommenger – Kohlmeyer 1998, app. 4). All vessel types in U:32äBK already existed by phase IIIa. Hence, a dating of the material to this phase seems more justified.

[189] Shaft-grave 25/48:7 also had two vessels which may belong to seriation group 6 (phase IIIa).

II. Analysis

partially excavated or otherwise badly damaged.

No *extramural* burial places are known from this phase. This phenomenon will be discussed later on.

II.4. The demographic analysis

During the excavations, the anthropologist W. Wolska carried out a preliminary examination of the skeletons. The final results will be published in a separate volume on the records from physical anthropology.[190] However, age and gender determinations for most of the graves are already available.

The following summary on age and gender representation cannot be taken as a definite palaeodemographical analysis. Too much data is missing in order to evaluate the anthropological remains in direct comparison to the age distribution of the living population. Even an estimation of population size is delicate.[191] This chapter will focus on finding a connection between the age and gender representation and, whether or not it influenced burial custom. The calculation of life expectancy[192] may naturally only be taken as an approximation due to the restrictions imposed by the small sample size.

The aged skeletal remains are grouped into eight categories: baby (0-1 years), child I (1-7 years), child II (7-14 years), *subadultus* (14-20 years), *adultus* (20-30 years), *maturus* I (30-40 years) *maturus* II (40-50 years) and *maturus* III (50-60 years).

The tombs dating from phase I-IIIb produced 121 skeletons suitable for age identification. The proportion of babies and children is over 45% which seems to be representative of that time.[193] It is however atypical that the peak of the child-mortality rate falls within the child I category[194] rather than within the baby category (Fig. 8).

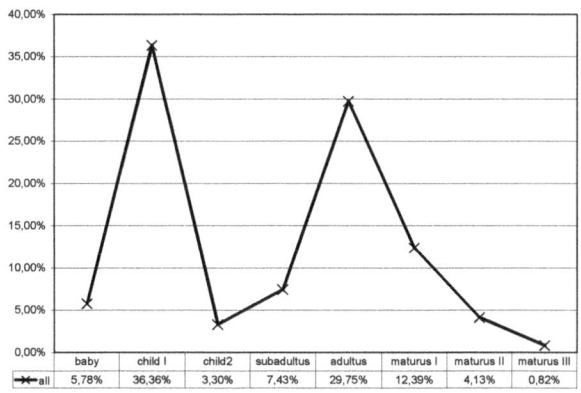

Fig. 8 The mortality rates in Tell Bi'a during phase I-IIIb

Among the adult population, the mortality rate was highest between the age of 20 and 30. For the whole period, from phase I to IIIb, life expectancy was at 17,15 years. The expected life-span in the over 14 population increased to 28,15 years. These estimations will be refined in the next chapters.

II.4.1 Phase I

Fifty-nine skeletons from this phase were identified, 32 (54%) from the six *intramural* mausolea[195] and 27 (46%) from the graves of cemetery U. The age of four skeletons (6%) could not be determined. The proportion of male and female skeletons was balanced (21 skeletons each), although 17 skeletons (29%) did not qualify for gender identification.

The mortality rate reached its peak in the *adultus* group (21 skeletons, 35%) (Fig. 9). The mortality rate of children was 25% (15 skeletons), which is lower than observed in comparative materials.[196]

The lower representation of children in the archaeological sample can be explained in several ways. It can result from poor conservation of the bones of small children, or age specific burial traditions connected with particular burial areas. Because of the underrepresentation of children, the calculated life expectancy is quite high: 22,13 years. The life expectancy in the population over 14 increases to 28,12 years.

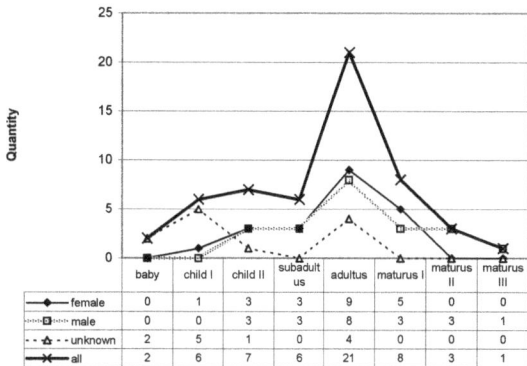

Fig. 9 The mortality rates in phase I

---

[190] It will be volume IX of the final report.
[191] A formula for estimating the living population has been given e.g. by Acsádi – Nemeskéri 1970, used e.g. for A...mad al-"attū in Eickhoff 1993, 56.
[192] The methods which I used for calculating life-expectancy are described by Littleton 1998 with further bibliography.
[193] The expected under 15 mortality is between 30-70% according to Littleton 1998, 41 cf. Buikstra – Mielke 1985.
[194] Compare with the analysis of Littleton 1998 esp. page 41, Fig. 6.1

[195] G1 and G2 was only partially excavated, G6R3 was eroded.
[196] See Chapter II.4. and note 191.

	female		male		unknown gender		Σ
	intra-mural (mausoleum)	*extra-mural* (cemetery)	*intra-mural* (mausoleum)	*extra-mural* (cemetery)	*intra-mural* (mausoleum)	*extra-mural* (cemetery)	
baby						*Sh:2*	15
child 1	1					*P:1* *Sh:4*	
child 2	3		3			*Sh:1*	
sub-adultus	2	*Sh:1*	3				6
adultus	6	*Sh:2+1?*	5	*Sh:3+* *Shs:1?*		*P:1* *Sh:4*	34
matu-rus I	2	*Sh:3*	3				
matu-rus II			1	*P:1* *Sh:1*			
matu-rus III			1				
un-known age		*Sh:1?*			2	*Sh:1*	4
un-known num-ber					G6R1, G2R3, G4R1 G3R3	V:1,2,3,4,5;	
Σ	14	6+2?	16	5+1?	2	13	59

Fig. 10 Age and gender distribution of the burials in phase I

Mauso-leum	Chamber	Number of burials	Ages	Gender
G1	R3	no data	no data	no data
G2	R3	multiple	no data	no data
G3	R1	6	3 x child II 1 x *adultus* 1 x *maturus* I 1 x *maturus* III	3 male 3 female
	R2	0		
	R3	multiple	no data	no data
G4	R1	no data	no data	no data
	R2	0		
	R3	17	1 x child I 3 x child II 4 x *subadultus* 7 x *adultus* 2 x *maturus* I	6 x male 11 x female
G5		4	1 x *adultus* 2 x *maturus* I 1 x *maturus* II	4 x male
G6	R1	min.2	no data	min.2
	R2 (23/46: 2&3)	2	1 x *subadultus* 1 x no data	1 x male 1 x no data
	R3	1+ (eroded)	no data	no data

Fig. 11 Age and gender distribution in the mausolea

In looking at the life-expectancy of the male and female populations separately,[197] we notice that it was more than three years higher among males. This means that at birth males could expect to live to an age of 23,8 years, but females only to 20,5 years. The difference remained the same in the over 14 population where life expectancy for men was 29,8 years, and for women only 26,4.

In order to answer the question of whether gender or age specific burial costumes influenced the place of the burial, we have to probe the age and gender

distribution in the *intramural* mausolea and *extramural* cemetery separately (Fig. 10).

The mausolea contained 32 skeletons identified as to age and sex. No babies are contained in this group. However, there were seven children (22%), five *subadultus* (16%), eighteen *adultus* and *maturus* (56%) and two of unknown age (6%). There were fourteen (44%) female and sixteen (50%) male skeletons, the gender of two of them (6%) was undeterminable. This distribution fits in well with the general age and gender representation of this phase.

A comparison of the figures from the mausolea among each other renders a less homogeneous picture (Fig. 11).

Only the skeletons of three chambers were fully aged and sexed. G5 contained exclusively male adults, whereas in G3R1 male and female were equally represented, and in G4R3 there were almost twice as many females than males.

In two mausolea (G3 and G4), no human remains were found in the vestibules, but several skeletons were discovered in the two side-chambers. Two skeletons were found in the vestibule of G6. Only one was intact; as to the other no anatomical order was detected.

The number of individual remains recorded in the burial chambers varied a lot from two (G6R2) to seventeen (G4R1). Such differences are best explained with significant divergences in the functional periods of the buildings, or by possible customised purposes of the chambers.

In all, twenty-seven skeletons from the *extramural* cemetery were identified. There were two babies (7,5%), six children (22%), one *subadultus* (4%), sixteen (59%) *adultus* and *maturus*. Only two skeletons (7,5%) were not aged. Eight (30%) were acknowledged as female and six (22%) as male. However, almost half of the skeletons (13 skeletons=48%) could not be sexed.

The age and gender of the remains do not seem to be connected with the different *subterranean* grave forms. The skeleton of a child (U:24), an adult (U:10) and a mature man (U:49) were found in individual pit-graves. All the others had been buried in shaft-tombs.

There does seem to be any connection between the size of the graves and the age of their occupants. The graves of the babies and children under 14 were 0,80-1,40 m long. The population over 14 were buried in tombs between 1,70 and 2,80 m long. There seems to be no difference between the dimensions of the female and the male graves (Fig. 12).

A grave shorter than 1,70 m would be large enough to bury an adult person in a fœtal position. For example grave U:20[198] was 1,7 m long and the northeastern chamber of U:43[199] was only 1,40 m long. However, the tombs had to have enough space to contain grave goods, a circumstance which needed to be taken into consideration during the preparation of the grave. Some of the shaft-graves, especially those with two chambers, were intended to hold several bodies.

Only one grave, U:34alt1, being the longest, does not fit into this pattern. It contained more than one body. A baby was the first occupant, the two later ones, a male child (II) and an adult female individual, were deposited at some later date. The length of the grave (2,80 m) suggests that it originally was intended to contain an adult, indicating that some of the graves may have been dug before the identity of the deceased individual was known.

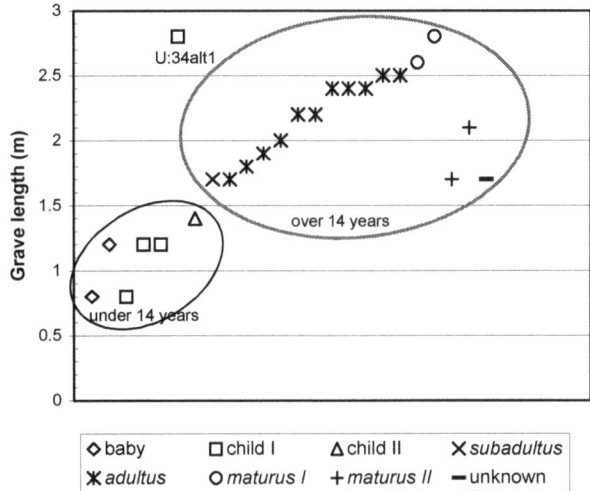

Fig. 12 The lengths of the subterranean graves during phase I

II.4.2 Phase II

The sample from this phase is very small, only ten skeletons were recovered. No burial evidence was found on mound E. *Subterranean* tombs were discovered in depression H, near the city wall and in cemetery U. All the new graves were *shaft-graves*.

---

[197] To the data of the female and male half of the unspecified skeletons were added.

[198] Strommenger – Kohlmeyer 1998, pl. 113
[199] Strommenger – Kohlmeyer 1998, pl. 130

	female		male		unknown gender		Σ
	near the city-wall	extramural (cemetery)	near the city-wall	extramural (cemetery)	near the city-wall	extramural (cemetery)	
baby							1
child I						1	
child II							
sub-adultus							0
adultus		1					4
maturus I				1			
maturus II				2			
maturus III							
unknown age					2	3	5
unknown number						2	
Σ	0	1	0	3	2	3	10

Fig. 13 Age and gender distribution in phase II

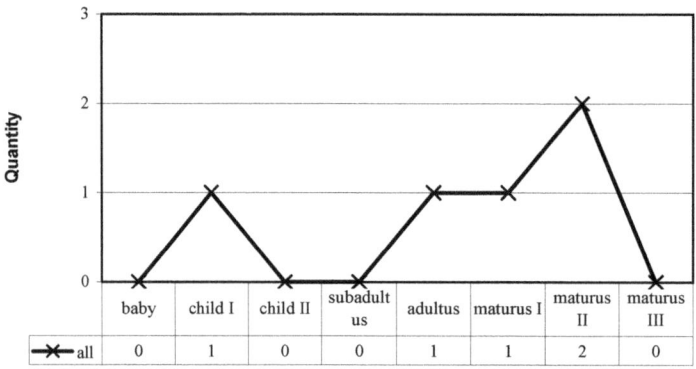

Fig. 14 The mortality rates in phase II

	female			male			unknown gender			Σ
	intra-mural	near the city-wall	extra-mural (cemetery)	intra-mural	near the city-wall	extra-mural (cemetery)	intra-mural	near the city-wall	extra-mural (cemetery)	
baby							P:1+ ?1		P:1	30
child I				Sh:2			P:10+ Sh:?1	1+ P:2	Sh:3+ P:1 Shs:4	
child II		Sh:1		P:2						
subadultus		Sh:1		P:1+ Sh:1						3
adultus	P:1 Sh:?1			Sh:?1	Sh:?1	Sh:?2	P:1		Sh:1+ Shs:1	15
maturus I	Sh:2			Sh:1	P:1	Sh:2				
maturus II										
maturus III										
unknown age							P:1+ Sh:4	P:1	Sh:3	9
unknown number							by 5 ensemble were remained from the skeletons			
Σ	4	0	2	8	2	4	19	4	14	57

Fig. 15 Distribution of burial types and age and gender representations in phase IIIa

Assessing the age and gender percentages of phase II is hardly worth-while. Only one child, one adult female, three adult males and five skeletons of unknown age and gender were recovered (Fig. 13).

The established life-expectancy of 30,8 years is longer than that established for the earlier phase, given that the peak occurs in the *maturus* II category (Fig. 14). This is probably due to the small sample-size.

The child's grave has a length of 1,60 m which fits into the pattern established for phase I. The adult graves were longer varying from 1,9 to 2,5 m.

II.4.3 Phase IIIa

Fifty-seven skeletons from this sub-phase were identified. Thirty-one (55%) were found within the city walls (mound B, C and E), six (10%) near the city-walls (mound E and *depression H*) and twenty (45%) outside the city in cemetery U (Fig. 15).

Forty-seven skeletons were categorised according to age. They comprise three (7%) babies,

twenty-one (47%) children I, three (7%) children II, three (9%) *subadultus*, and fifteen (30%) adult skeletons. A majority, consisting of 32 skeletons (64%), was apt for sex determination. Only six (12%) female and thirteen (24%) male graves were recorded (Fig. 16).

- child mortality increased, resulting from epidemics.
- phase IIIa included burials from mounds B and C, where most of the recorded tombs belonged to children, while lacking material from the preceding phases.
- The children began to be treated differently than in earlier phases.

More attention will be given to these thoughts in the following chapters. It is evidently it hard to archaeologically verify the break-out of an epidemic. However, in the case that the tendency towards higher child mortality rates persists through the next phases, preference should then be given to the possibility that this was a cultural phenomenon rather than a pathological one.

The life expectancy at birth was very low, only 12,77 years. This is partly due to the improved perceptibility of children in the archaeological record. The population older than 14 years had a life-expectancy of 27 years, one year less that of phase I.

A similar pattern can be discerned in phase I in comparing the grave sizes with the age distribution of the dead. Children were buried in graves measuring from 0,7 to 1,5 m, and adults in graves from 1,6 to 2,2 m (Fig. 17).

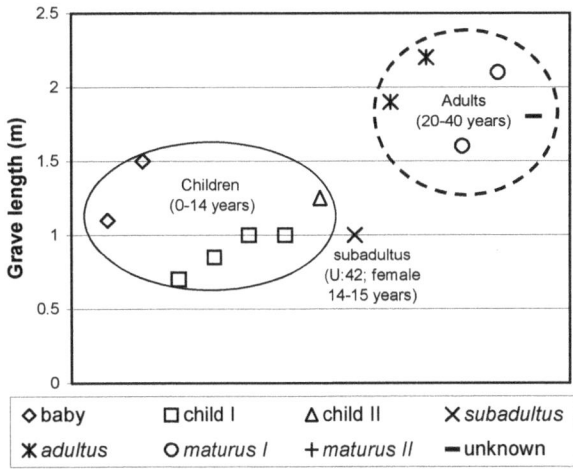

Fig. 17 The lengths of subterranean graves in phase IIIa

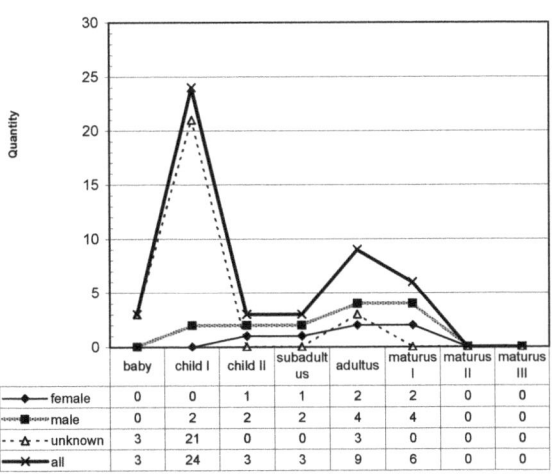

Fig. 16 The mortality rates in phase IIIa

Babies were found buried only in pit-graves. The older children and adults were buried in both shaft- and pit-graves as well as in some of the shafts in cemetery U as secondary burials (Fig. 15).[200]

The increased occurrence of children may have a number of explanations:

Grave U:42 (Plate 9) contained a skeleton of a 14-15 year old girl. The grave measured only 1 m, which indicates that she had been buried in the manner of a child. The transition from childhood to adulthood seems to have taken place at an older age. It is difficult to assess from only one sample to what extent marital status might have influenced the manner of how a young woman was buried.

II.4.4 Phase IIIb

All 23 skeletons identified in this sub-phase were recovered from the city area (mounds B, C, E, F, K).

---

[200] In Fig. 15 the distribution of the burial types is also noted: *P = pit-grave, Sh = shaft-grave* and *Shs = shaft-grave used secondarily*. The number that follows is the number of burials belonging to each category.

	female			male			unknown gender			Σ
	intra-mural	near the city-wall	extra-mural (cemetery)	intra-mural	near the city-wall	extra-mural (Cemetery)	intra-mural	near the city-wall	extra-mural (Cemetery)	
baby							*P:*2 *Pot:* 1			17
child I				*P:*1			*P:*13			
child II										
subadultus										0
adultus							*P:*2			2
maturus I										
maturus II										
maturus III										
unknown age							*P:*4			
unknown number										
Σ	0	0	0	1	0	0	22	0	0	23

Fig. 18 Distribution of burial-types and of age and gender in phase IIIb

Babies and children (seventeen skeletons) made up 71% of the recorded individuals. The adult population, consisting only of two individuals, represented 12 % (Fig. 18).

The archaeological visibility of the children thus increases from 62,5% to 71%. As already proposed, the explanation for this phenomenon is most likely not due to pathology. Only two adult tombs were cleared on mound C and on plateau F. Mounds B, E and K contained child graves are represented. This is in so far as unusual that there were just as many buried adults recorded on mound E in phase IIIa as children.

This apparent physical separation of children and adults in the burial practice may reflect an alteration of status of the children within the community. This practice, if at all, is hardly perceptible for phases I and II, but a certain tendency in that direction had already begun in phase IIIa. Other than the two burials mentioned above, we are unaware of any other burial site for the remaining adult population. Hence also the difficulties of carrying out any further assessments. It is probable that another, yet unknown cemetery was established in this phase, though this time outside the city walls.

Not much can be said about the life expectancy of the people recorded from this phase, given that the data for the adult population is missing. However, it is likely that it didn't differ significantly from the ones established for the earlier phases.

The burial forms cannot be separated according to age categories, since only one *pot-grave* was unearthed. It contained the bones of a baby. All other graves were *pit-graves*.

There is not enough data to analyse the grave lengths.

II.5 Detailed examination of the spatial organisation of the graves in cemetery U and on mound E

In the preceding chapters some attention was given to the relation of the graves to the city walls. Presently, focus will be set on the spatial organisation of the graves in their relation to each other as well as to their immediate surroundings.

Generally in cemeteries graves may be organised in rows or around a significant feature in the landscape. They may also be arranged together in groups or evenly scattered. In settlements they are found under the floors of houses, or even under streets. It is interesting to observe which rooms were used for burial purposes.

Analysing all these aspects is not yet possible, given that the settlement is not completely excavated. However it is possible to take a closer look at cemetery U and mound E, wherever the data is judged adequate.

II.5.1 Phase I

The reasons standing behind the choice of designating a particular location for a burial site are an interesting issue to examine.

Cemetery U lies about 300 m north of the tell (Plate 4), near the slope of a gravel terrace. It is not clear how far the cemetery extended. However it is probable that the graves within the area of the Abbasid-Palace (Palace V) belong to the same graveyard.[201] In view of the fact that the coordinates of one grave were 25/92,[202] the cemetery must have extended at least 450 m to the west.

---

[201] Strommenger – Kohlmeyer 1998, 117
[202] Strommenger – Kohlmeyer 1998, 118

II. Analysis

It is possible that the cemetery stretched entirely along the northern gravel terrace. The terrace is approximately triangular in shape (Plate 4, marked with red and white bands) and covers about 14 ha.[203] The excavation area only included 0,7 ha, which corresponds to only 0,5% of the terrace's surface.

The gravel-conglomeration is very hard so that at first it does not seem practical to use this terrain for burial purposes. But on the other hand it allowed for shaft-graves to be used over longer periods of time, the solidity of the ground thus preventing the vaults from collapsing. Some of the graves were hence probably intended to be used several times.

Beyond the practical reasons, it is possible that the landscape also played a role in the choice of the cemetery's location. The northern slope falls down to a depression, forming possibly some kind of branch or drain leading to the Balīḫ.[204] The proximity of water could therefore also have played some symbolic role referring to images of the netherworld.

On any account, it is noteworthy that the same area was used many times over again for the same purpose. During the excavations even Roman graves were found, and today the terrain still serves as a cemetery.[205]

The graves in cemetery U are oriented either from east to west (in the western part of the excavation area) or from north to south (in its eastern part) (Plate 7). The excavators suggest that the direction of the slope was the main factor in determining the graves' orientation.[206]

All the skeletons were uncovered lying in a flexed posture, either on the left or the right side, persistently facing the shafts. There doesn't seem to be any specific bipolarisation. Men, women and children were all found in both positions (Plate 11/1). This posture was the general *practice of lying in state* at Tell Bi'a. The arrangement of the body was likely to have taken place either before the onset of *rigor mortis* which commences shortly after cessation of life (2-8 hours after death), or after the rigidity had dissipated (2-3 days later depending on atmospheric conditions).

In spite of the differences in orientation, the arrangement of the graves is not fully unsystematic. Although they are not organised in rows or any recognisable geometrical form, they seem nevertheless to cluster in groups in varying in distances from each other. In the excavated area at least six such groups can be made out. In Plate 7 they are assigned with the roman numerals I-VI and marked with circles. The distance between the neighbouring graves of one group varies between 0,5 m to 2,80 m and from 3,70 m to 8,0 m between the groups.

As for the graves' orientation with respect to the different cluster groups, we notice that only the graves of group VI were oriented near to the NS axis (Plate 11/1). The ones in which the skeletons were lying in a flexed position on the left side, displayed a 10° deviation from this axis. The graves in which the skeletons were lying in a flexed position on the left side exhibited a counter-clockwise maximum limit of 40° deviations from the NS axis. Thus, there is a maximum of 35° difference in the grave orientation within this spatial group.

The graves of groups I-V were oriented close to the EW axis. The deviations are aligned 12° clockwise and 18° counter-clockwise in relation to this axis. These values were exceeding in only two instances within group IV[207] (both 35° counter-clockwise). Thus, the maximum difference in the grave orientation was 45°, but generally it varied around 30° (Plate 11/1).

The deviation from the East-West axis may be explained with the shifting azimuth.[208]

In this sense the south-north orientation might hint to a different tradition, though probably originating in a similar religious belief. In these graves if the corpses were deposited in a flexed position on the left side, they either faced the sunrise[209] or the sunset.[210]

It has to be taken into account that the area is not completely excavated in the south and to the West, and that some graves are likely to have been eroded at the northern and eastern parts. Assuming that all groups had a similar extent,[211] then from group I roughly 80%, and from group III more than 50 % of the graves would be missing. Group II and groups IV-VI are more complete. A maximum 10−30 % of the graves disappeared because of erosion or other disturbances.

If it is agreed that the choice of the burial place in these groups was taken deliberately, and didn't happen by chance, then it is reasonable to ask the question according to which ordering principles these groups had developed.

The groups are small, as they contained only 5-7 burials in phase I. The age and gender composition is mixed,[212] therefore an age- or gender-based order is out of discussion. The similar composition of age and gender would rather suggest that small families or nuclear households[213] had their own respective burial places.

---

[203] A. Becker and K. Kohlmeyer suggested that the cemetery extended to a max. length of 800 m and max. width of 350 m in MDOG 116 (Arns et al.), 58, and probably designed the same territory.
[204] Strommenger − Kohlmeyer 1998, 82-83, 117-118, pl. 1
[205] Strommenger − Kohlmeyer, 82
[206] Strommenger − Kohlmeyer 1998, 83.

[207] Burials U:22, the skeleton had a flexed position on the left side and U:14, the skeleton had a flexed position on the right side.
[208] The azimuth here is the angle between the point at the horizon, where the sun rises and the south. This point depends on the geographical coordinates as well as the season, see also Ahnert 1983.
[209] Burials U:45 and probable U:50, where the body was lying in a flexed position on the left.
[210] Burials U:43, U:44, U:49 and U:51, where the body was lying in a flexed position on the right.
[211] The largest distance between two burials is 12,5 m in Group IV and 12,1 m in group V.
[212] 4-5 adults per group, roughly equal amount of male and female ones, plus 1-2 children − see table on Plate 7.
[213] For the definition of nuclear families and households in the Ancient

The final publication of the anthropological material will hopefully produce some results as to possible blood relationships between the skeletons, based for instance on hereditary symptoms observed on the skeletons. A systematic examination on kinship will only be possible on the evidence from DNA-analyses.

Grave U:15 seems to yield proof that it was used by a family. In the chamber an adult male was buried, then sometime later but still in phase I, a corpse of a female *maturus* I was deposited inside the shaft. The reason for this behaviour excludes the lack of free space, since even in later periods new graves were dug inside the group. It is more likely that a direct familial relationship, possibly matrimonial, had motivated this decision.

In taking a closer look at group IV, of which almost all adult skeletons were anthropologically determined, we notice a group of people consisting of 2 children, a female *subadultus* (19-22 years old), two female adults (28-30 and 30-40 years old) and 2 male adults (25-28 years old, the second being still undetermined). On the basis of the mentioned hypothesis that the buried were representatives of nuclear families or households, we may presume that people were buried over 2 generations in phase I.

The reconstruction of the spatial organisation of the mausolea in relation with each other has yet to be carried out as some have not been fully excavated, and their architectural environment too is missing. Therefore it is still unknown how many of these mausolea had once existed, and what by what structures they were enclosed.

The most apparent element is the SN orientated, narrow (just 1,20 m–1,50 m wide) alley ("SN alley 1") running between the rows of mausolea and originally leading to an open square in the south[214] (Plate 12/1). This axis leads further to the north along *G2* and *G1*. However, due to the circumstance mentioned above that some mausolea were only partially excavated, we don't know, whether the alley, and with it too the extension of the mausolea, ended at the northern limits of *G1* and *G2*. Future investigations will thus have to clarify as to what kind of building or architectural feature (open square, street, surrounding wall, public buildings etc.) joined upon the mausolea.[215]

The entrance way to *G4* leads from the mentioned alley, but *G3* situated on the East side of the alley, was inaccessible from this alley. It was most likely entered from another SN alley ("SN Alley 2 (?)" on Plate 12). The small, one-chambered building *G5* was erected on the open square, its entries located on its West and East sides(Plate 12/1 – white colour).

Finally, *G6* was built, obstructing the west door of *G5* and virtually creating *cul-de-sac* from the "SN alley 1", just leaving a very narrow, 0,5 m wide EW passage (Plate 6 and Plate 12/2). The view into the "SN alley 1" was thus blocked from the open square.

It has already been alluded to the higher social status of the mausoleum builders and their descendants as opposed to the families who inhumed their members in cemetery U.[216] The superposition of the mausoleum makes it even more likely that the status of their holders were at even levels with the leadership of Tuttul. The mausolea had been erected on top of two monumental buildings of fundamental importance in the city's public life.[217] Thus, in the case that this event had no radical impact on the city's layout, accordingly the significance of these new structures for public life in Tuttul at any rate equalled that of their forerunners.

II.5.2 Phase II

During this phase in cemetery U new tombs were erected (Plate 8). They were built inside the spatial groups (U:13 in group II, U:23 and U:25[218] in group IV:, U:33 in group V), otherwise just outside them and therefore enlarging their respective areas (U:27 in group II , U:30 in group III[219] and U:36 in group V). In some cases secondary burials inside shaft-graves were recorded as well (U:34 in group V, maybe also U:7[220] in group II). The later tombs did not impair the earlier graves even if they had been lowered down very close to them, as in the case of U:14 and U:25[221] (Plate 10).

The pattern observed here of erection of new burials fits well into the one observed for phase I. The horizontal and vertical enlargement of the graves respected the borders of the earlier groups. In this case too, it therefore seems highly probable that kinship was the main criterion behind the spatial organisation within the cemetery.

During this phase one to three new burials containing no more than two new individuals older than 14 years were at the origin for each group (Table on Plate 8) (e.g. group V). This is suggestive of a short time-span, no longer than one generation for phase II.[222]

Mesopotamia see in Gelb 1978.
[214] Strommenger – Kohlmeyer 1998, 48.
[215] The excavators supposed an adjoined palace to the north (Strommenger – Kohlmeyer 1998, 48, repeated Strommenger – Kohlmeyer 2000, 9) but the excavation didn't extend far enough to the north to justify it.

[216] Chapter II.3.1.
[217] Strommenger – Kohlmeyer 2000, 5-8. As to the function of the buildings, be it administrative, representative or economic, nothing can yet be said because of the limited excavation. However, the large 1,9-2,4 m thick walls and the 2,2 m wide entrance seem to exclude that it had been built for simple domestic use.
[218] Strommenger – Kohlmeyer 1998, 94-96: no skeletons are associated with the pottery from this phase.
[219] U:30 lies between the newly dug graves U:13 (belonging to group II) and U:23 (belonging to group IV), but the distance to U:13 is just half of what is it to U:23. (Plate 8).
[220] In the filling of the grave a pottery collection was found which belonged to seriation-group 3 (Strommenger – Kohlmeyer 1998, 87-88, pl. 107).
[221] The chamber of U:25 only touched the chamber of U:14 , see Strommenger – Kohlmeyer 1998, 83. The only example from the cemetery U in which a new tomb destroyed an older one, is grave U:47. Strommenger – Kohlmeyer 1998, 83.
[222] Even if some of the tombs belonging to this phase could not be

No burials dating to phase II were recorded within the excavated area of mound E. The erection of a new official (representative) building, Palace B, shows as suggested above, that the buildings in this section still had a central importance within public life.

Just prior to the construction of Palace B the mausolea still remained intact and in use. The levelling then happened promptly in a planned action. The resting-place of the ancestors was as a consequence sealed for good.

II.5.3 Phase IIIa

In the latest phase of cemetery U new tombs occurred in group II (U:6, U:8, U:11 and U:42). One tomb (U47) enlarged the area of group VI. Most of the new burials, however, were secondary burials in earlier shaft-graves (U:7 in group II; U:30 in group V; U:25 in group IV; U:31, U:32 and U:34 in group V; U:43 and U:47 in group VI).

As time went on, the number of secondary burials increased, so filling the cemetery to the verge of saturation. However no new pattern was applied to seek a solution because the boundaries between the spatial clusters, or kin groups still remained unviolated, which meant that the tradition of multiple use of the shaft-graves going back to the very beginnings of the cemetery could be held up.

No more than four adults were buried per group during phase IIIa (table in Plate 9), which suggests a time-span of two generations for this phase. Had the graves which produced imprecise seriation results (Plate 10, graves marked with broken lines) nevertheless proved to belong to this phase, the time-span would have been prolonged by another generation. All in all this would end up to a total functional period for cemetery U of at least five, and at most six generations.[223]

Altogether 63 burials in 46 tombs were recovered during the excavations. Ideally, if the graves in the estimated cemetery[224] had the same regularity as in area U, the gravel terrace could have been able to receive up to 12600 burials. This would have come down to 2100–2500 burials per generation, or a burial place for 800-900 families. But even the other large cemeteries at the Euphrates Big Bend do not display such ideal patterns of grave distribution. They too, seem rather to have been organised in larger sections.[225]

This calculation does not represent the complete living population, as it does not include contemporary *intramural* burials.

In phase IIIa new graves were dug on mound E above Palace B (see Plate 31). The graves seem to be arranged into groups, in a similar way as observed in cemetery U. However, there are differences. On mound E it is commonly observed that the graves overlap and that their orientation does not follow any recognisable pattern. This would suggest that space was extremely limited and probably even located below buildings.

Indeed, the layers between Palace B and Palace A included scarce architectural remains that had been heavily damaged by the deep foundations of Palace A. The connection between the graves and the architectural remains could not be reconstructed anymore.[226] Also, whether they had served domestic or in some instances even funerary purposes, remains unsure,

Half of the graves contained adults of both genders, and the other half children similarly to the demographic picture revealed in cemetery U. Both, the concentration of graves as well as the age and gender composition again point to the clusters as a reflection of family- or household-related burial traditions. The group in quadrant 25/48 contained six adult graves indicating a duration lasting for three generations, which would correspond with that of cemetery U.

Because of the "public" character of mound E in earlier times, we can only speculate about the graves in this area as being somehow more important than those in cemetery U.

II.5.4 Phase IIIb

It seems that after the *Pfeilergebäude* was abandoned, the area finally lost its particular importance. The graves on its top now contained children and were otherwise lacking special features.

This persisting decline seems to have begun after the destruction of Palace B. It is indicative of a fundamental change in the settlement structure and possibly even in the administration. From this perspective, the erection of Palace A could be seen as an act of "ideological restoration" of the area, symbolising the re-establishment of the "traditional" structure before the destruction of Palace B.

Only in area 28/45 an adult burial seems to display some continuity of the tradition observed in phase IIIa. The evidence is less suitable for estimating the duration of this phase, since there are no control groups suggesting the presence of only one generation. However, with only two building levels between the *Pfeilergebäude* and Palace A, it is reasonable to suggest that they covered only a short period.[227] The thin-walled buildings apparently belonged to small-scale domestic architecture.

---

dated by means of the seriation, this still remains valid (Plate 10, graves marked with broken lines).

[223] Looking at the quantity of adults in the table of Plate 10, the result would be similar according to the corrections suggested in Chapter II.6.1.

[224] 14 ha, see chapter II.5.1.

[225] E.g. Tawi (Kampschulte–Orthmann 1984, 6 fig.2) or Abu Hamed (Krasnik 2005)

[226] Some graves are cutting the tiny walls, e.g. 24/49:6 (Strommenger – Kohlmeyer 2000, pl. 71).

[227] See e.g. Strommenger–Kohlmeyer 2000, app. 9 and 10. However the stratigraphy between the *Pfeilergebäude* and Palace A had been disturbed by erosion as well as by the building of an Early Byzantine

Height of WT/F	Min. (cm)	Max. (cm)	Average (cm)	Quantity
Children	12,9	21,7	15,3	8
Men	16,7	25,5	22,1	8
Women	12,5	25,0	20,7	22
Adults of unidentified gender	13,5	23,7	19,9	6

Fig. 19 The heights of open-mouth pots and jars in cemetery U during phase I

II.6 The grave goods

More than 200 burials were presented in the final publication. It is therefore not the aim of this study to discuss again the grave goods one by one.

First of all, an overview over the different artefact types from the particular phases will be given. Much attention is paid to artefact function within the funerary ritual which is scrutinised according to the aspects already mentioned in chapter I.1.5, while basing mainly on the work of J.–W. Meyer.[228]

The typology for the seriation was carried out by E. Strommenger and K. Kohlmeyer.[229] It is essentially based on a combination of observations on wares,[230] shapes and sizes, including both, vessels and metal objects.[231] Given that this work is based on their typology and seriation, it was deemed more judicious to maintain the German terms and tags instead of creating new typology labels.

Most artefacts were neither decorated nor marked in any form. However, vessels with pottery marks were quite common in the graves. This aspect will be discussed separately in chapter II.7.

II.6.1 Phase I

The most frequent grave good was pottery. In all 35 different vessel types were identified (Plate 13-16). Most of them were manufactured from the so called "simple-ware". In general terms, round bases and unprofiled rims were characteristic for the simple ware vessels of this phase.

Most types continued to be used in later phases. The significant types, which do not appear in later assemblages, are separated in the upper part of the plates (e.g. Tg2, S/N *mit Schnurösen*, WT/F1, WT/F2, *Zweihenkelige* F1, TT1, SR, L1 and Na1 see Plates 13-17).

The *extramural* cemetery U contained individual burials. They provide a very good base for the observation of the grave good inventory.

All graves contained at least one vessel.[232] In all except for one,[233] at least one open-mouth pot or jar was recorded (Plate 14, types WT/F 1, 3 and 5-7). The volume of those pots or jars was larger in adult graves than in ones containing children (Fig 19).

In the settlement similar sized open-mouth pots and jars were used in food processing and short term food storage.[234] In the funerary context they also inherited a secondary or *ideal function*. The vessels are not decorated, but have pottery marks in a high proportion (Fig. 21). A more detailed examination of the marked pottery will follow in chapter II.7.

Some botanical[235] and animal remains were recovered from the graves, but not from inside the pots. This seems to suggest that the open-mouth pots and jars contained liquids and already processed food.

Their interpretation as "prestige objects" may be ruled out as they were the most common types, even in the secular context. However they were nevertheless included in the interment ritual practices or were given such purposes because of cultic-religious reasons. Because the vessel's size and thus the quantity of the food or liquid contained inside was determined by the age of the deceased, an interpretation as "supply" for the journey to the netherworld or afterlife is more likely.[236]

One or more drinking vessels were added to the pots and jars in most graves[237] (Plate 13, types Tg 1-6 and "N *mit Schnurösen*"). The volume of the drinking vessels is invariable in adult and child burials. The only peculiarity is that no looped cups were recorded in the graves of men

---

cloister.

[228] Meyer 2000.

[229] For the definition of the single types see Strommenger – Kohlmeyer 1998, 121-129. The abbreviations here were established after the German terms.

[230] The definition of the different wares can be found Strommenger – Kohlmeyer 1998, and Orthmann – Rova 1991, 71-76.

[231] See the seriation principles in Strommenger – Kohlmeyer 1998, 121-122.

[232] Burial U:32alt1 probably also contained some vessels that were associated with later graves (see e.g. Strommenger–Kohlmeyer 1998, Pl. 121/ 4, 8). This burial as well as the graves from cemetery V are excluded from the following overview.

[233] Burial U:44, a "luxury" pot, although probably with the same function as the "simple-ware" pots.

[234] See P.M. Rice for the functional classification of vessels generally, and Hempelmann 2004 and 2005 adapting it for Near Eastern assemblages at the Euphrates Big Bend.

[235] E.g. in burial U:9 some carbonised cereal grains were found near the scull, but not in the pots.

[236] Also Meyer 2000, 24.

[237] Only the burials U:15alt and U:20 did not contain any drinking vessels or looped cups. In the case of U:15 it is possible that one of the cups of the later burials belonged to the older one.

(Plate 13, type "N *mit Schnurösen*"). Some cups were found in bowls.[238]

In half of the graves round based bowls were also found (Plate 13, type "*Rundbodige* S1-4"), in two cases with stands[239] (Plate 13, type "*Rundbodige* S2") or with tripods[240] (Plate 13, type "S/Sa *mit Tüllenfüßen*"), and once with a loop[241] (Plate 13 type S/Na *mit Schnurösen*). The bowl heights without stand vary between 8,2 and 12,2 cm revealing no differences between graves of children and adults.

Because the smallest pottery set included a pot and a drinking vessel, it is probable that at least some of the pots, contained liquids. The association of drinking vessels and deep bowls with round bases in some graves seems to suggest that these bowls were used for mixing such liquids.

One third (9 graves) of the graves included "luxury vessels", mostly jars of the "Euphrates-ware" (Plate 16 Type Lu 3; 5 specimens) and the "stone or metallic-ware" (Plate 16 Lu2a and Lu5a; 6 in the graves of women). They had globular bodies, straight necks and usually pronounced horizontal lips. However their bases differ. Whereas the Euphrates-ware vessels had ring-bases, the vessels of the "stone-ware" had round bases. Other types (Lu1, Lu4 on Plate 16) do not appear in the examined graves of cemetery U, but they are known from cemetery V.

No grave containing "luxury vessels" belonged to a child. This means, that about half of the adult graves (in total 17 adult burials) contained up to three "luxury" vessels (Fig. 20). It is worthwhile to note that their distribution is uneven. Whereas each adult member from Group VI – and Group IV – was allotted one "luxury" jar, adults in the Groups II and V had none (Fig. 20 and Plate 7).

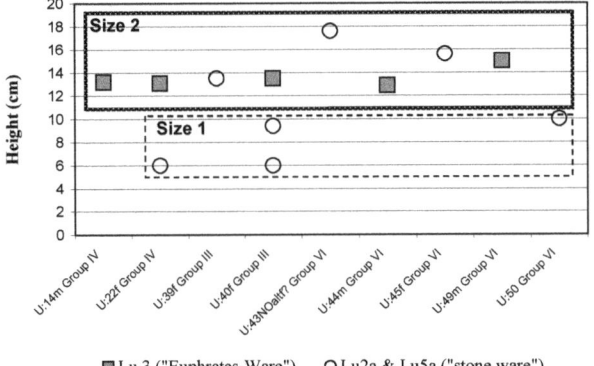

Fig. 20 *The heights of the "luxury vessels" in cemetery U in phase I*

The sizes of the luxury jars or pots varied little. Especially the Euphrates-ware pots seem to be standardised. Their heights varied between 12,9 and 15 cm. The pots and jars of "stone-ware" belonged to two size categories. The smaller ones (Fig. 20, Size 1) were between 6 and 10 cm high and accompanied a "Euphrates-ware" pot. The bigger ones had approximately the same volume as the "Euphrates-ware" vessels. Their heights varied between 13,5 and 17,6 cm (Fig. 20, size 2).

These vessel types were labelled as "luxury" because of their special ware and characteristic surface treatment. They are furthermore uncommon. For this reason they are designated as "prestige objects" or cultic-religious artefacts. Most such "luxury" vessels also stem from secular contexts,[242] but their percentage in the total ceramic assemblage remains low.

Nevertheless, the "Euphrates-ware" vessels only appear in funerary contexts along the Euphrates,[243] in graves and in special buildings of the ancestral worship.[244] This suggests that the vessels played an important role in the funerary practices. However, in Tell Bi'a only five adult burials contained pots of the Euphrates-ware (Fig. 20, grey quadrate).

How are we to interpret this phenomenon? On one hand, it is a fact that a special pottery was manufactured only for funerary purposes, also it is not probable that it only functioned as a prestige object. On the other hand, this pottery had an uneven distribution, so it cannot be asserted *ad hoc* that its presence was obligatory for the funeral. More than one working hypothesis is needed to find the most plausible interpretation for the meaning and function of this special pottery.

- The first assumption is that the "Euphrates-Ware", and luxury ware in general, was imported. It contained particular substances that were produced in the same area as the pottery. Consequently, the presence of such pottery in graves leads to suggest close contacts with the area of its production.[245] These contacts could either have been of familial or commercial nature. In this case the pottery testifies to the practice of giving additional artefacts for cultic-religious or social-personal reasons (*"Beigabe"* or *"Mitgabe"*), e.g. social status. The question, however, why other luxury ware vessels of the same size category (size 2) never are found associated with the Euphrates-ware, cannot be answered with this hypothesis.

- The second assumption is that the "Euphrates-ware" was necessary for the fulfilling of special rituals

---

[238] Burials U:14, U:18 and U:28.
[239] Burial U:18.
[240] Burial U:44.
[241] Burial U:24.

[242] This is the case e.g. for the stone or metallic-ware etc. See e.g. Pruß 2001.
[243] Porter 1999, 312, 316 and Hempelmann 2004.
[244] Hempelmann 2001, 158-160.
[245] Production of the "Euphrates-ware" has been confirmed from the Euphrates Big Bend area for Tell Banat (Porter 1999, 313). The production area of the "stone-ware" has to be sought north of Tell Bi'a, in the Syrian Ğazīra (Rova 1996, 25 and Pruß 2000).

Pottery	Number of vessels	Number of graves	Max. number per grave
WT/F 1, 3 and 5-7	49 38,5%	25 96%	4
Tg 1-6 + N *mit Schnurösen*	40 31,5%	23 88%	3
Rundbodige S 1-4 + S/Sa *mit Tüllenfüßen* + S mit Schnurösen	15 12%	13 50%	2
Lu 2a, 3 and 5a	12 9,5%	9 34%	3
Zweihenkelige F1	2 1,5%	2 7%	1
other pottery types	9 7%		
Σ:	**127** *100%*	**26** *100%*	**10**
marked pottery (WT/F 1, 3 and 5-7 +*Zweihenkelige* F1)	19 15% (30,1% from WTF + Lu + Zweihenkelige F1)	13 50%	3

Fig. 21 Distribution of vessels in cemetery U in phase I

during the interment *("Beisetzungssitte")*. In that case, the vessel type itself conveys a distinctive cultic-symbolic connotation. Less than one third of the adult burials contained such vessels. Consequently, only these burials enjoyed that particular attention. The reasons for carrying out that kind of ritual were not connected to gender. A special status of the deceased within the family cannot be conceived either, because in some family-groups there were no "Euphrates-ware" vessels at all. A motivation for carrying out a special ritual might for example have arisen from the possible hapless circumstances of the death or even an ill-fated oracle. For this assumption it hardly matters, whether the vessels were made on the site or whether they were imported.

- The third assumption is that the shape of the "Euphrates-ware" vessels was especially well suited for containing a particular substance used during the burial ritual *("Beisetzungssitte")*. Consequently, emphasis is set on the substance rather than on the container. Logically, a different pottery type could just as well have served the purpose. The most adequate seems to one whose shape resembles most to the Euphrates vessels, in other words, the pots and jars belonging to the stoneware. This is also supported by the circumstance that their capacities (size 2) approximately are the same. The uneven distribution between the groups may be explained with the possible presence of diverging traditions in the funerary ritual, be it for example for reasons of any particular family's social ranking or specific origin.
- The fourth assumption builds on the third. If "size 2" pots of the Lu5a (Plate 16) type were used for containing that particular substance, then similar shapes of the simple-ware might have been considered apt to fulfil the same task as well. Open-mouth pots and jars (WT/F on Plate 15) with heights between 12 and 18 cm seem to be the most adequate. In all graves, including the ones of children (Figs. 19 and 22), there was a pot this size, or a slightly larger one.[246] Consequently, the core of the funeral tradition was the same for everybody. Whether this basic funeral practice occurred *during the interment ("Beisetzungssitte")*, e.g. in the form of a ritual meal at the place of burial, or for cultic-religious reasons *("Beigabensitte")*, remains unclear. However, the disparities in the vessels' qualities might reflect on one hand differences in wealth among the families, and on the other status differentiation within a family itself. We may therefore assume a low status of children in general. This would mean, that luxury vessels had a secondary function as status symbols in the after-life (*"Mitgabe"*).

From the four hypotheses the latter seems the most plausible because it provides an answer to most of the problems which occurred during the examination of luxury vessels.

Other vessel types too, were recovered from the graves (e.g. jars with two handles, cooking pots etc.), but their distribution is too sporadic as to being able to detect any pattern in their occurrence (Fig. 21).

The number of vessels per grave can vary between one and ten (Fig. 21). The vessels had been deposed at a certain distance from the corpses in the western parts of the graves.[247] They were arranged in assemblages, usually above the heads,[248] at the backsides,[249] or in front of the

---

[246] Burials U:9–18,6 cm; U:10–21,9 cm; U:12 – 21,7 cm; U:15alt–19,5 cm; U:31alt–20,6 cm; U:37–20,7 cm.
[247] In the N-S oriented burials U:45 and U:51 the vessels were lying on the north side.
[248] Burials U:9, U:12, U:14, U:15alt, U:20, U:22, U:28, U:37, U:39, U:40, U:41, U:45 and U:51.
[249] Burials U:44 and U:10.

II. Analysis

bodies.[250] The corpses had been placed in the eastern parts of the tombs, though in group VI in the south. As it seems, a codified sequence of depositing the corpses and the objects seems to have been observed almost everywhere. As a rule the corpse was laid down first into the grave, and then the vessels with their contents.[251] The varying quantity of pottery may give a hint as to the number of the *dramatis personae* present at the funeral.

Bronze pins (Plate 16 types Na 2 and 3) were found in half of the graves. In one grave[252] a straight bone pin was recovered, probably with the same function as the bronze pins. No pins were found in child graves.

Men's graves usually[253] only contained one bronze pin lying near the chest,[254] or the face.[255] In one grave[256] there were three pins, and in another male adult grave[257] there was none.

In women's graves there was generally[258] more than one pin.[259] They were lying near the shoulders[260] and the chest,[261] or near the face.[262]

Four other graves[263] of adults of undetermined gender were excavated, of which two had one bronze pin,[264] one a bone pin,[265] and one without a pin.

All pins were found near the upper part of the bodies (chest, shoulder, neck, face and scull), because they were part of the burial costume.[266] Children's costumes generally differed to those of the adults in that none had pins. The varying pin numbers in adult graves also point to different costumes. This might have been dependent on gender, as women usually had more than one pin, social status, fashion, or simply on season.[267]

Beads and pendants were recorded in nine graves. Five of them belonged to women,[268] two to adults of unspecified sex,[269] one to a man[270] and one to a child.[271] They were made from different materials (clay, snail-shell, frit, bronze, crystal and semi-precious stones), and had different shapes (round, cylindrical, zoomorphic etc.). The beads and pendants were found lying near the upper parts of the bodies, near the sculls or the arms. They belonged to the costumes, either as parts of separate necklaces or bracelets, garment decorations, or simply hanging down from the pins. The small frit cylinder seal with a geometrical design in burial U:43NOalt recorded near a left elbow probably too was suspended in the same way, given that beads were recorded from an area between the pins and the seal.[272]

All daggers[273] (Plate 17, DL) were recovered from men's graves. They were found lying near the upper parts of the bodies, usually close to the sculls, in one instance below the scull.[274] It is hard to imagine any practical reason for this position as being part the costume. It might therefore have resided within the cultic-religious sphere (a gender specified *"Beigabensitte"*) or else marked a personal attribute (an indication of their profession as soldiers, or of rank etc., *"Mitgabe"*). The presence of daggers in graves might also have given some information as to the circumstances under which an individual had passed away, in this case one would thus be tempted to assume through violence.

Some "special objects" do not belong to the mentioned categories. In two graves terra-cotta models of chariots with wheels were found. Their interpretation as toys (also an artefact with a personal meaning: *"Mitgabe"*) is hardly plausible, since only one originates from a child burial.[275] The other chariot model was found in a grave of an elderly man.[276] In the child burial the model was placed near the face of the body. In the grave of the man the chariot was found together with the vessels. A magical-religious interpretation (*"Beigabe"*) for these objects seems quite credible.[277]

Another, such "special object", a bronze diadem stems from the burial of a mature woman.[278] It was found on the scull, thus assigning it to her funeral costume. The special costume could hint to the women's high social rank in her life-time. The above assumption that the

---

[250] Burials U:34alt, U:43NOalt and U:49.
[251] Except possibly burial U:44, where the position of the skeleton may have caused some trouble for the subsequent deposition of the pottery.
[252] Burial U:9.
[253] Burials U:14, U:15alt, U:32 alt1, U:37.
[254] Burials U:14, U:15 and U:37.
[255] Burial U:32alt 1.
[256] Burial U:49.
[257] Burial U:44.
[258] Burials U:22, U:39, U:40, U:43NO, U:45.
[259] In the graves U:20 and U:31alt only one pin was found respectively. In U:20 was a lead staff, maybe used as a pin or a make-up staff. Burial U:15jung did not contain any pin.
[260] Burials U:22 and U:45, artefact U:302,4.
[261] Burials U:20, U:40 artefact U:270,2, U:43NO, U:45
[262] Burial U:39
[263] Burials U:7alt, U:9, U:10 and U:35.
[264] Burials U:7alt and U:10. In U:10 the pin was lying near the face.
[265] Burial U:9, the pin was lying at the shoulder.
[266] Pins around the shoulder and chest were most probably attached to the garment. One pin in U:43 NOalt was lying above the head which may hint to a veil or head-dress.
[267] A multi-causal explanation for this finding is also plausible.
[268] Burials, U:22, U:39, U:40, U:43 NOalt and U:45.

[269] Burials U:9 and U:10.
[270] Burial U:15alt.
[271] Burial U:12.
[272] Such a costume is depicted on an inlay piece from Mari, see Kohlmeyer 1985, 155 fig. 39.
[273] In burials U:14, U:15alt, U:37 and U:49. Also in U:32alt1 which was excluded from the analysis of other artefacts, because its inventory seems to be incomplete — see note 233.
[274] Burial U:37.
[275] Burial U:41; the chariot model and the four wheels were made from unbaked clay. Moorey 2001 rejects their function as toys for adults, but doesn't exclude it in the case of child burials.
[276] Burial U:49, maturus II; only one wheel was found.
[277] In this sense Meyer 2001 who proposes a similar interpretation for boat models recovered from graves. For diverging interpretations see Moorey 2001.
[278] Burial U:40.

"luxury vessels" had a secondary function as status symbols would correspond with the suggested higher status of some individuals, in view of the fact that as many as three luxury vessels were recorded from this grave (Fig. 21).

As already mentioned, the graves also produced some botanical and zoological remains. In general they may be identified with organic remnants from food provisions.

However, the shaft of grave U:22 was sealed with mud bricks after the deposition of a female adult corpse and some pots. A donkey skeleton and a small cup were then placed over the mud-bricks. This is the only grave in Tell Bi'a displaying this practice, thus obstructing any possibility of interpretation. Anyhow, it seems probable that this deposition had a cultic–religious meaning.[279]

In sealing of the grave entrance with mud bricks the interment process was concluded in most cases. Occasionally, pottery was recorded inside the shafts which might either point to a closing ritual of the interment,[280] or possibly to some later activity as part of ancestral worship.

These remarks end the overview of the grave goods from the cemetery U. It provided very useful comparative material for the analysis of the mausolea.

Except in the case of G6R2, it is not possible to separate the grave goods according to their respective burials. It needs to be stressed again that most mausolea had been disturbed and possibly even looted. The majority of the artefacts that brought wealth to the robbers have escaped analysis. Nevertheless 251 complete and 69 fragmentary vessels have been recorded. This is twice as many as from cemetery U, so there is enough reason to hope for results, at least by comparing them.

In the mausolea the distribution of different pottery types varies considerably among the chambers (Plate 31/2). For example the antechamber (*R2*) of *G3* apparently contained no pottery.[281] I will come back to this issue later on in this chapter.

Vessels made from simple-ware were the most common ones (Plate 29-31), especially pots and jars (Plate 29, 53%). They had the same shape types as in cemetery U i.e. open-mouth pots and jars (Plate 14). However, in every room, apart from G5 and G3R2, vessels of much larger capacities than those from cemetery U were recovered (Fig. 22).

The variability of "luxury" vessels is greater than that from cemetery U. Besides the already known forms of the

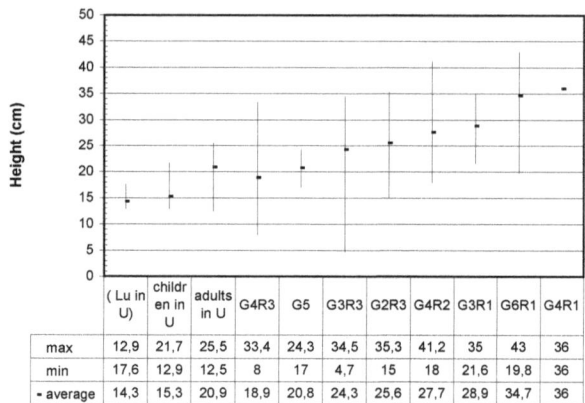

Fig. 22 The heights of WT/F in phase I

"Euphrates-ware" (Plate16, Lu3) and the "stone-ware" (Plate 16, Lu2a and Lu5a) there appears a new "stone-ware" type with round base and wide, horizontal lips (Plate 16, Lu4) as well as a new ware type called the "black-ware"[282] (Plate 16, Lu1). The ratio of luxury vessels is somewhat higher than observed for cemetery U: 10,2 % of the total pottery amount (Plate 29), of which most consists of "stone-ware" (7,4%). The distribution is very uneven as half of the luxury vessels are from G3R3 (Plate 29).

The dimensions of the luxury vessels form three size categories. Small pots are between 5 and 11 cm high (Fig. 23, size 1). Most of the vessels belong to this category (16 complete vessels). Medium-sized ones (size 2) are luxury vessels with heights between 12 and 19 cm. Only four complete vessels belong to that group. The heights of the largest luxury pots vary between 20 and 40 cm (size 3). Five of them have been preserved. In cemetery U no luxury vessel of this size was found. In recollection most of the simple-ware-pots and jars belong to this large category.

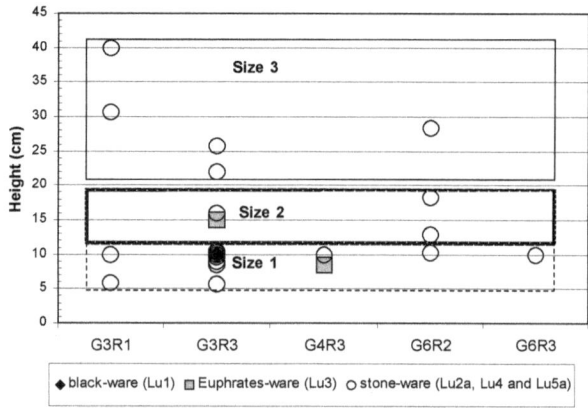

Fig. 23 The heights of the luxury vessels in the mausolea

---

[279] A short overview about graves combined with donkey depositions in EBA Syria is given by Magen 2001, 252-253 with further bibliography.

[280] The same has been suggested for the burial with the donkey skeleton on top of it (U:22).

[281] Some sherds and a drinking vessel were recovered, though which probably got there from the neighbouring rooms.

[282] In earlier publications the definition and labels of this ware vary. For the most recent summary see Pruß 2000, 413-417.

This size distribution contrasts to that in cemetery U, where most of the luxury vessels belong to the second category (compare Fig 20 and Fig. 23). It is also interesting that only one small pot (Size 1) from "stoneware" belonged to the only intact skeleton (23/46:3).

Again several explanations for the above mentioned differences between the mausolea and the cemetery can be given.

- The mausolea were robbed. Because the "luxury" vessels and maybe their contents might have been considered valuable, they were stolen. This of course does not explain the case of burial 23/46:3 which apparently was not robbed.
- Another assumption is that the different distribution of objects including the luxury vessels in the mausolea can be connected with the different stages of the funeral rites before the buildings were finally sealed. It is conceivable that the person buried last in 23/46:3 did not receive the full funerary treatment as the building had been sealed e.g. after the "laying in state". Otherwise the "obligatory" pot occurs in every fulfilled ritual, only its volume was generally bigger than in cemetery U. The number of small "luxury" pots of size 1 could have contained other valuable substances (e.g. aromatic oils, balm etc) than the larger pots of size 2 and 3. They were not obligatory for the basic ritual but symbolised the wealth of the mourners as well as the high status of the dead.

The higher ratio of pots and jars in the mausolea than that in cemetery U too requires some explanation. Again, more than one interpretation is possible.

- Compared with cemetery U, more elaborate rituals took place in the mausolea. It is conceivable that such rituals required more ingredients.
- The dead buried inside the mausolea received more supplies for their journey to the netherworld and for afterlife and had more offerings for the gods than those buried in the cemetery.
- At least some of the pots and jars were connected with ancestor worship which also included the tradition of offering meals and drinks. This explanation is plausible at least in the case of G4R2, because in this room no skeletal remains were found. Similarly the deposition of five caprine sculls and feet bones in G3R2 may be interpreted as a symbolic meal offering.[283]

As in the case of cemetery U, drinking vessels and different types of bowls were the second most common objects after the pots.

The stands (Plate 15 SR) functionally belong to the pots and jars with round base, because they held them in an upright position. In cemetery U no stand was found, which contrasts to the findings in the mausolea where 11,1% of all the pottery consisted of stands (Plate 31). One of them was found *in situ* in a niche of G3R1. In G3R1 and burial 23/46:2 in G6R2 the number of stands amounts almost to that of the pots. In the other rooms however not every pot belonged to a stand.

Drinking vessels and bowls were usually also found in the mausolea (Plate 30), but their ratio was somewhat lower than in cemetery U (see Fig. 21).

Some metal objects were found in the mausolea, however not as many as expected (e.g. in G4R3 thirteen people over 14 were buried, but only 7 pins were recorded). Most metal objects were made from bronze, but some small silver and gold artefacts, probably belonging to the costume (beads, rings, pins) had escaped looting, thus indicative of the lost wealth of the graves and witnessing the lavishness of garments in comparison to those worn in cemetery U.

An ornamented bone tube was found in room 3 of mausoleum G3.[284] It contained a black substance with a vertical hole (diameter 0,3 cm), probably kohl, as observed in one case at Tell Banat.[285] Such bone tubes were used most probably as containers for cosmetics, the vertical hole could have held a thin make-up spatula. The original position of the object is not known, however it could have belonged to a costume hanging from a necklace or a bell, as both its extremities had suspension holes. Whether it belonged to a man or a woman cannot be determined, though both tubes from Tawi had been found near the remains of women.[286] Whether or not the deceased wore make-up is speculative, but the utensil's presence inside a tomb does make it probable. Another such tube was also recovered from cemetery U, although from a grave which had previously been destroyed by a dredge.[287]

As for the weapons, the situation is different. An undisturbed grave 23/46:3 of a young man contained next the common bronze dagger, a bronze axe-blade, a shaft-axe and the rounded end of a bronze quiver. He seems to have worn his dagger in a belt while holding the axes in his hands. The quiver was placed at his shoulder.[288] It is evident that these items belonged to his costume.

It is possible to reconstruct the costume of this warrior (Plate 32/2) with the help of roughly contemporary inlays

---

[283] The term "symbolic" seemed adequate because the parts mentioned are not the most appreciated ingredients in meals, and would thus have been deposited as *pars pro toto*.

[284] Strommenger – Kohlmeyer 1998, 60-61 and pl. 76/16.
[285] Porter 1995, 8-9. Similar objects have been found at several Syrian sites like Amuq (Phase J – Braidwood – Braidwood 1960, 340, 392-393 Fig. 300, pl. 76/1), Hammam et-Turkman (van Loon – Meijer 1987, 1-2 fig. 5), Hama (Thuesen 1988, 171 pl. 12/64), Tawi Tombs 70 and 71 (Kampschulte – Orthmann 1984, pl. 33/16 and 34/15) and Jerablus Tahtani (Peltenburg 1999a, 102 fig. 3).
[286] Kampschulte – Orthmann 1984, 93-97, 98-102, pl. 43.For the anthropological examination see: Kunter 1984, 115-119.
[287] Artefact U:48, Strommenger – Kohlmeyer 1998, 111, pl. 146/3 and pl. 167/1.
[288] The excavators suggested a positioning of the quiver over the chest (Strommenger – Kohlmeyer 1998, 74).

and carvings from Mari and Ur (Plate 32/3-5). Depictions of axes are quite common, and sometimes warriors hold short swords or blades in their hands, but quivers are rarely represented as part of the infantry equipment. Although in one case, a standing individual is shown on an Akkadian stele from Tello (Girsu) shooting with a bow and wearing a quiver on the back.[289] Another bowing foot soldier is also depicted on a carving from Mari dated *a priori* to the Akkadian presence, but a quiver cannot be recognised on the panel (Plate 32/4).

Warriors are always depicted with helms, but no evidence of them is known from the graves. It is quite probable that the helm was made from leather. The question remains why no arrowheads from stone or bronze were found in the burials. One is tempted to think of cultic-religious or superstitious prescriptions which prohibited arrows in graves. However such finds are also rare in the contemporary settlements and graves in Syria.[290] This absence leads to suggest that they were made from a perishable material, for example hardened wood. Hence the same would also apply to the bow.

On the depictions warriors never wear as many weapons as recorded in G6R2. The explanation for this is simple in that a bow and axe are impossible to use at the same time. It is conceivable that the representations concentrated only on those weapons which were essential for the scene. Another interpretation is that "superfluous" weapons in graves were not part of the normal equipment, but they were offered to symbolise status or rank (*"Mitgabe"*) or as a gift for the gods.

E. E. Rehm suggests another possibility for interpreting weapons in graves.[291] She argues that blades and axes could have been seen primarily as working instruments and used as weapons in the case of need. On the other hand not everybody possessed a blade or an axe, so they also symbolised rank or status. Next to their role in warfare bows and arrows were also used in hunting, so they may be seen as luxury artefacts too. Rehm goes on in attempting to explain the absence of arrowheads in graves. She argues that arrows, bows, helms, spears and shields might have been army and not a private property.[292]

She assumes that the graves which contain weapons did not belong to soldiers but to members of a social group, who at some stage of their lives were involved in warfare, their weapons thus being the symbols of this membership.[293] She categorises weapons found in graves as personal property and therefore regards them as part of the costume.[294]

Inlays were also found in the mausolea. They were non-figurative ornaments (triangles, rosettes, an eye etc.) decorating the sides of wooden furnishings or boxes. All mausolea contained some remains of mother of pearl or eggshell inlays, of which reconstructions were proposed for G5 and G6R1.[295] It is quite probable that they served as prestige objects (*"Mitgabe"*).

II.6.2 phase II

Twenty-one (60%) pottery types of the older phase continued to be in use in phase II, but fourteen (40%) new types also appeared for the first time (Plates 18–21). Flat bases were the characteristic feature of the new types, but numerous vessels still kept their round bases. The most common ware type remained to be the "simple-ware".

There was a change in the portions of the most common shapes and functional classes. While the most frequent form used to be the open-mouth-pot, followed by drinking vessels, the latter had by now become twice as frequent as the former (Fig. 24). Except for burial 59/78:1, all graves contained at least one drinking vessel but no more than five. The explanation for this phenomenon might reside in alterations in the ritual process and activities at the burial site. Anyhow at least some affirmation can be given to changes in using different substances, although the contention that the sample is too small for statistical substantiation still persists.

Open-mouth pots are still common (Fig. 24). They were not contained in three burials,[296] but in two their function might have been replaced with a luxury vessel[297] or a different pot-type.[298] The heights of the open-mouth pots and jars vary between 12 and 36 cm. There are several pots with greater volumes than those found in cemetery U in phase I (compare with Fig. 19). It is impossible to compare the heights of pots and jars in the graves of children and adults because here again the sample is too small.

Most graves also contained a bowl, in only two graves[299] they were absent. This is probably connected with the general use of drinking vessels.

The proportion of the "luxury" pots remained unchanged, but the "black-ware" became the most common ware type (Fig. 24 and 25). Kohlmeyer dated one "Euphrates-ware" jar to phase II. If he is right, it would have belonged to an earlier burial in shaft-grave U:30 and consequently be the only vessel of that ware in phase II.[300] The heights of the vessels vary between 6 and 18 cm without any clear cut size-categories (Fig. 25).

---

[289] Orthmann 1985, Pl. 102a. The angular end of the quiver is different to that of the rounded one from Tell Bi'a.
[290] Apart from the tombs 241-242 in Mari.
[291] Rehm 2001, 189-199.
[292] Rehm 2001, 170-171 and 198. Waetzold 1990, 1-38 referring to Ebla.
[293] Rehm 2001, 199.
[294] Rehm 2001, 218.

[295] Strommenger – Kohlmeyer 1998, pl. 93-94, 96 and app. 1-2.
[296] Burials 59/78:1, 59/78:2 and U:27.
[297] Burial 59/78:1.
[298] Burial U:27, type *Große* T1 on Plate 19.
[299] Burial 59/78:1 and U:36.
[300] Strommenger – Kohlmeyer 1998, 122.

Pottery	Altogether	Number of graves	Max. number per graves
WT/F 3 and 5-7	18 *20%*	7 *70%*	5
Tg 1, 3-5, 9-10 and 12	35 *38,8%*	9 *90%*	8
Rundbodige S 1-6 + S/Sa *mit Tüllenfüßen* + Sa 6	10 *11,1%*	8 *80%*	2
Lu 2a (3?) and c, 4 and 6	9 (10?) *9,9%*	6 *60%*	3
M1	4 *4,4%*	3 *30%*	2
TT2	3 *3,3%*	3 *30%*	1
T *mit Riefen*	3 *3,3%*	2 *20%*	2
EF1	2 *2,2%*	2 *20%*	1
other pottery types	8 *8,8%*		
Σ:	90 (91?) *100%*	10 *100%*	17
marked pottery (WT/F 3-7)	14 *15,6% (51,8% from WTF+Lu)*	8 *80%*	6

Fig. 24 Distribution of vessels in phase II

A small jar type with a very narrow neck (EF1 on Plate 21), the so-called "Syrian bottle", appears for the first time in this phase. Usually it belongs to the "black-ware" but sometimes also to the "simple-ware".[301]

Bronze pins were common as well (Na2 and 3 on Plate 22). They were not contained in some graves as for example the ones belonging to children. Similar to the previous phase, one burial contained no more than three pins. The pins were recovered from the upper parts of the bodies in the same way as observed earlier on. Beads and pendants also belonged to some costumes. Among the few recorded rings, one was made of silver.[302]

Only one grave contained a bronze blade. Because its position within the grave was not recorded, it is impossible to tell whether it belonged to the costume or whether it was a cultic-religious or socially motivated offering.

Burial U:1 yielded a number of unusual objects. Among them a bird-shaped rattle and two lid-shaped objects proposed to be castanets. In Tell Bi'a these finds are without parallels, hindering further interpretation.

II.6.3 Phase IIIa

The great diversity of pottery types is characteristic for this phase in the EBA burials at Tell Bi'a. Forty-five (71%) pottery shapes were new in this phase,[303] and only twenty (31%) types persisted since phase II[304] (Plates 23-26). Merely nine (14%) types were customary since phase I,[305] though corresponding to only 5%[306] of the total pottery quantity. New elements were e.g. ring bases and multiply ribbed rims.

Similarly to cemetery U in phase I, jars and pots[307] are the most frequent vessel types in the graves[308] (Fig. 26). The occurrence of drinking vessels is somewhat lower than in the phases before, but the number of bowls

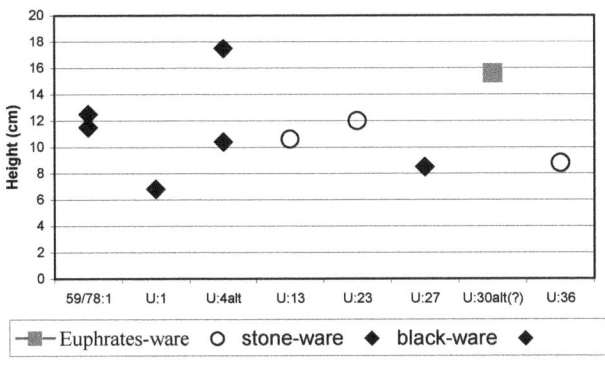

Fig. 25 The heights of "luxury vessels" in phase II

---

[301] See also Pruß 2001.
[302] In Burial U:1.
[303] However 81% of all vessels have a new shape.
[304] 19% of all vessels belong to them.
[305] Tg6, WT/F5, WT/F7, KT *mit Griffleisten*, *Zweihenkelige* F2, Sa3, Lu5a, M1 and Si.
[306] 22 pieces.
[307] 38,5 % of all pottery belonged to the WT/F (Fig. 21).
[308] First of all the jars F1-11 on Plate 25 and bigger pots "*Große* T1-7" on Plate 24. The former common type, the open-mouth pots (WT/F 5 and 7 on Plate 24) became rare, only 7 of them have been found.

Pottery	Intramural burials and near the city-wall			cemetery U			Σ:
	Total	number of graves	Max. piece per grave	Total	number of graves	Max. piece per grave	
pots and jars (WT/F, F, Große T, zweihenkelige F, TT)	109 36,5%	30 83%	11	46 32,2%	13 76%	11	155 35%
smaller pots (WT1+KuT+T mit Fenster)	7 2,3%	5 14%	2	4 2,8%	3 17,6%	1	11 2,5%
Drinking vessels (Tg)	44 14,7%	25 69%	3	23 16%	12 70%	3	67 15,2%
bowls (Sa+S+S mit Rinderfüßen)	72 24%	29 80%	7	44 30,8%	15 88%	7	116 26,2%
black, stone and simple-ware (Lu)	26 8,7%	13 36%	4	12 8,4%	7 41%	3	38 8,6%
"Syrian-bottle" (EF)	8 2,7%	5 14%	2	8 5,6%	5 29%	2	16 3,6%
other pottery types	33 11%			6 4,2%			39 8,8%
Σ:	299 100%	36 100%	26	143 100%	17 100%	24	442 100%
marked pottery	8 2,7% (7,3 % pots and jars whose H>14 cm)	5 14%		2 1,4% (4,3 % of pots and jars whose H>14 cm)	2 12%		10 2,2% (6,4 % of pots and jars whose H>14 cm)

Fig. 26 Distribution of vessels in phase IIIa

doubled (26%), whereas 44 graves (83%) contained at least one bowl.

Changes can also be noticed in the appearance of the luxury vessels. The most ordinary shape is the pot with loops at the sides (Lu 8-13 on Plate 26) and often belonging to the "black-ware" or "simple-ware". Only one "stone-ware" pot was recorded for this phase (Fig. 27). It was found in a shaft-tomb[309] which also contained a burial from phase I.

The occurrence of luxury vessels with child burials is also

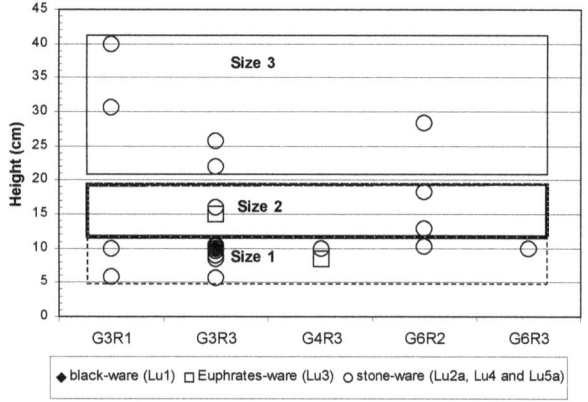

Fig. 27 The heights of "luxury vessels" in phase IIIa

---

[309] Burial U:43.

new (Fig. 27). They have the same shape and volume (size 1 and 2 in Fig 27) as the vessels found in the adult graves.

The distribution of luxury vessels in cemetery U is quite even. There is no concentration on one particular group (Fig. 27). However, similar to phase I, only one third of all burials contained luxury vessels.

The narrow-necked or Syrian-bottles (EF 1-4 on Plate 26) may be included to the "luxury" vessels. They have a round or pointed base, a globular or ellipsoid body and a pronounced, narrow neck. Their manufacture was similar to that of the luxury vessels, and they were made of "black-ware" and "simple-ware" In four graves "Syrian-bottles" were found together with luxury vessels.[310] In six other graves they were the only "luxury" types.[311] Not only graves of adults contained Syrian bottles but those of children as well. The closed vessel shape indicates that it probably contained a liquid unlike the open luxury vessel with loops (Lu 8-13 in Plate 26).

Most of the burials (83%) usually contained more than one bowl. This tendency already began in phase II (Fig. 24). By contrast in phase IIIa the number of drinking vessels in graves drastically decreases.[312] However, still

---

[310] Burials 25/48:11, U:25Nord, U:43SW and U:47.

[311] Burials 24/49:6, 24/49:10, 25/48:3, 25/48:10, U:6 and U:42.

[312] In phase I 31,5% of the pottery in cemetery U were drinking vessels which was equivalent with 23,3% of all the pottery from burial contexts in that phase. In phase IIIa only 15,2% of all the pottery were

II. Analysis

70% of the graves contained a drinking vessel. As already suggested in the last chapter, the explanation for this has to be connected with a change of the ritual process and activities at the burial site, or at least with a change of the used substances.

The most common metal object in the graves were straight pins either from bronze or silver[313] (Na 3-5 on Plate 27), in all 22 in number distributed over 13 graves.[314] Pins were found in the graves of men and women as in the older phases, however now they began to be added to the costumes of children.[315] They are found located near the upper part of the corpse, mostly near the chest and the scull in the same way as observed for the older phases. In one case[316] a pin was found at the hip suggesting that it was fixed on some sort of kilt.

Different weapons were found in the graves including dagger blades, spearheads, a knife, and an axe-blade (B and DL on Plate 27). It is possible that rectangular metal sheets (Bl on Plate 27) also served as axe-blades. These metal artefacts were found in four graves.[317]

Nine graves, mostly of men, contained weapons,[318] but one belonged to a female *subadultus*.[319]

Three graves contained only one weapon: a male *maturus* had a spear-head,[320] a grave without skeleton a dagger-blade,[321] and the above mentioned female *subadultus* an apparently unsharpened axe-blade.[322] No more than three different weapons were found in one grave. They usually[323] consisted of a dagger-blade, a spearhead and an axe-blade. In one case a knife was found instead of a spearhead.[324]

The positions the daggers in the graves varied. They were either located near the hip,[325] the arm[326] or together with the vessels.[327] In the first two cases the daggers were probably part of the burial costume, in the latter they belonged to the *Beigaben* or *Mitgaben*. I find it more probable that it was a *Beigabe* since the daggers were situated among other objects at some distance from the body.

In two burials[328] the spearheads lay at the feet suggesting that the spears were held in the hands in a downward position and that they belonged to the burial costume.

In one case even an axe-blade was found near the feet.[329] Its position compares with that of the spearheads, but it is probable that the context was different. It is hard to imagine how it could have belonged to the burial costume. It could represent a *Beigabe* or a *Mitgabe*. However it is probable that this axe was offered for social reasons (*Mitgabe*) thus maybe symbolising rank, since it was located close to the body and not among the other objects like some of the daggers. We do not have any data about the positions of the other axe-blades, hence keeping us from making any more statements as to their function inside the graves.

In three graves containing weapons, silver headbands with leaf-like decorations were found on the skulls.[330] However they were not exclusive to graves with weapons since three skeletons buried without weapons as well had such headbands.[331] This artefact belonged probably to male burial costumes, since the three sexed skeletons with headbands were men.[332] Each grave containing silver headbands was *intramural* and located on mound E.

Some unusual objects are worth discussing. Only one cylinder seal was found in a grave of an adult person.[333] The style of this seal has been classified as mature Akkadian.[334] A. Otto noticed some regional components as well.[335] The seal was lying next to the skeleton at the backside of the hip. At the front side of the hip were some beads, a pendant and a fragmentary pin. The cylinder seal and the beads could have hung from the pin as suggested for the case from phase I, though with the difference that the pin had been fixed to the skirt. It seems to have belonged to the costume.

In a grave of a child[336] a model of a plain frit cart was found among the pottery vessels near the skull.[337] The possible function of chariot or waggon models in graves

---

drinking vessels.
[313] In two graves: 24/49:3; 25/48:5.
[314] Burials 21/62:4, 24/49:3, 24/49:, 24/49:8, 24/49:9, 25/48:1, 25/48:5, 42/23:7, U:2, U:8, U:25*Süd*, U:25*Nord* and U:43SW.
[315] Burials 24/49:9 *child*, 42/23:7 *child*, U:8 *baby* and U:25Süd *child II*.
[316] Burial 24/47:4.
[317] Burials 24/47:4, 25/48:11, U:25Nord and U:47.
[318] Burials 17/35:4, 24/47:4, 24/49:4a, 25/48:8, 25/48:11, U:2, U:25Nord, U:42, U:47
[319] Burial U:42.
[320] Burial 17/35:4.
[321] Burial 24/49:4a; this grave was partially excavated. Therefore, it is possible that it also contained other weapons.
[322] Strommenger – Kohlmeyer 1998, Pl. 127/21.
[323] Burials 24/47:4 *adultus* and 25/48:11 male *subadultus* and probably U:47.
[324] Burial 25/48:8.
[325] Burial 25/48:8.
[326] Burial 25/48:11.
[327] Burials 24/47:4 and 24/49:4a.

[328] Burials 25/48:8 and 25/48:11.
[329] Burials 25/48:11.
[330] Burials 17/35:4, 27/47:4, 25/48:8.
[331] Burials 24/49:3, 24/49:5, 25/48:1.
[332] However an undecorated head-band appeared in the burial U:40 of an older woman.
[333] Burial 24/47:4.
[334] Strommenger in MDOG 123, 18 uses the term "reichsakkadisch". Otto 2004, 15 follows Boehmer 1965 and dates into the period Akkadian I-II.
[335] Otto 2004, 15.
[336] Burial U:6.
[337] Another plain frit waggon (Object U:296,1.2 in Strommenger – Kohlmeyer 1998, 115) was picked up in the area of cemetery U without known grave context.

Pottery	Intramural burials and at the city-wall		
	Total	Number graves	Max. number per grave
pots and jars (F, Große T)	7 *7,5%*	7 *28%*	1
small pots (WT+*Kleiner T*)	45 *48%*	19 *76%*	6
Drinking vessels (Tg+N)	14 *15,5%*	10 *40%*	2
bowls (Sa+S)	12 *13%*	10 *40%*	2
Miniature vessels (M)	12 *13%*	7 *28%*	2
black-ware (Lu)	3 *3%*	1 *4%*	3
Σ:	93 *100%*	25 *100%*	7

Fig. 28 Distribution of vessels in phase IIIb

as *Beigabe* (e.g. magic) or *Mitgabe* (e.g. toy) has already been discussed.[338]

II.6.4 Phase IIIb

The pottery shapes vary less in this phase than in the previous ones. From 27 different pottery shapes eight (29%) were new,[339] and nineteen (71%) had remained in use since phase IIIa.[340]

The most common pottery types are rather small pots with open mouths (WT 1-5 on Plate 28). Almost half of the vessels belong to this type (Fig. 28). The use of miniature vessels also increased markedly.

The use of bigger pots and jars as well as bowls had decreased since the earlier phase (Fig. 28). Luxury vessels appeared only in one grave.[341]

In general terms, the offered vessels and other artefacts (*Beigabe* and *Mitgabe*) had become less comparable to the ones from the earlier phases.[342]

Pins were the most frequent metal objects, and were recorded in eight graves[343] at the chests,[344] shoulders[345] or necks[346] of the deceased. The aged graves belonged to babies[347] and children,[348] revealing that the children's burial costumes had become similar to those of the adults.

Not one single grave contained a weapon. Precious metal artefacts (gold, silver) are missing too.

II.7 The marked pottery

The last analytical aspect of my study[349] is the analysis of the symbolism of decorated and marked artefacts in the graves. In order to increase the possibilities of encoding any symbolism, a vast sample of comparable illustrations is necessary. In an ideal situation such illustrations appear in a largest possible number on artefacts with identical functions.

In the graves of Tell Bi'a decorations appear on different artefacts like seals,[350] wooden furniture or boxes,[351] headbands,[352] stone vessels[353] waggon models,[354] and pottery vessels. However, apart from the pottery, the sample of different artefact types is rather small.

In dealing with the pottery vessels, it is necessary to differentiate between decoration types like slips,[355] paintings,[356] and engravings. Engravings may further be classified into decorations applied around the vessels[357] and single marks.

In total 118 pottery marks are known from the funerary context, a quantity which makes further analysis possible. All marks were carved on the upper part of the body, below the neck of the jars or pots. It is therefore probable that the marks were intentionally applied to the visible

---

[338] Chapter II.6.1.
[339] However over 40% (40 pieces=43%) of all pottery belongs to the new types.
[340] 57% (53 pieces) of all pottery.
[341] Partly excavated burial 38/24?:1.
[342] At most seven vessels belonged to one grave, however only six graves (24%) had more than four vessels: burials 37/22:1, 37/22:8, 37/23:1, 37/23?:1, 42/23:6 and F:1.
[343] Burials 16/35:2, 16/36:5, 24/47:3, 25/48:7, 29/43:2, 37/22:8, 38/24?:1 and 41/23:1.
[344] Burials 24/47:3 and 25/48:7.
[345] Burial 29/43:2.
[346] Burial 16/35:2.
[347] Burials 16/35:2, 16/36:5.
[348] Burials 24/47:3, 29/43:2, and 41/23:1.

[349] Chapter I.1.5.
[350] In burials 24/47:4, U:43NOalt and SWjung.
[351] In the mausolea G5 and G6.
[352] Burials 17/35:4, 27/47:4, 24/49:3, 24/49:5, 25/48:1 and 25/48:8.
[353] Burials 24/49:5, 25/48:1, 25/48:2, 25/48:11 and U:47.
[354] Burial U:6.
[355] A widespread surface treatment on the Euphrates-ware vessels.
[356] In mausoleum G4R2 and in burial U:25.
[357] Figurative decoration appears on a pot in burial U:47 and simple incised bands on the potteries with combed decoration e.g. in burials 25/45:1 and F:1.

parts and that they conveyed some intelligible information to the observer.

The term "pottery mark" was preferred to the more commonly used "potter's mark" as it is more neutral and less bound to interpretation than latter expression. In the following analysis questions are raised pertaining to:

- which pottery types were signed with a pottery mark.
- the stage within the pottery manufacturing process at which the signs were carved into the clay.
- whether the habit of offering marked pottery stood in any relation with the gender or age of the deceased person.
- any information on the vessel contents the marks might have given.
- conceivable relationships between the different pottery marks and the vessel volumes.
- possible identities of the manufacturer furnished by the marks.
- whether the marks might have had some role in cultic symbolism.
- whether the marks might have been signs of ownership

II.7.1 Phase I

Only a limited number of pottery types were marked. Apart from three vessels[358] all belonged to the open-mouth pots or jars (WT/F 1-7 on Plate 14): in other words, only vessels which served as containers were marked,[359] but not those used for eating or drinking.

In cemetery U marked pottery was found in half of the graves. The habit of offering marked pottery in a burial was independent from the gender and age of the deceased person since the vessels were found indiscriminately inside graves of men,[360] women,[361] and children[362] (Plate 7).

All pottery marks were carved into the wet clay before the firing process. In the case that the marks indicated the content, the contained substance would already have been predetermined before manufacture. In this case the pottery mark would not represent an *ideological* information but rather a *functional* one. Further we would expect that vessels with identical marks and therefore identical function would thus also have the same technical and functional features, and *vice-versa*.

However, two marked jars with handles display for instance different pottery marks and in contrast a marked stoneware pot had the same mark type (Nr.14 on Plate 33) as two simple-ware vessels. This functional interpretation is therefore relatively unlikely.

The same mark types can appear on vessels with different dimensions[363] and, on the opposite, jars and pots of the same dimensions were signed with different marks.[364] Therefore it is also improbable that any volume related system stood behind the pottery marks.

Altogether 94 marked vessels were found in the tombs, 73 in the mausolea, 19 in the graves of cemetery U and two in area V. This means that 20,4% of all vessels and 34,3% of all pots and jars were marked. This is a much higher proportion than usually observed in contemporary profane contexts, be they of domestic or palatial nature.[365] In the case that pottery marks only hinted to the potter, one would not expect such a large discrepancy between the settlement and burial finds.

On the other hand, this disparity would seem less unreasonable, in the case that the ideal component of the pottery mark were more important, accordingly playing a more meaningful role during rituals than in daily life. The distribution of marks in the graves can give hints as to whether they were symbols purely within cult and religion, as for instance symbols for deities, or mere signs of ownership.

In all 22 different pottery marks with several variations are known from the vessels (Plate 33). Their distribution is not even. This means, there are mark types that occur only once[366] and others that are represented on more than ten vessels.[367] Furthermore, in cemetery U there were five graves containing more than one vessel with a pottery mark.[368] In three of them vessels bearing identical signs were found[369]; in the two remaining ones however, two different signs occur on the pots and jars.[370]

If we interpret the marks as signs of ownership, then the graves containing pots with two different pottery marks would suggest that the signs did not inform about the deceased but rather about the mourners from whom the vessels originated.

But if we view the marks as cultic symbols, then they would probably hint to certain deities who were important in the burial ritual. Seen from this angle, the vessel and its content would then have been a present for a particular god in the netherworld.

---

[358] Two jars with two handles (Zweihenkelige F1 on Plate 15) and one luxury pot (Lu 2a on Plate 16).
[359] The height of all marked vessels is above 14 cm.
[360] Burials U:15, U:37, U:45 and U:49.
[361] Burials U: 39, U:40 and U:44.
[362] Burials U:12, U:22 and U: 34.
[363] E.g. motive 17 on Plate 33 appears on jars with heights of 21,0 cm, 25,4 cm, 27,4 and in one case even 38,0 cm. In this context it needs to be mentioned that the elaboration of the pottery marks varies. This may open prospects for discussing a breakdown of the marks into singular motive groups. Even less sure is the assignment of the fragmentary signs.
[364] E.g. jars with heights between 28-29 cm were marked with the Type 5, 6, 9, 14, 1 (Plate 33).
[365] Most pottery publications from contemporary sites along the Euphrates contain no statistical data.
[366] E.g. motives 1, 2, 16, 18, 20, 21, 22 on Plate 33.
[367] E.g. motives 5 and 6 on Plate 33.
[368] Burials U:7, U:9, U:10, U:39 and U:40.
[369] Burials U:9, U:10 and U:39.
[370] Burials U:7 and U:40, however in the last one three pots were marked, two with motive 6 and one with motive 9.

In both cases the question arises how to interpret the different mark frequency and their uneven distribution.

It is possible to correlate each grave group in cemetery U with a characteristic combination of pottery marks. As for the single mausolea the sign combinations were less consistent.[371] Nevertheless we can detect a pattern: a special combination of signs is also characteristic for these buildings.

A seriation of the pottery marks in the mausolea and grave-groups increases the legibility of the relationships between them (Fig. 29). The mausolea are all located close to each other in the middle of the seriation table. Further, mausoleum G3 is closely connected with grave-groups II and III in cemetery U. Similarly mausoleum G4 is also directly connected with groups IV and V. Only the graves of group VI had special marks which could not be correlated with any other tomb. This group will be left out from the following discussion for the time being.

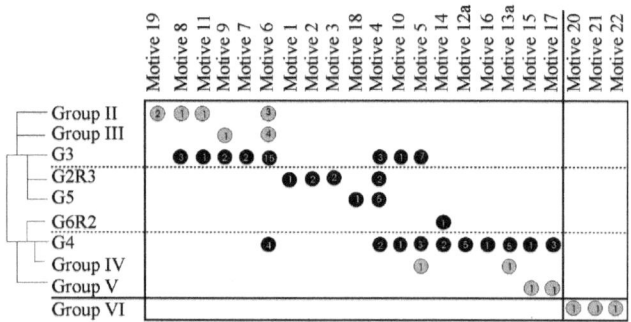

Fig. 29 Relationships between the mausolea and the grave groups in cemetery U as perceived from the pottery marks

Accepting the hypothesis that the marks symbolise ownership, we recognise family relationships in a wider sense between these groups. Furthermore, because in the particular sites the motive variation of the marks is much lower than the expected quantity of the living population, it is probable that the particular pottery marks do not refer to individuals or even small families symbols but rather to kin-groupings or lineage.[372] Consequently, the range of pottery marks in one tomb is an indication of the extension of connections.

As for the hypothesis that the marks were cultic symbols, we would conclude that some aspects of the burial rituals, e.g. the invoked gods, were very diverse between the particular families. However, the similarities concerning all other aspects (spatial organisation, grave orientation, flexed posture, burial costume, grave goods etc.) between the grave groups in cemetery U show a quite uniform ritual behaviour.

As a last step it is possible to return to group VI in cemetery U whose pottery marks showed no relationship

---

[371] E.g. in G3 were 34 marked vessels with seven different signs or in G4 were 27 marked vessels with ten different signs (Plate 33).
[372] Or any degree of relationship like family, clan or tribe.

with the other groups. A simple explanation of this phenomenon could be that only a part of the mausolea and graves of cemetery U had actually been excavated. However this is the only group which in addition had differences in some other aspects, e.g. a south-north alignment of the graves and an over-proportionate quantity of luxury vessels. Therefore we may suspect with caution the possibility that a family did not follow local traditions but foreign ones.[373]

II.7.2 Phase II

Eight graves contained marked pots and jars (WT/F 3-7 types on Plate 19). Fourteen vessels were signed with eight different pottery mark motives (Plate 34/a) which corresponds with 15,6% of all vessels in the graves.[374] The pottery marks were carved into the wet clay on the upper part of the body before the firing process. All marked pots and jars were just like in phase I taller than 14 cm.

There are as many motives already known from phase I[375] as new motives.[376] In cemetery U appear one or two marked vessels per grave-group (Fig. 30).

	All motives	Recurring motives	New motives
Group II	4		4
Group III	9	9	
Group IV	23		23
Group V	9+24		9+24
Without group	4+6+10?+25		

Fig. 30 Distribution of pottery marks in cemetery U in phase II

From the continuity and change in the pattern we underline the presence of strong family connections without being able of specifying their exact nature due to the small sample size.

In the graves of cemetery U there were usually only one or two marked vessels, however in one grave there were six.[377] Five signs depict a bird (motive 25 on Plate 34) and one probably a snake (motive 10 on Plate 34).

The frequent appearance of one motive in one particular grave strengthens the argument that the appearance of marked pottery in the graves is not unintentional.

---

[373] In this respect the appearance of a clay vehicle model in the grave of an adult person could hint to cultic practices connected with mercantile traditions. Therefore it could be a burial place of a family of merchants originating from other cities.
[374] And 51,8% of all open-mouth pots and jars and luxury vessels (Fig. 24). The discrepancy to phase I could be due to the smaller sample.
[375] Motives 4, 6, 9 and 10 on Plate 34.
[376] Motives 23-26 on Plate 34.
[377] Burial U:4.

II.7.3 Phase IIIa

Marked pots or jars[378] have been found only in seven graves.[379] The shapes of the vessels are quite different from the older ones, however only pots and jars taller than 14 cm were marked. One mark was scraped on the pot after its firing,[380] the others were all carved into the wet clay.

On the whole, ten marked vessels were recorded from the graves. This is equivalent to 2,2% of all pottery grave goods and only to 6,4% of the taller pots and jars. This exhibits a strong decrease compared to the proportion in earlier phases. In the following sub-phase IIIb not one grave contained marked pottery.

Four different motives appear on the vessels, one of which was new,[381] and two variations of motives already known from phase I.[382] On one pot from grave U:32 there is a mark (motive 6) known from phases I and II.[383] Four *intramural* graves contained pottery marked with the same motive. These graves were divided into two groups[384] (Plate 34/c).

Depending on the interpretation of the pottery marks the unambiguous change in the use of marked pottery may reflect significant alterations

    a) in the social structure (in the case that the marks are only signs of the family relationships).
    b) in the ritual behaviour (in the case that the marks are signs with religious meaning)
    c) in both (in the case that the marks are signs with religious meaning related to the families, e.g. tutelary god).

---

[378] F7 and F8 on Plate 25 and Große T4-6 on Plate 24.

[379] 13% of the graves (Fig. 26) in contrast to the older phases where more than the half of the single graves contained marked vessels (Figs. 21 and 24).

[380] Motive 13b in grave 25/48:5 (Plate 34/b).

[381] Motive 27 (Plate 34/b).

[382] Motive 12b is a variation of motive 12a rotated 90° and 13b is a variation of motive 13a rotated 180° (compare Plate 33 and Plate 34/b).

[383] But this pot is maybe primarily from the burial context of phase I according to Strommenger-Kohlmeyer 1998: 99

[384] The problems of interpreting this arrangement has been discussed in Chapter II.5.3.

III. Summary and conclusions

III.1 Summary of the analysis

In the preceding analysis it has been possible to distinguish between three main settlement phases dating the EBA, all of them containing burial evidence. It has also been possible to allocate most of these graves to these phases by means of stratigraphy and seriation.

With respect to which aspects were observed for a particular phase was dependent upon the quantity and sometimes the quality of the burials. However, it has been possible to follow the development of the grave groups in cemetery U as well as the changing significance of an area within mound E including the changing importance of the burials themselves.

In order to give a more general overview of each phase it is necessary to sum up the particular aspects that were discussed separately in the preceding text.

III.1.1 Phase I

Two clearly discernible groups of burials were detected, i.e. the individual graves in the extramural cemetery U and the mausolea on mound E.

Subterranean graves – shaft-graves or pit-graves – were grouped in area U into six spatially separated grave groups. Four grave groups (II and IV-VI) were established as being representative. However, we have to keep in mind that 10-30% of the graves are lost, even within the groups, due to erosion or other destruction. Each group had similar dimensions.

It has been suggested previously that the grave groups may be interpreted as burial places of nuclear families or households

- because of the similar age and gender composition of each group (five to seven burials occur in each group: one or two children and three to five adult burials with an even sex distribution).
- because of the analogous development of the burials in each group also in the following phase;
- because of some particular characteristics of the groups, e.g. specific pottery marks, an exceptionally high proportion of "luxury" vessels, or even a specific grave orientation (see group VI).

There exist differences between the particular burials, as for instance the smaller dimensions of children's' graves, the absence of pins in the children's graves (age-specific burial customs) or the fact that weapons only appear in graves of adult men (gender-specific burial custom).

However, between groups I-V there are no significant differences concerning valuable grave goods or burial practices, thus suggesting that the families which buried their members there belonged to the same rank or social class.

Group VI is somewhat different since all adult burials contained "luxury" vessels and the graves were orientated north to south. This difference can be explained with a foreign origin from and an intensive contact with the main territories of the Euphrates ware and metallic ware production. We can imagine e.g. a family of merchants (ga-raš and maš-kim ga-raš) originating from another city or at least another lineage than all the other families.

Apart from these differences, several common customs have been observed in all groups. As part of the *Aufbahrungssitte* the dead were found dressed in burial costumes (probably depending on the season and on the age, gender, and status of the deceased) and the body arranged into a flexed position. To the burial costume belonged pins – with the exception of the children's burials – joining together the dress or maybe also a veil or headdress, jewellery, sometimes cylinder seals, and in one case an undecorated bronze headband. It is possible that at least some of the deceased wore make-up and even carried a small bone tube filled with kohl on a chain. The weapons from the five male burials were deposited near the scull, which makes it unlikely that they belonged to the costume.

Part of the *Beisetzungssitte* is the choice of the burial place in the cemetery next to other family members, i. e. inside the grave-group or even within the same shaft-grave.[385] The graves were dug into the gravel soil; for the children at a length of up to 1,5 m, for the adults they were longer than 1,7 m. Some of the large shaft-graves were deliberately designed for multiple use. The pit-graves were used only for single burials.

First the body was placed in the Eastern part of the tomb – in group VI in the southern part. After that the grave goods were arranged in an assemblage above the head, behind the back or in front of the body. Hereafter, most of the graves were closed with mud-brick and filled with earth. Sometimes a vessel and once the skeleton of a donkey were placed into the filling as an indication for a closing ritual of the interment. It is not possible to decide exactly when these depositions took place, so some of them could belong to the sphere of later ancestral worship at the burial place.

Between one and ten vessels were found in each grave. The varying quantity of the pottery could give an indication, whether directly or indirectly, as to the number of the *dramatis personae* involved in the interment.

It is not easy to differentiate between *Beigaben* and *Mitgaben*. In several cases a single artefact might have had both functions as in the case of the most common artefacts, the vessels. Only in the case of uncommon artefacts can we suggest a differentiation, e.g. it has been suggested that there was a religious reason for putting

---

[385] Because the babies and children are underrepresented, it is quite probable that they were buried in the domestic part of the contemporary settlement under courtyards or houses, as has been demonstrated for phase III.

Summary and conclusions

chariot models into the graves.

Some of the pots or jars had special markings depending on the lineage of the mourners. The intra and interfamilial relationships can be seen in the combination of pottery marks (Fig. 29). The distinctive position of group VI again is apparent, since it has no pottery marks in common with the other groups.

The duration of phase I in cemetery U was about two generations. Contemporary to cemetery U were the above ground mausolea that were unearthed on mound E. At least six of them had been built on top of public buildings.

The socially higher position of the owners of the mausolea with reference to the families in cemetery U is advertised on all four[386] symbolic levels as

- location: the prominent position of the burial place (on a place which had traditionally a communal significance and as always being visible and present as above ground facilities).
- grave form and monument: mud brick buildings of great dimensions (which had to be constructed in a cooperative action) and the elaborated structures of the buildings, e.g. the plastering of the inner and the outer walls.
- grave goods: the more sophisticated furnishing and the valuable grave goods.
- marked objects: larger variation of pottery marks (showing an extended family relationship).

The construction of the mausolea took a period of time; however, all of them ended with the foundation of Palace B.

It seems, because of stratigraphical reasons, that their construction occurred from north to south: first G1 and 2, after that G3 and 4, then G5 and finally G6.

The mausolea were multiply used tombs as is shown for example by the two floor levels in G2 or the evidence of intact and disturbed skeletons in G6R2. The quantity of the people buried as well as their age and gender composition seem to be different in each room; however, only a part of them was anthropologically determined. It is clear anyhow that the tripartite buildings had a mixed age and gender composition just like cemetery U. This makes it likely that we are dealing with family vaults. However, if they were the burial places of families or households of the elite, their family structure was quite different from the nuclear families seen in cemetery U.

The evidence of G4R3 with seventeen individuals, among them three male and twice as many female adults, can be explained in different ways:
- G4 was the burial place of an extended family including e.g. cousins and nephews, but some of the male relatives were not buried inside the same room (they might be e.g. in the anthropologically not yet determined Room 1). The existence of the single-room building G5 with only male burials could indicate that.
- Polygamy was possible among the elite. Also, in G3R1 more female than male adults had been buried.

The final publication of the anthropological remains might bring some light to some of these questions.

The similar, tripartite construction of the mausolea suggests a similar functional division to each room. The entrance into the mausolea had always been from the east side into the central room (R2).[387] The northern (R1) and southern (R3) rooms could be entered only through room 2.

It seems that the entrance room played a role in different stages of the funeral:

- The only intact skeleton with rich burial costume but scanty grave goods in G6R2 makes it probably that the first stage after death took place in that room (marginal state). Several rituals could have been carried out during the time of transformation from a dead person to an ancestor (e.g. funeral banquets). At the last stage (rite of aggregation) the skeleton was deposited with complete utensils into the southern or northern rooms.
- With this act begins the ancestral worship which took place – at least partly – in the entrance room. Remains of such practices have been found in G3R2 with the deposition of selected bones of five goats and in G4R2 where several vessels – including their contents – had been placed. It is quite probably that the offerings in the different buildings happened at about the same time, just before the foundation of Palace B. The differences between the mausolea can be explained by different family traditions.

The picture of a stratified society is evident from the above sketched differences between the subterranean and above ground tombs. The existence of huge public buildings, already in the older levels, show us that we are not dealing with the very beginning of stratified urban society here. The forthcoming publications can provide us with some more hints about the earlier development of the city.

The evidence of the pottery marks has shown that not only vertical stratification existed but also a horizontal diversity between kin-groups. The portrayed social structure agrees with the model of the "conical clan" system (Fig. 31) "in which the degree of relationship to a real or fictive common ancestor served as a basis for internal tendencies towards stratification[388]". The conical

---
[386] see Chapter I.1.5.
[387] However, G2 had an entrance into R3 from the south before the construction of G4. Therefore, the following description and functional analysis of the rooms refers to the final stage of use.
[388] Adams 1966, 94.

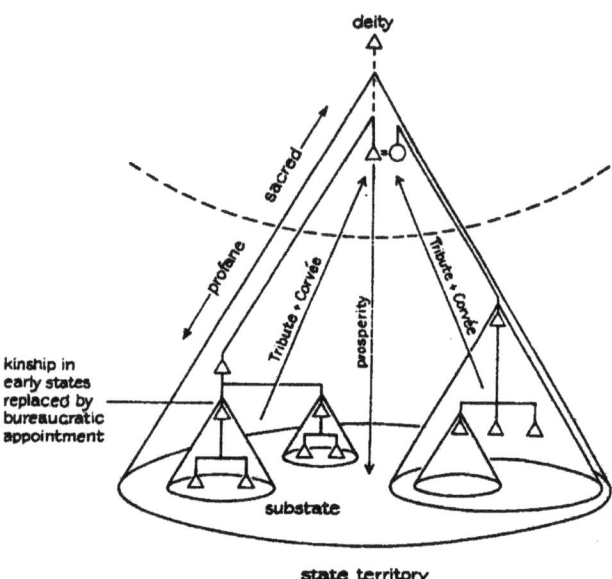

Fig. 31 Diagram of the conical clan system (according to Breuer 1990, 59 fig. 4 with reference to Friedman 1979, 258)

clan system has been described as one of the possible social structures in early state formation,[389] but in many cases the clan or tribal organisation survived even in societies of further developed, territorial states.

The spatial organisation of the mausolea in two parallel rows with a south-north alley between them leading into an open square – symbolised the relative equality of the builders of G1 to G4 and their successors. The picture changed with the building of G6. It was built into the open square blocking the view and the entrance of the alley from the south and blocking the western entrance of G5. This seems to be a symbolic claim for primacy at least towards the owners of *G2, G4* and *G5*.

This time of internal crisis reached its climax and came to a solution by the construction of Palace B on top of all mausolea in phase II. It is a meaningful coincidence that the last person buried was an "over-equipped" young man.

III.2.1 Phase II

There seems to have been a change in the power structure, whereby palace B on top of the mausolea proclaims the seizure of power and its legitimacy. In terms of political organisation it could mean a change from kin-groups, whose members had a more or less equal chance to rise to the highest authority, towards a dynastic structure.

However, the family and kin organisation seems to have continued, since no fundamental changes occurred in cemetery U, considering the horizontal and vertical enlargement of the graves. The use of pottery marks continued as well. The appearance of new pottery marks in the particular grave groups is a sign of vivid social interactions.

Palace B came to a violent end. It cannot be decided by the archaeological evidence, whether it was a result of external destruction or of internal crisis, but the abrupt change in material culture may hint at an outside influence.[390] An approximate synchronicity with the destruction level of Palace G in Ebla can be proposed which would allow further historical interpretation.[391]

III.1.3 Phase IIIa

In this phase the burial pattern in cemetery U is similar to the earlier phases, only the number of secondary burials increased, probably because the cemetery had been filling up, having been used by two or three generations before it came to an end.

The marked vessels became less frequent in the graves, thus hinting at a gradual change starting in this phase. However, the interpretation of this phenomenon requires further examination in future studies.

It is not clear whether the burials within the layers above palace B belonged to a new cemetery or to some buildings. The graves were concentrated in groups, but superpositions occurred and, unlike those of cemetery U, some graves cut through others. Space seems to have been more limited than in cemetery U. Half of the graves belonged to adults of both sexes, half of them to children, similar to the demographic situation in cemetery U. Both, the concentration of graves and the age and gender combination, again make an interpretation as family or household burial places seem probably. The group in quadrant 25/48 contained six graves of adults suggesting a duration of three generations.

Five burials above Palace B contained marked vessels. Only two pottery marks appear on eight vessels,[392] both are variations of marks known since phase I. In that phase both appeared only in one mausoleum, G4.[393]

Some special artefacts from precious metals (e.g. ornamented silver head-bands) marked a specific men's costume differing from the burial costume of men in cemetery U. Also the positioning of the graves in a place with a traditional communal significance makes it probably, that we are dealing with burials which belonged to people with a certain position different from those buried in cemetery U.

Other intramural burials were found on mounds B and C in domestic areas or near the city wall. Almost all belong

---

[389] Examples for the existence of the conical clan organisation in Mesopotamia are described e.g. by Adams 1966, Breuer 1990,174-178 and Postgate 1994², 82-83.

[390] E.g. the scale of change in pottery types was much greater than between the other phases. See also Chapter II.6.3.
[391] See also Chapter III.2.
[392] Motives 12b and 13b on Plate 34/b.
[393] See Plate 33.

to children showing that certain infants had a specific burial place. Probably this was not a new phenomenon, because children are under-represented already in the earlier phases and the excavations in those areas did not yet reach those earlier levels. It is not yet possible to say which children were buried within the grave groups and which received a specific treatment.

III.1.4 Phase IIIb

We do not know where the adult population was buried, since almost all known burials belonged to children. cemetery U was not in use anymore and the domestic areas contained mostly burials of children just as in phase IIIa.

In general, fewer artefacts were put into the graves. The vessels chosen for burial purposes were not marked anymore, but marked vessels were still in use in the contemporary settlement. This change in burial customs – for whatever reasons – was not a sudden affair but a gradual process. The proportion of marked pottery decreased since phase IIIa.

We can try to imagine several explanations for this phenomenon, but as long as the contemporary burial place – most likely a cemetery – of the adult population remains unknown all interpretation will remain vague and insecure.

The pot grave, a new burial form, appeared in this phase. Later this burial form was common at least for intramural children burials during the MBA, represented by the burials of seriation groups 8-11. This shows the transitional character of phase IIIb between the EBA and the MBA.

It seems that after the *Pfeilergebäude* had been abandoned the area finally lost its special importance; the graves on its top belong to children and they are without any peculiarities. Only in area 28/45 an adult burial seems to have taken place showing a continuity of tradition since phase IIIa.

The evidence is less solid for estimating the duration of this phase, because there are no control groups to suggest only one generation. However, it is probably, that it was in fact a short period of time, with only two building levels between the *Pfeilergebäude* and Palace A.[394] The thin walled buildings apparently belonged to small-scale domestic architecture.

The end of this phase is marked by the construction of Palace A. This building seems to symbolise the beginning of a new epoch in the settlement structure of Tell Bi'a and possibly also in the political organisation. After the gradual loss of the area's importance during phase III the builders of Palace A decided to bring about an "ideological restoration" here. In this sense the Palace symbolised the re-establishment of the "traditional" structure before the destruction of Palace B.

III.2 Relations to the Syrian and Mesopotamian Socio-cultural history

So far, these social processes have been observed only at Tell Bi'a, but of course the social, political, economical environment known from archaeological and written sources influenced them.

Further study would be necessary for a systematic comparison of contemporary sites to define the degree of similarities in material culture (e.g. pottery assemblages), in ritual behaviour (e.g. burial tradition) or in ideological components (e.g. expression of lineage by pottery marks) and to interpret the reasons for such similarities.

Therefore, in this study we can only point out some analogies to different sites in the Euphrates region which show similarities in particular aspects. Contemporary evidence will, however, be a key criterion, as well as in the use of written sources.

The difficulties in comparing the archaeological to the literary relative dating system have been discussed in the first part. However, the analysis has yielded some results which can be used to attempt such a comparison.

III.2.1 The chronological consequences: piecing together the archaeological and the literary relative dating systems

Interpreting the spatial groups in cemetery U of Tell Bi'a as burial places of nuclear families has helped to give an estimation for the duration of the particular phases in terms of generations (Fig. 32). In this respect, only the burials of individuals older than fourteen years have been taken into account.

The demographic analysis[395] has shown that in phases I to IIIb the average life expectancy of the population older than fourteen years was generally 28,15 years. This could vary between 25 and 30,8 years in the particular phases (Fig. 32).

	Duration on the base of cemetery U	Life-expectancy
Phase I (young)	2 generations	28,12 years
Phase II	1 generation	30,8 years
Phase IIIa	2-3 generations*	27 years
Phase IIIb		25 years
Σ	5-6 generations	28,15 years

*The contemporary intramural burials were used during three generations.

Fig. 32 Duration of cemetery U

This gives a solid basis for the suggestion that cemetery U was in use for 125 years at least and for 180 years at

---

[394] See e.g. Strommenger–Kohlmeyer 2000, app. 9 and 10. The stratigraphy between the *Pfeilergebäude* and Palace A has been disturbed by erosion as well as by an Early Byzantine monastery.

[395] Chapter II.4.

	Hypothesis I						Hypothesis II					
	1			2			1			2		
	A	B	C	A	B	C	A	B	C	A	B	C
Length of one generation (in years)	25	28,15	30	25	28,15	30	25	28,15	30	25	28,15	30
Akkadian Period	181 years						197 years					
Destruction of Palace G in Ebla	by Sargon (30th year of reign)			by Narām-Sîn			by Sargon (30th year of reign)			by Narām-Sîn		
Relation of Palace G in Ebla and Palace B in Tuttul	roughly at the same time (less than 30 years)											

Fig. 33 Working hypotheses for the comparison of archaeological and historical data of the Akkadian period

This gives a solid basis for the suggestion that cemetery U was in use for 125 years at least and for 180 years at most.[396] The correct value must be somewhere in between. Presumably, when taking into account the duration of the intramural burials and the general life expectancy, it must have been rather closer to the higher proposition.

The basis for an estimate of the duration of phase IIIb is less reliable. However, it is unlikely to have lasted for more than two generations.

No objects or inscriptions that can be dated exactly have been found in Tell Bi'a from the EBA.

A *terminus ante quem* for the end of phase IIIb (EBA) is given by the erection of Palace A. B. Einwag suggested dating it to the Ur III period or to the very beginning of the Isin/Larsa period.[397] The reasons given are: a surface plan which is very similar with the so-called *Šakkanakku*-Palace in Mari, the evaluation of the pottery assemblage and the find of seal impressions.[398]

A seal and seal impressions in phase IIIa of Akkadian style cannot be further specified. They belong most likely to the Akkadian III style according to R. M. Boehmer.[399] However, as R. Dittmann has shown recently, this style represents a very long interval from the reign of Narām-Sîn until the reign of the Ur III kings.[400] Therefore, the appearance of such seals and impressions can only help to constitute a *terminus post quem* which seems not earlier than Narām-Sîn.

A better chronological comparison is possible between Palace G in Ebla and phase II in Tell Bi'a. Not only the surface plan of Palace B in Tell Bi'a is similar to the Palace G in Ebla, but also various almost identical artefacts – some of them imports found in Tell Bi'a – suggest the coexistence and direct contact between both palaces (Plate 35).[401] Since phase II in Tell Bi'a represents about one generation, we can assume that less than thirty years passed between the destruction of both palaces.[402]

As we have seen in Chapters I.3.1[403] and I.3.2, the question of who destroyed Palace G in Ebla – Sargon or Narām-Sîn – is widely discussed. Recently, Sallaberger[404] dated the end of the Ebla archives close to the thirtieth year of Sargon's reign.[405] Other studies[406] argue in favour of a destruction by Narām-Sîn without suggesting a concrete year. A suggestion, however, was made that his Syrian campaign took place after he had secured his rule over the revolting cities in southern Mesopotamia.[407]

The sequence of the Akkadian kings and the length of their reigns are known from the Sumerian King Lists. Two main variations exist which depend essentially on the duration of the reign of Narām-Sîn, who either ruled for 37 or for 56 years.[408] Therefore, the Akkadian period lasted for 181 or 197 years.

Some working hypotheses can be postulated for the comparison of the archaeological with the historical data on the base of the data mentioned above (Fig. 33 and Plates 37-38).

---

[395] Chapter II.4.

[396] A minimum of five generations with an average mortality rate of 25 years and a maximum of six generations with an average mortality rate of c.30 years.

[397] For the following it is important, that the foundation did not take place at the beginning of the Ur III period.

[398] Einwag 1995, 45 fig. 10, 49 and 51 fig. 15 with additional arguments. Compare Krebernik 2001, 15-18.

[399] Boehmer 1965. Otto 2004 correlates with Akkadian Ic-III styles, however some of the early dated seals and impressions show local Syrian notes, which makes a sure dating difficult.

[400] Dittmann 1994.

[401] See also the correlation by Hempelmann 2005, 93 table 11.

[402] One could start a controversial debate about problems, e. g. if the phase IIB1 in Ebla was a much longer period than the Phase II in Tell Bi'a and if the palace of Tuttul was destroyed earlier than Palace G. But until now there is no hint to a long interval of Mardīḫ IIB1 and the published material from the burned layer of Palace G is very much like that from palace B of Tell Bi'a.

[403] Especially note 71.

[404] Sallaberger 2004.

[405] Hempelmann 2004, Table 2.

[406] See note 71.

[407] E.g. Gelb–Kienast in the commentary on Narām-Sîn C1.

[408] Hempelmann 2004, especially Table 3.

Summary and conclusions

Beginning with hypothesis I/1. (Plate 37) it can be seen that phase IIIb should start at the latest at the beginning of the reign of Šarkališarrī (I/1.C),[410] more than sixty years before the end of the Akkadian period. In hypothesis II/1. (Plate 38) this is even a longer interval, almost eighty years owing to the longer reign of Narām-Sîn (II/1.C). Consequently, a longer period of time elapsed until the erection of Palace A which took place not before the Ur III dynasty (and not at its very beginning). However, phase IIIb hardly lasted for more than two generations.

According to hypothesis I/2., phase IIIa finished at the latest after the Akkadian period in Mesopotamia (I/2.C), at the beginning of the Ur III dynasty. In hypothesis II/2. phase IIIa ended at the latest during the reign of Šū-Durul, less than fifteen years before the end of the Akkad Dynasty. If we calculate with one or two generations (min. 25 – max. 60 years) for phase IIIb, its end would correspond with the suggested erection of Palace A.

Even if we change any of the uncertain components in these hypotheses, it seems to be more likely to date the destruction of the palaces rather to the reign of Narām-Sîn than to the reign of Sargon.

According to the hypotheses I/2.A–C and II/2.A–C, phase II in Tell Bi'a is contemporary to the reign of Narām-Sîn and his predecessors,[411] while phase I ended in the earlier Akkadian period, but started already in the time of Mesopotamia's Early Dynastic kings.

III.2.2 Intramural above ground funerary monuments

Some above ground funerary monuments like Tomb 302 in Ğerablūs Taḥtāni,[412] White Monuments I–III in Tell Banāt,[413] the mausolea in Tell Bi'a and elite tombs in Umm el-Marra on the Ğabbūl-Plain[414] have been unearthed at the Euphrates over the last decades. In the light of such new information, some tombs from former excavations have been re-evaluated and identified as above ground facilities like the *Hypogeum* in Tell Aḥmār[415] and probably Tomb 300 in Mari, without a documented *dromos*.[416]

Most of these tombs – if not all – have been constructed in EBA III according to the Syrian chronology (or Period IV in Tell Banāt, phase I in Tell Bi'a etc. Plate 2). On several sites[417] other than Tell Bi'a the tombs were still in use in EBA IV A (Bi'a phase II/EBA IVa) or even later.

---

[410] And at the earliest – according to hypotheses I/1.A – the end of Maništūsu.

[411] In the extreme case, if the destruction of the Palace B happened in the last years of Narām-Sîn, the existence of Palace B overlaps with his reign.

[412] Peltenburg 1999b.

[413] McClellan – Porter 1999.

[414] Schwartz – Curvers – Stuart 2000, Schwartz *et al.* 2006 and Schwartz 2007.

[415] Roobaert – Bunnens 1999.

[416] Jean-Marie 1990 and 1999. It is quite probable that tombs 21, 22, 241 and 242 were also similar above ground constructions, but a sure reconstruction is not possible anymore.

[417] E.g. Tell Aḥmār, Umm el-Marra.

In Ğerablūs Taḥtāni a modification in function has been observed for the later period, a change from a funerary place to a place for post-interment funerary offerings as indication for ancestor worship.[418] This reminds us of Tell Banāt where the White Monument A (Banāt Period III)[419] encased some tumuli. White Monument included secondary burial deposits which took place during the construction of the funeral monument; none of those occurred later.[420]

Mortuary Monument II in Tell Banāt incorporated some individual *tumuli* under one great mound.[421] Tomb 302 in Ğerablūs Taḥtāni had a main chamber and a deepened annex, its walls were built from limestone blocks and covered with a mound with a similarly corrugated surface as in Banāt.[422]

The *Hypogeum* in Tell Aḥmār was a half deepened, stone built chamber with a stairway on its western side probably leading to another chamber.[423] The tombs in Mari were also built from stone and might at least have been partially above ground. However, they had only one chamber. In Tell Bi'a the mausolea were completely above ground and built from mud bricks.

The mode of construction was different on all sites, but shows some common characteristics:

- They were, at least partially, above ground facilities and, therefore, visible to the living.
- They were located in a dominant place of the settlement, usually intramural with the exception of Ğerablūs Taḥtāni, but in any case visible from the riverside – according to E. Peltenburg a "visible landmark"– and incorporated into the settlement's communication network.[424] Mortuary Monument II and the White Monuments in Tell Banāt seem to be located outside the urban centre as well.[425]
- They were "collective burial programs".[426]

N. Laneri summarised the possible symbolism of intramural burials of "the wealthiest members of the community"[427] as follows:

(1) "a copy of the domestic dwelling (with the *dromos*, the entrance door and the room itself) and in particular of that part of home which is depository of the socio-economical and ideological-ritual values that are expressed through the archaeological

---

[418] Peltenburg 1999b.

[419] Porter 2002b, 12.

[420] McClellan – Porter 1999, 108.

[421] McClellan – Porter 1999, 107, Porter 2002a and b.

[422] Peltenburg 1999b, 431, Cooper 2006, 239.

[423] Roobaert – Bunnens 1999, 164-165.

[424] Peltenburg 1999b, 429-430.

[425] McClellan – Porter, 1999, 108.

[426] Peltenburg 1999b, 428-429.

[427] Laneri 1999, 232.

material cultural specific to the region;
(2) a small ancestral temple, where to bury the individuals of the family of highest lineage;
(3) a place that testifies to an affiliation to the group and stands as a social territorial marker[428];
(4) a way to keep in contact with the dead, by enhancing, through spatial proximity, the feelings of separation and despair typical of the ritual moment of the "rite of passage";
(5) the legitimation of the transfer of power (inheritance) within the group[429];
(6) the attempt to reconstruct a family tree that includes the ancestors."[430]

Which of these aspects could be applied to which of the particular tombs needs to be discussed in the context of each specific site.[431] The analysis of the mausolea in Tell Bi'a has shown that they can at least be seen as examples for the theses (2) to (5).[432]

The appearance of elaborate above ground funerary monuments in urban societies is a particular feature of the upper Euphrates sites during the EBA III period.[433] This phenomenon can be connected with intra and interregional changes within the social and power structures[434] in the course of urbanisation and state formation.[435]

In Tell Bi'a the change from mausolea to a palace characterises a striking stage in a process in which course "pre-existing elites were integrated into larger alliance systems".[436] This created an unstable social structure which ended with the introduction of dynastic succession.[437]

III.2.3 Pottery marks

Pottery marks in burial contexts served also as traditional social territorial markers on different levels of the society.[438] In this sense, similar pottery marks found at different archaeological sites can point to interrelationships (Plate 39).

In domestic and palatial contexts their function was more practical: to mark the origin of wares, similar to the seal impressions.[439] The appearance of pottery marks in settlement features can indicate economical exchange of wares, but the pottery marks in burial contexts should be interpreted in terms of social connections.[440]

The material basis, however, is not yet large enough to enable us to carry out a comparative study between economical and social connections on the Upper Euphrates.

III.2.4 The Ebla texts: political organisation, burials and ancestor worship

It has been discussed above that the time of the Ebla archives mainly overlapped with phase II in Tell Bi'a, though some texts refer to earlier periods.

The texts were partially compared with the archaeological evidence, e.g. by Mazzoni[441] in order to understand the economic system in Ebla or by Meyer[442] to reconstruct the settlement system on the upper Euphrates and in central Western Syria. Meyer in his reconstruction using the hierarchic "Christaller-model" suggested that in the later EBA in North-Syria from the Orontes to the meeting of the Balīḫ and Euphrates rivers there were some central sites of the highest level (administrative, religious and economic centres): Ebla, Ḫalab, Emar and Tuttul.

The written sources give some, rather incomplete, information on the power structures in the 3rd millennium BC in Ebla, Emar and Mari, even if most of the terms are still under discussion, e.g. e n, l u g a l or ABx.ÁŠ.ABx.ÁŠ.[443]

It seems that these expressions were used differently in the contemporary South-Mesopotamian texts. However, the existing sources show us the e n ("king" or "head of the organisation[444]"), l u g a l ("prince"[445] or "high officer"[446]) and ABx.ÁŠ.ABx.ÁŠ ("elders") as playing important roles in the distribution system of Ebla as well as in the external exchange with Mari[447] and Emar.[448] In other words, they had a special status in the socio-political and economical structures.

---

[428] Also Peltenburg 1999b, 429-430 for Ǧerablūs Taḫtāni and McClellan – Porter 1999, 111 for Tell Banāt.
[429] Also Peltenburg 1999b, 428-429: "The introduction of collective burial program in an above ground, large-scale facility that exceeded the practical requirements of burial was an assertive act that symbolised and fostered new notions of social structure. Further, in view of the likely prevalence of long-term funerary cults, it was erected in full cognizance of its role in future generations."
[430] Laneri 1999, 232 with references to the particular theses.
[431] An overview gives Cooper 2006, 202-256 and recently Peltenburg 2008.
[432] The validity of the first thesis – similarity to parts of the domestic architecture – can be examined only after the publication of contemporary domestic architecture.
[433] Also Hempelmann 2005, 159, McClellan – Porter 1999, 111 and Peltenburg 1999b.
[434] Peltenburg 1999b, 428.
[435] E.g. McClellan 1999, 419 and Peltenburg 1999b, 429.
[436] Peltenburg 1999b, 429.
[437] Suggested also for other Syrian EBA palaces and Tell Banāt by McClellan 1999, 419. For the theoretical backgrounds on the transformation of the archaic state see Breuer 1990, 68-75.
[438] In different times or cultural contexts pottery marks can express other things. Therefore, here only the EBA Syro-Anatolian territory is referred to.
[439] Mazzoni 1988: 89.
[440] Finds in kilns or potters' quarters should also be taken into consideration interpreted with them.
[441] e.g. Mazzoni 1988.
[442] Meyer 1996, esp. 144-155.
[443] See e.g. Archi 1982, Geller 1987, Michalowski 1988, Hallo 1992.
[444] Michalowski 1988, 270.
[445] Archi 1982, 203-204.
[446] Grégoire-Renger 1988, 219.
[447] Archi 1981.
[448] Archi 1990.

Whatever power the e n symbolised, it seems from the Ebla texts that this office was not hereditary before the time of the last two e n.[449] According to A. Archi[450] it is remarkable that the elements "Damu" and "Lim" appeared in the names of eight out of ten persons in ARET 7, 150 as well as in the names of family members of Ibrium and Ibbi-Zikir. Therefore, he maintains that the social structure in Ebla had tribal elements[451] or was at least founded mainly on kinship. Also, the manner of economical production seems to have been determined by a combination of congenial relationships and village communities in a patrimonial state.[452]

The texts give us information about the family organisation of the higher officials. Michalowski[453] when comparing the personal-names of the d u m u . n i t a e n ("male children of the e n), d u m u . m u n u s e n (female children of the e n) with those of d u m u . n i t a or d u m u . m u n u s ib-rí-um or i-bí-zi-kir found that they do not correlate well to each other; therefore, it is very unlikely that they were the en. But all of these had a large number of "children".[454] He suggested three solutions to explain those terms[455]:

- If e n means king, "the title d u m u . n i t a e n was borne for life by the male child of any king, alive or dead."
- "One could posit also, that the rulers had numerous wives and concubines and all their offspring were referred to as children of the king."
- According to Civil's suggestion,[456] based on the lack of an expression for "cousin" in the Sumerian language, one could assume a system comparable to the Hawaiian system for the articulation of kinship system. "If one accepts this hypothesis then as a result one must assume that the numerous "children" of Ibrium and the e n are not in fact all daughters and sons of that person, but members of the same generations in Ibrium's family."

In the Ebla documents from Palace G only a limited number of such large extended families appear: those of the e n, Ibrium and Ibbi-Zikir. The family structure on the basic level of society was much more the small or the nuclear family structure.

As a result of his analysis, Michalowski concluded: "I do not think, that we can say with any certainty that Ibrium was the king of Ebla, but we can point out that one or more large corporate kin groups were of great importance in the activities of the state that were recorded in this particular archives."[457]. Therefore, "instead of concentrating on the 'royal family' as such" one can take a "closer look at the kin groupings of the elite of the city"[458] – just as we have been able to observe in the archaeological material of phase I in Tell Bi'a.

In the texts there are also some references to the cultic activities of the elite can be found. Lists of offerings to the ancestors and a group of texts concerning the ÉxPAP are the most interesting for the study presented here. The first group includes texts which mention the dead en or en-en (Plural), sometimes in connection with laments (si-du$_3$-si-du$_3$).[459] In some texts the terminus dingir (god) appears before the word en, interpreted as a genitive connection (god of the en = tutelary god)[460] or as a determinative for deities, thus expressing that the title holder was dead and had become a god.[461] The latter expression can be seen in a greater context of ancestral worship which played a great role in the public cult.[462] The texts mention first of all offerings of animals connected to the ancestral cult.

The texts concerning the term ÉxPAP seem to have been in direct connection with the burial itself. Pettinato explains it as a burial place or a cemetery but Archi argues for a translation as a "burial ritual".[463]

Different objects were given to the ÉxPAP: diverse textiles; some mines of gold, silver or bronze; silver pins with golden heads, "amorite" daggers etc.[464]

Most of these objects are well known from the burial records of the Euphrates region. Objects of silver or gold have been found mostly in the contemporary and earlier above ground tombs and in some subterranean constructions,[465] but not in the common pit or shaft-graves.

A. Archi found a connection in several cases between the ÉxPAP and a "purification ceremony" (ì-giš-sag, literally

---

[449] Pettinato 1981 suggested that the kings of the city were originally elected for a short period of time and also that they were a kind of "primus inter pares". Archi 1986, 206 denied the existence of such an election. At the same time, by the interpretation of ARET 7, 150 he stressed, that the office of e n was not passed on from father to son and not even inside a family except in the case of the last two kings.

[450] Archi 1986.

[451] Already Archi 1982, 207. Archi 1986, 216 note 17 shows that also in Emar in the 3rd millennium Damu was the tutelary god for the family (dynasty) of the e n.

[452] Grégoire – Renger 1988, 219-22. They interpret the term e$_2$-duru^{ki} as a group of persons in the village community related by kinship to each other. The evidence of the signed pottery can be connected with this organisation. Mazzoni 1984 and 1988, 89 suggested that the sealed pottery originated from the villages of the rural environment of Ebla. In the case of the pottery marks we can think of dues of greater congenial groups or lineages.

[453] Michalowski 1988, 270-276.

[454] According to the evaluation of the Ebla archives by Michalowski 1988 Ibrium had fourteen male and fourteen female "children", Ibbi-Zikir had eleven male and three female. Hallo 1992 writes of twenty-five sons of Ebrium (according to Archi 1988b, 222-235).

[455] The following quotations are from Michalowski 1988, 270-271.

[456] Civil 1976, 142.

[457] Michalowski 1988, 272.

[458] Michalowski 1988, 272.

[459] E.g. Xella 1988, 357.

[460] E.g. Archi 1988b.

[461] E.g. Xella 1988, 357-358.

[462] E.g. Xella 1988.

[463] Pettinato 1988, 313; Archi 1996, 17.

[464] See e.g. the texts in Pettinato 1988, 314–316.

[465] Like Tomb 7 in Tell Banat. The entrance to the dromos seems to have been visible, but the chambers were subterranean according to McClellan – Porter 1999.

"oiling of the head").[466] The utensils used in this ceremony are not mentioned; however, we can think of some special vessels found in contemporary burial contexts – first of all the "Syrian bottle".

The sign ÉxPAP is so far only known from the Ebla texts. It neither appears in the earlier texts from Fara and Abu Salabikh nor slightly later in Mari or Tell Beydar. It was possibly a technical term used only in a specific period and a particular cultural region.

The above ground funerary monuments were similarly special cultural phenomena, limited to more or less the same time and territory. The objects known from the ÉxPAP texts seem to refer to the burial costume.

However, the term ÉxPAP did not necessarily designate the place of the interment. Another possibility could be disclosed by comparing the texts to buildings connected to the dead or ancestral cult (as opposed to places of the interment). Such buildings have been identified e.g. in Halawa A and Tell Chuēra,[467] but dealing with them unfortunately would exceed the limits of this study.[468]

---

[466] Archi 1996, 17-18.
[467] Hempelmann 2001, 158-160.
[468] An evaluation of about 120 passages published regarding the ÉxPAP is planned for the future.

Abbreviations

AHW II
von Soden, W. 1972: Akkadisches Handwörterbuch – Band II. Wiesbaden

Akkadica
Akkadica. Périodique bimestriel de la Fondation Assyriologique Georges Dossin. Brüssel

Amurru 1
Durand, J.-M. (ed.) 1996, *Mari, Ébla et les Hourrites dix ans de travauxc - Première partie*. Actes du colloque international (Paris, mai 1993). Paris

AoF
Altorientalische Forschungen. Berlin.

ARES
Archivi Reali di Ebla – Studi. Roma

BaM
Baghdader Mittelungen. Berlin, Mainz.

BAR IntSer
British Archaeological Reports International Series. Oxford

BASOR
Bulletin of the American Schools of Oriental Research. Philadelphia

CDOG
Colloquien der Deutschen Orient-Gesellschaft.

FAOS
Freiburger Altorientalische Studien. Stuttgart

Levant
Levant – Journal of the British School of Archaeology in Jerusalem. London

MARI
Mari Annales de Recherches Interdisciplinaires. Paris

MDOG
Mitteilungen der deutschen Orient-Gesellschaft zu Berlin. Berlin

Mesopotamia
Mesopotamia, Rivista di Archaeologia, epigrafia e storia orientale antica, Torino

OBO
Orbis Biblicus et Orientalis. Publié au nom de l'Institut Biblique de l'Université de Fribourg Suisse, du Seminar für biblische Zeitgeschichte der Universität Münster i.W. et de la Société Suisse pour l'Etudedu Proche Orient Ancien. Ed. Keel, O. Freiburg (Schweiz) – Göttingen

OIP
The University of Chicago Oriental Institute Publications. Chicago

OxfEnc
The Oxford Encyclopedia of Archaeology in the Near East. Meyers, E. M. (Ed.) 1997, New York – Oxford

RAI
Rencontre Assyrologique Internationale

RGTC 1
Répertoire Géographiques des Textes Cunéiformes. Band 1:
Edzard, D. O. – Farber, G. – Sollberger, E. 1977, *Die Orts -und Gewässernamen der präsargonischen und sargonischen Zeit*. Wiesbaden (TAVO Beihefte B 7/1)

RGTC 12/1
Répertoire Géographiques des Textes Cunéiformes. Band 12/1: Bonechi, M. 1993, *I nomi geografici dei testi di Ebla*. Wiesbaden (TAVO Beihefte B 7/12)

RIME
The Royal Inscriptions of Mesopotamia. Toronto – Buffalo –London.

RlA
Reallexikon der Assyorologie (ab 1957) und Vorderasiatischen Archäologie. Berlin, Leipzig, New York.

TAVO
Tübinger Atlas des Vorderen Orients. Wiesbaden

TUAT II/4
Texte aus der Umwelt des Alten Testaments. Ed. by Kaiser, O. Band II Lieferung 4: Butterweck, Chr. et al.: Grab-, Sarg-, Votiv- und Bauinschriften. Gütersloh 1988

WA
World Archaeology.

WVDOG
Wissenschaftliche Veröffentlichung der Deutschen Orient-Gesellschaft.

ZA
Zeitschrift der Assyorologie. Zeitschrift für Assyriologie und Vorderasiatische Archäologie. Berlin, New York.

References

Ahnert, P.
1983
Kleine praktische Astronomie. Leipzig

Albright, W. F.
1932
The excavation of Tell Beit Mersim in Palestine I: The pottery of the first three campaigns. (AASOR 12), New Haven

Albright, W. F.
1933
The excavation at Tell Beit Mersim 1A: The Pottery of the Fourth Campaign. (AASOR 13), New Haven

Anbar, M
1991
Les tribus amurites de Mari. (OBO 108) Freiburg – Göttingen

Arbeitman, Y. L. (ed.)
1988
FUCUS– A Semitic/Afrasian gathering in remembrance of Albert Ehran. Amsterdam – Philadelphia

Archi, A.
1981
I rapporti tra Ebla e Mari. in: *Seb 4*, 129-166

Archi, A.
1982
About the Organisation of the Eblaite State. in: *Seb 5*, 201-220

Archi, A.
1986
Die ersten zehn Könige von Ebla. in: *ZA 76*, 213-217

Archi, A.
1987
Les titres de en et lugal à Ebla et des cadeaux pour le roi de Kish. in: *MARI 5*, 37-52.

Archi, A.
1988
Cult of the ancestors and tutelary god at Ebla. in: *Arbeitman (ed.) 1988*, 103-112

Archi, A.
1990a
Tuttul-sur-Baliḫ à lâge d'Ebla. in: *Tunca ed. 1990*, 197-207

Archi, A.
1990b
Imâr au IIIeme millénaire d'après les archives d'Ebla. in: *MARI 6*, 21-38

Archi, A.
1996a
Chronologie relative des archives d'Ébla. in: *Amurru 1*, 11-28

Archi, A.
1998
The Regional State of Nagar According to the Texts of Ebla. in: *Subartu IV/2*, 1-22

Archi, A. – Piacentini, P. – Pomponio, F.
1993
I nomi di luogo dei testi di Ebla. (ARES II) Roma

Ariès, P.
1974
Western Attitudes Towards Death from the Middle Ages to the Present. Baltimore

Astour, M. C.
1988
The Geographical and Political Structure of the Ebla Empire. in: *Hauptmann – Waetzold (eds.) 1988*, 139-158

Bartoloni, G – Benedettini, M. G. (eds.)
2008
Sepoltri tra i vivi – Buried among the living. Roma

Bietak, M. (ed.)
2000
The Synchronisation of Civilisations in the Near Eastern Mediterranean in the Second Millennium B.C. – Proccedings of an International Symposium at Schloß Haindorf, 15th – 17th of November 1996 and at the Austrian Academy, Vienna, 11th– 12th of May 1998. Wien

Binford, L. R.
1971
Mortuary practices: their study and their potential. in: *Brown (ed.) 1971*, 6-29

Boehmer, R. M.
1965
Die Entwicklung der Glyptik währen der Akkad-Zeit. Berlin

Braidwood, R. J. – Braidwood, L. S.
1960
Excavations in the Plain of Antioch I – The Earlier Assemblages Phases A-J. (OIP 61) Chicago

Breuer, St.
1990
Der archaische Staat – Zur Soziologie charismatischer Herrschaft. Berlin

Brown, J. A. (ed.)
1971
Approaches to the social dimensions of mortuary practices. New York

References

Buchanan, B.
1966
Cylinder Seals. Volume I. (Catalogue of Ancient Near Eastern Seals in the Ashmolean Museum). Oxford

Buikstra, J. – Mielke, J.
1985
Demography, diet, and health. in: *Mielke – Gilbert (eds.) 1985*, 359-422.

Campbell, S.
1999
Archaeological constructs and past reality on the upper Euphrates. in: *del Olmo Lete – Montero Fenollós (eds.) 1999*, 573-583

Campbell, S.
2000
Questions of definition in the EBA of the Tishrin Dam. in: *Marro – Hauptmann eds. 2000*, 53-63

Campbell, S. – Green, A. (eds.)
1995
The Archaeology f Death in the Ancient Near East. Oxford

Chapman, R. W. – Kinnes, I. – Randsborg, K. (eds.)
1981
The archaeology of Death. Cambridge

Civil, M.
1976
Lexicography. in: *Liebermann (ed.)1976*, 123-158

Cooper, E. N.
1999
The EB-MB transitional period at Tell Kabir, Syria. in: *del Olmo Lete – Montero Fenollós (eds.) 1999*, 321-332

Cooper, L.
2006
Early Urbanism on the Syrian Euphrates. New York – London

del Olmo Lete, G. – Montero Fenollós, J.-L. (eds.)
1999
Archaeology of the Upper Syrian Euphrates the Tishrin Dam Area. Proceedings of the International Symposium Held at Barcelona, January 28th-30th 1998. (Aula Orientalis - Supplementa 15.) Sabadell (Barcelona)

Dittmann, R.
1994
Glyptikgruppen a Übergang von der Akkad– zur Ur III–Zeit. in: *BaM 25*, 75-117

Dossin, G.
1955
L'inscription de fondation de Iaḫdun-Lim, roi de Mari. in: *Syria 32*, 1-28

Durand, J.-M.
1985
La situation historique des šakkanakku: nouvelle approche. in: *MARI 4*, 147-172.

Edzard, D. O.
1981
Neue Erwägungen zum Brief des Enna-Dagan von Mari. in: *Seb 4*, 89-97

Einwag, B.
1998
Die Keramik aus dem Bereich des Palastes A in Tall Bi'a/Tuttul und das Problem der frühen Mittleren Bronzezeit. München - Wien

Falb, Chr. *et al.*
2005
Der Friedhof von Abu Ḥamed. (Gräber des 3. Jahrtausends v. Chr. im syrischen Euphrattal 4) Saarwellingen

Franke, S.
1995
Königsinschriften und Königsideologie: Die Könige von Akkade zwischen Tradition und Neuerung. Münster – Hamburg

Frayne, R. D.
1993
Sargonic and Gutian Periods (2334–2113). (RIME Early Periods Vol. 2) Toronto – Buffalo – London

Frayne, R. D.
1997
Ur III Period (2112–2004). (RIME Early Periods Vol. 3/2). Toronto – Buffalo – London

Frazer, Sir J. G
1934
The Fear of the Dead in Primitive Religion. Vol.II. London

Frazer, Sir J. G
1936
The Fear of the Dead in Primitive Religion. Vol. III. London

Frazer, Sir J. G.
1933
The Fear of the Dead in Primitive Religion. Vol. I. London

Frazer, Sir J. G.
1963 [1890]
The Golden Bough. New York (Original in 1890)

Friedman, J.
1979
System, Structure and Contradiction in the Evolution of "Asiatic" Social Formations. Copenhagen

Gasche, H. et al.
1998
Dating the Fall of Babylon. Ghent, Chicago

Geller, M.J.
1987
The Lugal of Mari at Ebla and the Sumerian King List. In: *Eblaitica 1*, 141-145

Giddens, A.
1979
Central problems in social theory: Action, structure and contradiction in social analysis. London and Basingstone

Görsdorf, J.
2000
Radiokohlenstoffdatierungen. in: *Strommenger – Kohlmeyer 2000,* 115-117.

Grégoire, J.-P. – Renger, J.
1988
Die Interdependenz der wirtschaftlichen und gesellschaftlich-politischen Strukturen von Ebla. Erwägungen zum System der Oikos-Wirtschaft in Ebla. In: *Waetzoldt – Hauptmann (eds) 1988*, 211-224

Hallo, W.W.
1992
Ebrium at Ebla. in: *Eblaitica 3,* 139-150

Hansen, D. P.
1980-1983
Lagaš – B. Archäologisch. in: *RLA 6,* 422-430.

Härke, H.
1997a
The Nature of Burial Data. in: *Jensen – Nielsen (eds.) 1997,* 19-27

Härke, H.
1997b
Final Comments: Ritual, Symbolism and Social Inference. in: *Jensen – Nielsen (eds.) 1997,* 191-195

Harrah, B. – Harrah, D. F.
1976
Funeral service: A bibliography of literature on its past, present and future, the various means of disposition and memorialisation. Metuchen

Harris, E. C.
1975
The stratigraphic sequence: A question of time. in: *WA 7,* 109-121

Harris, E. C.
1979
Principles of Archaeological Stratigraphy. London - San Diego.

Harris, E. C. – Brown III, M. R. – Brown, G. J. (eds.)
1993
Practices of archaeological stratigraphy. London

Hauptmann, H. – Waetzold, H. (eds.)
1988
Wirtschaft und Gesellschaft von Ebla. Akten der internationalen Tagung Heidelberg 4.-7. November 1986. Heidelberg

Hempelmann, R.
2001
Menschen- und tiergestaltige Darstellungen auf frühbronzezeitlichen Gefäßen von Halawa A. in: *Meyer, J.-W. – Novák, M. – Pruß, A. (eds.) 2001,* 150-169

Hempelmann, R.
2004
Die Keramik von Halawa A und ihre Bezüge zur Kulturgeschichte am mittleren Euphrat um 2000 v. Chr.. in: *Meyer, J-W. – Sommerfeld, W. (eds.) 2004,* 49-85

Hempelmann, R.
2005
Ausgrabungen in Halawa 3 – Die bronzezeitliche Keramik von Halawa A. Saarbrücken

Herfort-Koch, M.
1992
Tod, Totenfürsorge und Jenseitsvorstellungen in der griechischen Antike: eine Bibliographie. München

Hertz, R.
1960 [1907]
Death Ritual and the right hand. Aberdeen [First published in French 1907]

Herzog, I.
1993
Computer-aided Harris Matrix generation. in: *Harris – Brown III – Brown (eds.) 1993,* 201-217

Hilprecht, H. V.
1904
Die Ausgrabungen in Assyrien und Babylonien. Leipzig

Hirsch, H.
1963
Die Inschriften der Könige von Agade. in: *AfO 20,* 1-82.

Hodder, I.
1982
Symbolism in action. Ethnoarchaeological studies of material culture. Cambridge

Holland, T.A.
1976
Preliminary Report on Excavations at Tell es-Sweyhat, Syria, 1973-4. in: *Levant 8,* 36-70

References

Holland, T.A.
1977
Preliminary Report on Excavations at Tell es-Sweyhat, Syria 1975. in: *Levant 9*, 36-65

Hunger, H.
2000
The Current State of Research on Mesopotamian Chronology (Absolute Chronology III) in: *Bietak (ed.) 2000*, 60-61

Huntington, R. – Metcalf, P.
1979
Celebration of Death. The Anthropology of Mortuary Ritual. Cambridge

Jacobsen, Th.
1978-1979
Iphur-Kīshi and His Times. in: *AfO 26*, 1-14

Jean-Marie, M.
1990
Les tombeaux en pierres de Mari. in: *MARI 6*, 303-336

Jean-Marie, M.
1999
Tombes et nécropoles de Mari. (Mission archéologique de Mari, volume 5) Beyrouth

Jensen, C. K. – Nielsen, K. H. (eds.)
1997
Burial &Society. The Chronological and Social Analysis of Archaeological Burial Data. Aarhus-Oxford

Kampschulte, I. – Orthmann, W.
1984
Gräber des 3. Jahrtausend im syrischen Euphrattal: 1. Ausgrabungen bei Tawi 1975 und 1978. (Saarbrücker Beiträge zur Altertumskunde Band 38) Bonn

Klengel, H.
1992
Syria 3000 to 300 B. C. A Handbook of Political History. Berlin

Kohlmeyer, K.
1985
Mari (Tell Hariri). in: *Weiss (ed.) 1985*, 130-134 and catalogue Nr. 48-84

Koldewey, R.
1887
Die altbabylonischen Gräber in Surghul und El Hibba. in: *ZA 2*, 403-430

Krasnik, K.
2005
Analyse der Gräber. in: *Falb et al. 2005*, 13-75

Krebernik, M.
2001
Die altorientalische Schriftfunde. (Tall Bi'a/Tuttul–II) Saarbrücken

Kunter, M.
1984
Anthropologische Untersuchung der Skelettreste. in: *Kampschulte – Orthmann 1984*, 115-119

Laneri, N.
1999
Intramural tombs – A funerary tradition of the middle Euphrates valley during the IIIrd millennium BC.. in: *Anatolica 25*, 221-241

Leach, E.
1986[2]
Social Anthropology. Glasgow

Leach, E. R.
1976
Culture and Communication: the logic by which symbols are connected. Cambridge

Lebeau, M. et. al.
2000
Stratified archaeological evidence and compared periodisations in the Syrian Jezirah during the third millennium B.C.. in: *Marro – Hauptmann (eds.) 2000*, 167-192

Liebermann, S. J. (ed)
1976
Sumerological Studies in Honor of Th. Jacobsen on his Seventieth Birthday, June 7, 1974. (Assyrological Studies 20) Chicago

Littleton, J.
1998
Skeletons and Social Composition. (BAR IntSer 703)

Liverani, M.
1993
Model and Actualisation – The Kings of Akkad in the Historical Traditions. in: *Liverani (ed.) 1993*, 41-68

Liverani, M. (ed.)
1993
Akkad – The First World Empire. Padova

Magen, U.
2001
Der Wettergott als Eselsreiter? in: *Meyer, J.-W. – Novák, M. – Pruß, A. (eds.) 2001*, 246-259

Marro, C. – Hauptmann, H. (eds.)
2000
Chronologies des Pays du Caucase et de l'Euphrate aux IVe-IIIe millenaires. (From the Euphrates to the Caucasus: Chronologies for the 4th-3rd millennium B.C.) Actes du colloque d'Istanbul, 16-19 décembre 1998. Paris

Matthews, D. – Eidem, J.
1993
Tell Brak and Nagar. in: *Iraq 55*, 201-207

Matthews, D. – Gibson, McG. – McMahon, A.
1997
The Early Dynastic – Akkadian Transition. in: *Iraq 59*, 1-19

Matthiae *et al.*
1995
Ebla – Alle origini della civiltà urbana. Roma

Matthiae, P.
1997
Ebla. in: *OxfEnc Vol. 2,* 180-183.

Mazzoni, S.
1988
Economic Features of the Pottery Equipment of Palace G. in:*Waetzold – Hauptmann (eds.) 1988*, 81-105

Mazzoni, St.
1982
La produzione ceramica del Palazzo G di Ebla e la sua Posizione Storica nell orizzonte Siro-Mesopotamico del III Millennio A.C..in: Studi Eblaiti 5, 145-192

Mazzoni, St.
1985
Elements of the ceramic culture of Early Syrian Ebla in comparison with syro-palestinan EB IV. in: *BASOR 257*, 1-18

McClellan, Th. – Porter, A.
1999
Survey of excavations at Tell Banat: Funerary practices. in: *del Olmo Lete – Montero Fenollós (eds.) 1999*, 107-116

McManners, J.
1981
Death and the Enlightenment. Oxford

MDOG 116
(Arns et al.)
1984
Ausgrabungen in Tall Bi^{c}a 1982 und 1983. in: *MDOG 116*, 15-63

MDOG 118
(Strommenger et al.)
1986
Ausgrabungen in Tall Bi^{c}a 1984. in: *MDOG 118*, 7-44

MDOG 119
(Strommenger et al.)
1987
Ausgrabungen in Tall Bi^{c}a 1985. in: *MDOG 119*, 7-49

MDOG 119
(Meyer, J.-W.)
1987
Die Tonlebermodelle aus Tall Bi^{c}a. in: MDOG 119, 51-56

MDOG 119
(Schirmer, W.)
1987
Landschaftsgeschichte um Tall Bi^{c}a am syrischen Euphrat. in: *MDOG 119*, 57-71

MDOG 121
(Strommenger et al.)
1989
Ausgrabungen in Tall Bi^{c}a 1987. in: *MDOG 120*, 5-63

MDOG 122
(Krebernik, M.)
1990
Die Textfunde aus Tall Bi^{c}a. in: *MDOG 122*, 67-87

MDOG 123
(Kalla, G.)
1991
Das ältere Mosaik des byzantinischen Klosters in Tall Bi^{c}a. in: *MDOG 123*, 35-39

MDOG 123
(Krebermik, M.)
1991
Schriftfunde aus Tall Bi^{c}a 1990. in: *MDOG 123*, 41-70

MDOG 123
(Strommenger, E.)
1991
Ausgrabungen in Tall Bi^{c}a 1990. in: *MDOG 123*, 7-34

MDOG 124
(Otto, A.)
1992
Siegelabrollungen aus Tall Bi^{c}a. in: *MDOG 124*, 45-78

MDOG 125
(Görsdorf, J.)
1993
Vorbericht zu den Radiokohlenstoffdatierungen aus Tall Bi^{c}a. in: *MDOG 125*, 61-68

MDOG 125
(Krebernik, M.)
1993
Schriftfunde aus Tall Bi^{c}a 1992. in: *MDOG 125*, 51-60

MDOG 125
(Strommenger, E.)
1993
Ausgrabungen in Tall Bi^{c}a 1992. in: *MDOG 125*, 7-34

References

MDOG 126
(Krebernik, M.)
1994
Tall Biᶜa 1993: Die Schriftfunde. in: *MDOG 126*, 33-36

MDOG 126
(Strommenger, E.)
1994
Schriftfunde aus Tall Biᶜa 1992. in: *MDOG 126*, 11-31

MDOG 126
(Wolska, W.)
1994
Zwei Fälle von Trepanation aus der altbabylonischen Zeit Syriens. in: *MDOG 126*, 37-50

MDOG 127
(Kohlmeyer, K. – Strommenger, E.)
1995
Die Ausgrabungen in Tall Biᶜa 1994 und 1995. in: *MDOG 127*, 43-55

MDOG 129
(Riederer, J.)
1997
Ein Gipsgefäß und ein Tafelförmiges Bruchstück aus Ägyptisch-Blau aus Tall Biᶜa/Tuttul. in: *MDOG 129*, 29-31

Meyer, J.-W.
1991
Gräber des 3. Jahrtausends v.Chr. im syrischen Euphrattal – 3. Ausgrabungen in Schamseddin und Djerniye.(Shriften zur Vorderasiatischen Archäologie, Vol. 3) Saarbrücken

Meyer, J.-W.
2001
Zur Bedeutung der Bootsmodelle aus dem Alten Orient. in: *Richter, Th. – Prechel, D. – Klinger, J. (eds.) 2001*, 267-283

Meyer, J.-W.
1996
Offene und geschlossene Siedlungen. in: *AoF 23/1*, 132-170.

Meyer, J.-W.
1997
Djebelet el-Beda: Eine Stätte der Ahnenverehrung? in: *AoF 24/2*, 294-309.

Meyer, J.-W.
2000
Zur Möglichkeit einer kulturhistorischen Einordnung von Grabfunden. in: *AoF 27*, 21-37

Meyer, J.-W. – Novák, M. – Pruß, A. (eds.)
2001
Beiträge zur Vorderasiatischen Archäologie Winfried Orthmann gewidmet. Frankfurt am Main

Meyer, J.-W. – Sallaberger, W. (eds.)
2004
2000 v. Chr. – Politische, wirtschaftliche und Kulturelle Entwicklung im Zeichen einer Jahrtausendwende. (CDOG 3) Saarbrücken

Michalowski, P.
1986
The Earliest Hurrian Toponymy: A New Sargonic Inscription. in: *ZA 76*, 4-11.

Michalowski, P.
1988
Thoughts about Ibrium. In: *Waetzoldt - Hauptmann (eds.) 1988*, 267-277

Michalowski, P.
1993
Memory and Deed: The Historiography of the Political Expansion of the Akkad State. in: *Liverani (ed.) 1993*, 69-90

Mielke, J. – Gilbert, R. (eds.)
1985
The Analysis of Prehistoric Diets. New York

Miglus, P. – Strommenger, E.
2002
Stadtbefestigungen, Häuser und Tempel. (Tall Bi'a/Tuttul VIII. WVDOG 103) Saarbrücken

Miglus, P. – Strommenger, E.
2007
Der Palast A. (Tall Bi'a/Tuttul VII. WVDOG 114) Wiesbaden.

Moorey, P. R. S.
2001
Clay Models and Overland Mobility in Syria, c. 2350–1800 B.C. in: *Meyer, J.-W. – Novák, M. – Pruß, A. (eds.) 2001*, 344-351

Morris, I.
1987
Burial and ancient society. Cambridge

Morris, I.
1992
Death-Ritual and Social Structure in Classical Antiquity. Cambridge

Nasrabadi, B. M.
1999
Untersuchungen zu den Bestattungssitten in Mesopotamien in der ersten Hälfte des ersten Jahrtausends v. Chr.. Mainz

O'Shea, J.
1981
Social configurations and the archaeological study of mortuary practices: a case study. in: *Chapman – Kinnes – Randsborg (eds) 1981*, 39-52

O'Shea, J.
1984
Mortuary variability. New York

Orthmann, W.
1985
Der alte Orient. (Propyläen Kunstgeschichte Bd. 18) Berlin

Orthmann, W. – Rova, E.
1991
Ausgrabungen in Wreide. Saarbrücken

Otto, A.
2004
Siegel und Siegelabrollungen. (Tall Bi'a/Tuttul IV. WVDOG 104) Saarbrücken

Pader, E.-J.
1982
Symbolism, social relations and the interpretation of mortuary remains. Oxford

Peltenburg, E.
1999a
Tell Jerablus Tahtani 1992-1996: A Summary. in: *del Olmo Lete – Montero Fenollós (eds.)* 1999, 97-105

Peltenburg, E.
1999b
The living and the ancestors: Early Bronze Age Mortuary Practices at Jerablus Tahtani. in: *del Olmo Lete – Montero Fenollós (eds.)* 1999, 427-442.

Peltenburg, E.
2008
Enclosing the ancestors and the growth of socio-political complexity in Early Bronze Age Syria. in: *Bartoloni – Benedettini 2008*, 215-247

Pettinato, G.
1972
Il commercio con l'estero della Mesopotamia meridionale nel 3. millennio av. Cr. alla luce delle fonti letterarie e lessicali sumeriche. in: *Mesopotamia 7*, 43-166.

Pettinato, G.
1980
Bollettino militare della campagna di Ebla contra la città di Mari. in: *OA 19*, 231-245.

Pettinato, G.
1981
The Archives in Ebla: An Empire Inscribed in Clay. Garden City

Pettinato, G. – Waetzoldt, H.
1985
Dagān in Ebla und Mesopotamien nach den Texten aus dem 3. Jahrtausend. in: *OrNS 54*, 234-256

Pomponio, F. – Xella, P.
1997
Les dieux d'Ebla. Münster

Porter, A.
1995
Tell Banat – Tomb I. in:*DaM 8*, 1-50

Porter, A.
1999
The ceramic horizon of the Early Bronze in the Upper Euphrates. in: *del Olmo Lete – Montero Fenollós (eds.) 1999*, 311-320

Porter, A.
2002a
Communities in Conflict. Death and the Contest for Social Order in the Euphrates River Valley. in: *Near Eastern Archaeology 65/3*, 156-173

Porter, A.
2002b
The Dynamics of Death: Pastoralism and the Origins of a Third-Millennium City in Syria. in: *BASOR 325, 1-36*

Postgate, J.N.
1994²
Early Mesopotamia – Society and economy at the dawn of history. London – New York

Pruß, A
2000
The Metallic Ware of Upper Mesopotamia: definition, chronology and distribution. in: *Marro – Hauptmann (eds.) 2000*, 193-203

Pruß, A
2001
Die graue Gazira-Ware. in: *Meyer – Novák – Pruß (eds) 2001*, 412-429

Rehm, E. E.
2001
Untersuchung zur kulturhistorischen Bedeutung von Waffen als Grabinventar – Die Gräber des 3. und frühen 2. Jt.s v.Chr. in Mesopotamien und Syrien. Unpublished augural dissertation, Frankfurt am Main

Renfrew, A. C.
1985
The archaeology of cult: the sanctuary at Phylakopi. London (British School at Athens, Suppl. Vol. 18)

Renger, J.
1969
Untersuchungen zum Priestertum der altbabylonischen Zeit. 2. Teil. in: *ZA 59 (NF25)*, 104-230.

Rice, P.M.
1987
Pottery Analysis. London

References

Richter, Th. – Prechel, D. – Klinger, J. (eds.)
2001
Kulturgeschichten – Altorientalische Studien für Volkert Haas zum 65. Geburtstag. Saarbrücken

Roobaert, A. – Bunnens, G.
1999
Excavations at Tell Ahmar – Til Barsip. in: *del Olmo Lete – Montero Fenollós (eds.) 1999*, 163-178

Rova, E.
1996
Ceramic provinces along the middle and upper Euphrates: Late Chalcolithic - Early Bronze Age, a diachronic view. in: *BaM 27*, 13-30.

Sallaberger, W.
1996
Nagar in den frühdynastischen Texten aus Beydar. in: *Van Lerberghe – Voet 1996*, 393-407

Sallaberger, W.
2004
Relative Chronologie von der späten frühdynastischen bis zur altbabylonischen Zeit. in : *Meyer, J-W. – Sommerfeld, W. (eds.) 2004*, 15-43

Saxe, A. A.
1970
Social dimensions of mortuary evidences. Michigan

Schwartz, G.
2007
Status, Ideology and Memory in Third Millennium Syria: 'Royal' Tombs at Umm el-Marra. in: Laneri 2007, 39-68

Schwartz, G. et al.
2006
A Third-Millennium B.C. Elite Mortuary Complex at Tell Umm el-Marra, Syria: 2002 and 2004 Excavations. in *AJA 110*, 603-641

Schwartz, G. M. – Curvers, H. H. – Stuart, B.
2000
A 3rd-millennium BC élite tomb from Umm el-Marra, Syria. in: *Antiquity 74*, 771-772

Stannard, D.
1977
The Puritan way of death. Oxford

Steible, H.
1991
Die neusumerischen Bau- und Weihinschriften. Teil 1. (FAOS 9,1) Stuttgart

Strommenger, E.
1976
Fünfter vorläufiger Bericht über die von der Deutschen Orient Gesellschaft mit Mitteln der Stiftung Volkswagenwerk in Habuba Kebira unternommenen archäologischen Untersuchungen. in: *MDOG 108*, 5-22

Strommenger, E.
1977
Tall Bi'a bei Raqqa. in: *MDOG 109*, 5-13

Strommenger, E. – Hirmer, M.
1962
Fünf Jahrtausende Mesopotamien – Die Kunst von den Anfängen um 5000 v. Chr. bis zu Alexander dem Großen. München

Strommenger, E. – Kohlmeyer, K.
1998
Die altorientalische Bestattungen. (Tall Bi'a/Tuttul I. WVDOG 96) Saarbrücken

Strommenger, E. – Kohlmeyer, K.
2000
Die Schichten des 3. Jahrtausends v. Chr. im Zentralhügel E. (Tall Bi'a/Tuttul III. WVDOG 101) Saarbrücken

Thomsen, Ch. J.
1837 [1836]
Leitfaden zur nordischen Altertumskunde. Kopenhagen (Danish original 1836: Ledertraad til Nordisk Oldkyndighed.)

Thuesen, I.
1988
Hama, Fouilles et Recherches de la Fondation Carlsberg 1931-1938, I – The Pre- and Protohistoric Periods. København

Trigger, B. G.
1989
A History of Archaeological Thought. Cambridge

Tunca, Ö. (ed.)
1990
De la Babylonie à la Syrie, en passant par Mari. Mélanges offerts à Monsieur j.-R. Kupper à l'occasion de son 70e anniversaire. Liège

Tylor, E. B.
1871
Primitive Culture. London

Unger, E.
1928
Ausgrabungen. in: *RlA I*, 315-321

Valdés Pereiro, C.
1999
Tell Qara Quzaq. in: *del Olmo Lete – Montero Fenollós (eds.) 1999*, 117-127

Van Gennep, A.
1986 [1909]
Übergangsriten. Frankfurt – New York [French original 1909: "Les rites de passage"]

Van Lerberghe, K. – Voet, G.
1996
Languages and Cultures in Contact. At the Crossroads of Civilisations in the Syro-Mesopotamian Realm. Proceedings of the 42 RAI. Leuven

Waetzold, H.
1990
Zur Bewaffnung des Heeres von Ebla. in: *OA 29*, 1-38

Weiss, H. (ed.)
1985
Ebla to Damascus: Art and archaeology of Ancient Syria. Exhibition held at Walters Art Gallery, Baltimore, Md and others, Sept. 1985 – Sept. 1987. Washington

Westenholz, J. G.
1997
Legends of the Kings of Akkade. Winona Lake

Winckelmann, J.
1764
Geschichte der Kunst des Altertums. Dresden

Xella, P.
1988
Tradition and Innovation. Bemerkungen zum Pantheon von Ebla. in: *Hauptmann – Waetzold (eds.) 1988*, 349-358

Catalogue
List of burials in Tell Bi'a from 8/34:1 to V:5, dates and references to the final publication.

Burial	Phase	Strommenger-Kohlmeyer 1998	Burial	Phase	Strommenger-Kohlmeyer 1998
8/34:1		S81, Pl.102	25/48:7	IIIb	S43;Pl.33;50;51
9/34:1		S.81;Pl.102	25/48:8	IIIa	S44;Pl.33;50;51
10/34:1	IIIa	S.81/Pl.102	25/48:9	IIIa	S44f;Pl. 48,51
10/34?:1		S.81; pl.102	25/48:10	IIIa	S45f;Pl.9/2;33;48;51;52
16/33:1		S.11; Pl.19	25/48:11	IIIa	S46f;Pl.33;48;53;54
16/34:1	IIIa	S.11; Pl.19	25/48:12	IIIa	S47,Pl.33;54
16/35:1	IIIa	S.11; Pl.19	25/51:4		S24f;Pl.7/6;30
16/35:2	IIIb	S12;Pl.19	26/34:1		S10;Pl.19
16/35:3		S12;Pl.19	26/34:4		S10;Pl.19
16/35:4	IIIa	S12; Pl.7/1; 20	26/34?:1		S10;Pl.19
16/35:5		S13; Pl.20	26/49:10	MB	S27;Pl.29;31
16/35:6	IIIb	S13;Pl.20	27/33:1		S119;Pl.149
16/35?:1		S.13; Pl.20	27/33:2		S119;Pl.149
17/34:1	IIIa	S14; Pl.21	27/46:1		S.27;Pl.8/1;29;31
17/35:1	IIIa	S14; Pl.21	27/46:2		S119f;Pl.149
17/35:2	IIIb	S14; Pl.21	27/46:6		S27;Pl.8/2;29;32
17/35:4	IIIa	S15;Taf7/2;22	27/46:7		S27;Pl.7/5;29;31
18/34?:1	IIIb	S16; Pl.23	27/46:8		S27;Pl.873;29;32
21/62:1	IIIb	S26;Pl.30	27/46:9	MB	
21/62:3		S26;Pl.31	27/47:4		S120;Pl.10/2;149
21/62:4	IIIa	S26;Pl.31	27/47:5		S120;Pl.149
23/46:1	I	S76f;Pl.98	27/48:3	MB/LB	S28;Pl.29;32
23/46:2	I	S74f; Pl. 97			
23/46:3	I	S 75f; Pl.98	27/48:4	MB	S28;Pl.29
24/45:2	IIIb	S30; Pl.34	28/46:1	MB	S28;pl.29;32
24/45:3	IIIb	S30; Pl. 8/6;34	28/46:2	MB	S.28;Pl.29;32
24/47:1	IIIb	S30; Pl.33, 34	28/46:4	MB	S28;Pl.29;32
24/47:2	IIIa	S30; Pl. 33, 34	28/47:1		S28;Pl.29;32
24/47:3	IIIb	S31; Pl. 33, 35	28/47:2		S120;Pl.149
24/47:4	IIIa	S31f; Pl. 33;35;36	28/49:1	MB/LB	S29;32
24/49:1	IIIb?	S32			
24/49:2		S32	28/50:1		S25;Pl.29;30
24/49:3	IIIa	S32f; Pl. 33; 36-38	28/50:2		S25;Pl.29;30
24/49:4a	IIIa	S33; 36; 38	28/50:6		S29;Pl.29;32
24/49:4b	IIIa	S34f;Pl.33; 36; 39	29/40:1		S25
24/49:5	IIIa	S35f; Pl.9/1;33;36;39-41	29/43:1		S25
24/49:6	IIIa	S36;Pl.33;36	29/43:2	IIIb	S25;Pl.7/4;30
24/49:7	IIIa	S36;Pl.33;36;42;43	29/44:1		S25;Pl.30
24/49:8	IIIa	S37ff;Pl.33; 36;43-45	29/47:1	MB	S29;Pl.29;33
24/49:9	IIIa	S39;Pl.36;45	29/48:1		S29;Pl.29;33
24/49:10	IIIa	S.39f;Pl.36;45	29/48:2	MB	S29;Pl.29;33
25/45:1	IIIb	S40;Pl.45	29/48:3		S120;Pl.149
25/45:4	IIIb	S40;Pl.8,4;46	29/49:1		S29;Pl.29;24
25/45:5	(IIIa or) IIIb	S40;Pl.8/5;46	29/50:1	MB	S29;Pl.29
			31/16:1	IIIa	S16;Pl.23
			32/34:1	LB	S119;Pl.149
25/48:1	IIIa	S40f;Pl.33;46	34/20:1	IIIb	S16;Pl.23
25/48:2	IIIa	S41;Pl.33;47	34/52:1		S24;Pl.29
25/48:3	IIIa	S.41;Pl.33;47;48	34/52:2		S24;Pl.29
25/48:4	III?	S.42;Pl.9/4;33;48	34/52:3		S24;Pl.29
25/48:5	IIIa	S42f;Pl.9/4;33;48;49	37/22:1	IIIb	S17;Pl.23
25/48:6	IIIa	S43;Pl.33;48;50	37/22:2	IIIb	S17;Pl.23

Burial	Phase	Strommenger-Kohlmeyer 1998
37/22:8	IIIb	S17;Pl.23
37/23:1	IIIb	S17;Pl.23
37/23?:1	IIIb	S18;Pl.24
38/16?:1	IIIb	S20;Pl.26
38/23?:1		S18;Pl.24
38/24?:1	IIIb	S18;Pl.24
38/27:1		S19;Pl.24
39/23:1		S19;Pl.24/18,19;25
39/23:2		S19;Pl.24/18,19;25
39/24:1		S19f;Taf25
39/24:2		S20;Pl.26
40/24:1		S20;Taf26
41/23:1	IIIb	S21;Pl.26
42/23:1	IIIa	S21;Pl.26
42/23:2	IIIa	S21;Pl.26;27
42/23:3	IIIb	S21;Pl.26;27
42/23:6	IIIb	S22;Pl.26;27
42/23:7	IIIa	S22;Pl.7/3;26;28
42/23:8	IIIa	S23;Pl.26;28
42/23:9	IIIa	S23;Pl.26;29
59/78:1	II	S78;Pl.99
59/78:2	II	S78;Pl.100
60/41:1	IIIb	S79;Pl.101
61/41:1		S80;Pl.101;102
61/41:2		S80;Pl.101;102
61/41:3		S80;Pl.101;102
61/41:4		S80;Pl.101
61/41:5		S80;Pl.101
62/41:1	IIIb	S80;Pl.101;102
F:1	IIIb	S77;Pl.10/1;99
G2R3	I	S51-53;Pl.55-62
G3R1	I	S53-57;Pl.13/4,5;14/2,3;55-57;62-69
G3R2	I	S57;Pl.14/1;55-57;69
G3R3	I	S57-61;Pl.15/1,2;55-57;6269-76
G4R1	I	S61f;Pl.11/2,3;55-57;77;78
G4R2	I	S62-65;Pl.11/2,3;15/3;55-57;78-87
G4R3	I	S65-68;Pl.11/2,3;15/4;55-57;87-91
G5	I	S68-73;Pl.12/1,2;55-57;91-94;169/1011
G6R1	I	S73f;Pl.13/1,2;55-57;94-96;99;170/2,3
G6R2	I	S74-76;Pl.15/5,&;55-57;97;98
G6R3	I	S76f;Pl.55-57;98;99
H?:1	IIIa	S79;Pl.100;101
U:1	II	S84;Pl.103
U:2	IIIa	S85;Pl.104
U:3		S85;Pl.104
U:4alt	II	S85;Pl.18/3,4;104;105
U:4jung	IIIa	S86;Pl.18/6;105
U:5	nach	
U:6	IIIa	S86;Pl.106;App.3
U:7alt	I	S87;Pl.106;app.3

Burial	Phase	Strommenger-Kohlmeyer 1998
U:7jung	IIIa	S87f;Pl.107;App.3
U:7 Füllung	II	S88;Pl.107;App.3
U:8	IIIa	S88;Pl.107;App.3
U:9	I	S88;pl.17/1;107;108;App.3
U:10	I	S89f;Pl.17/2,3;108;App.3
U:11	IIIa	S89;Pl.109:App.3
U:12	I	S89f;Pl.109;App.3
U:13	II	S90;Pl.110;App.3
U:14	I	S90f;Pl.110;111;App.3
U:15alt	I	S90;Pl.111;112;App.3
U:15jung	I	S91;Pl.111;112;App.3
U:16	I	S92;Pl.112;App.3
U:17		S92
U:18	I	S92;Pl.18/2;112;App.3
U:19		S92
U:20	I	S92;Pl.113;App.3
U:21		S92;Pl.113;App.3
U:22	I	S93;Pl.17/6;113;114;App.3
U:23	II	S93f;Pl.114;115;Beilge3
U:24	I	S94;Pl.115;App.3
U:25süd	IIIa	S94f;Pl.18/5;115117;App.3
U:25nord	IIIa	S95f;Pl.18/5;117;App.3
U:25jung/Ein-steigeschacht	IIIa	S96;Pl.117;App.3
U:25?	II	S96;Pl.118;App.3
U:26	nach	S96
U:27	II	S96;Pl.118;119;App.3
U:28	I	S97;Pl.119;App.3
U:29		S97;Pl.119;App.3
U:30alt	II	S97;Pl.119;120;App.3
U:30jung	IIIa	S97f;Pl.119;120;App.3
U:31alt	I	S98;Pl.17/4;120;App.3
U:31jung1	IIIa	S98;Pl.121;App.3
U:31jung2	IIIa	S98;Pl.121;App.3
U:32alt1	I	S98f;Pl.121;App.3
U:32alt2	IIIa	S99;Pl.121;App.3
U:32jung	IIIa	S99;Pl.122;App.3
U:33	II	S99f;Pl.18/1;122;123;App.3
U:34alt1	I	S100;Pl.123;App.3
U:34mitte	I or II	S100;Pl.123;App.3
U:34jung	IIIa	S100;Pl.123;App.3
U:35	I	S100;Pl.124;App.3
U:36	II	S100f;Pl.124;App.3
U:37	I	S101;Pl.124;125;App.3
U:38		S101;Pl.125;App.3
U:39	I	S101f;Pl.125;App.3
U:40	I	S102f;Pl.126;App.3
U:41	I	S103;Pl.127;App.3
U:42	IIIa	S103f;Pl.127;App.3
U:43NOalt	I	S104;Pl.1128;130;App.3
U:43SWalt	IIIa	S105;Pl.129;130;App.3
U:43SWjung	IIIa	S105f;Pl.130;App.3
U:43jung	IIIa	S106;Pl.130;App.3
U:44	I	S106;Pl.17/5;130;App.3
U:45	I	S106;Pl.131;App.3
U:46		S106;App.3
U:47	IIIa	S106ff;Pl.132-134;App.3

Catalogue

Burial	Phase	Strommenger-Kohlmeyer 1998
U:48	later	
U:49	I	S108;Pl.134;135;App.3
U:50	I	S108f;Pl.135;App.3
U:51	I	S109;Pl.135;136;App.3
U:52	later	
U:53	later	S109;App.3
U:54	later?	S109
U:55		S109;App.3
U:56	later	
U:57	later	S109;App.3
U:58		S109f;Pl.136
V:1	I	S118;Pl.147
V:2	I	S118;Pl.147
V:3	I	S118;Pl.147
V:4	I	S118;Pl.148
V:5	I	S118;Pl.148

Plate 1

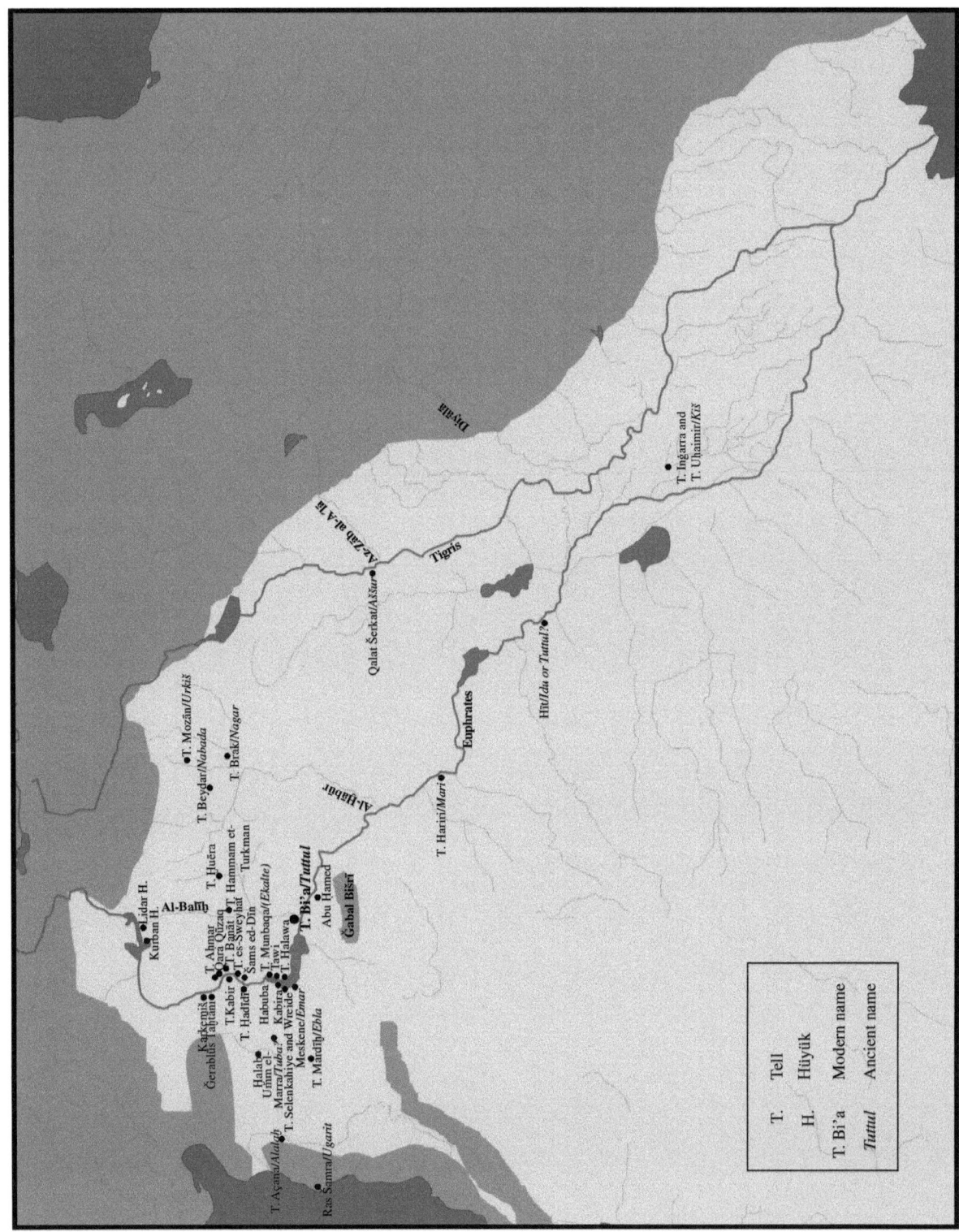

Situation of localities mentioned in text

Plates

Plate 2

Periods in Syria	Periods in South-Mesopotamien	Ebla	Halawa A Quadrant L/M	Halawa Quadrant Q	Lidar Höyük	Kurban Höyük	Hammam et-Turkman	Habuba Kebira	Wreide	Tell Hadidi	Tell Kabir	Tell Banat Period	Tell Banat North	Qara Quzaq	Munbaqa	Tell es-Sweyhat	Tawi	Scham seddin	Mari Chantier B	Mari Gräber	Tell Bi'a Phases	Tell Bi'a, Mound E	Tell Bi'a, sounding 21/62 West	Tell Bi'a, Graves
MBA I	Ur III	Mardikh IIIA	Bauschicht 2		Phase 1-2, 3 früh		Period VIIB	„Jüngstes Niveau"		„MBII" Siedlungs keramik				Schicht II								Ground-plan of the Palace A and its fundaments		
EB/MB transitional period		?	L/M3 jung	Q3A		III jung	Period VIIA				Schicht 6	I									IIIb	„level under the Palace A, silo, ovens		Group of seriation 7
EBA IVB	Akkad late	Mardikh IIB2		Q3B		III alt	Period VI west	Siedlungs keramik, Erdgrab	Gräber feld	Grab LI Siedlungs keramik „EB III/IV"	Schicht 7	II	White Monument I	Schicht III	Kuppe Schicht 1-5	Area IV	Grab T9, T16	Grab 2	Schicht 1-6	"Shakkanaku"-Gräber	IIIa	*Pfeilergebäude* Levels 4 - 2	Schicht 4-3	Groups of seriation 4-6
EBA IVA	Akkad early	Mardikh IIB1 (Palast G)	L/M 3 alt	Q3C							Schicht 8 jung	III			Kuppe, Schicht 6-7	Grube 17/3;	Grab T6	Grab 9 Grab 10		Grab 86	II	Palace B	Schicht 10-5	Group of seriation 3
End of EBA III	F D III	?				IV	Period V- VI east				Schicht 8 alt	IV	White Monument II?	Schicht IV		Oper.5, Gebäude mit Wand-gemälden ?	Grab T1, T4, T5, T20, T70, T71		Schicht 7-x	z.B. Grab 300	I (young)	Mausolea	Schicht 11-14	Groups of seriation 1-2

**Relative chronological correlation of sites along the Middle and Upper Euphrates
(according to Hempelmann 2005 with modification of Tell Bi'a)**

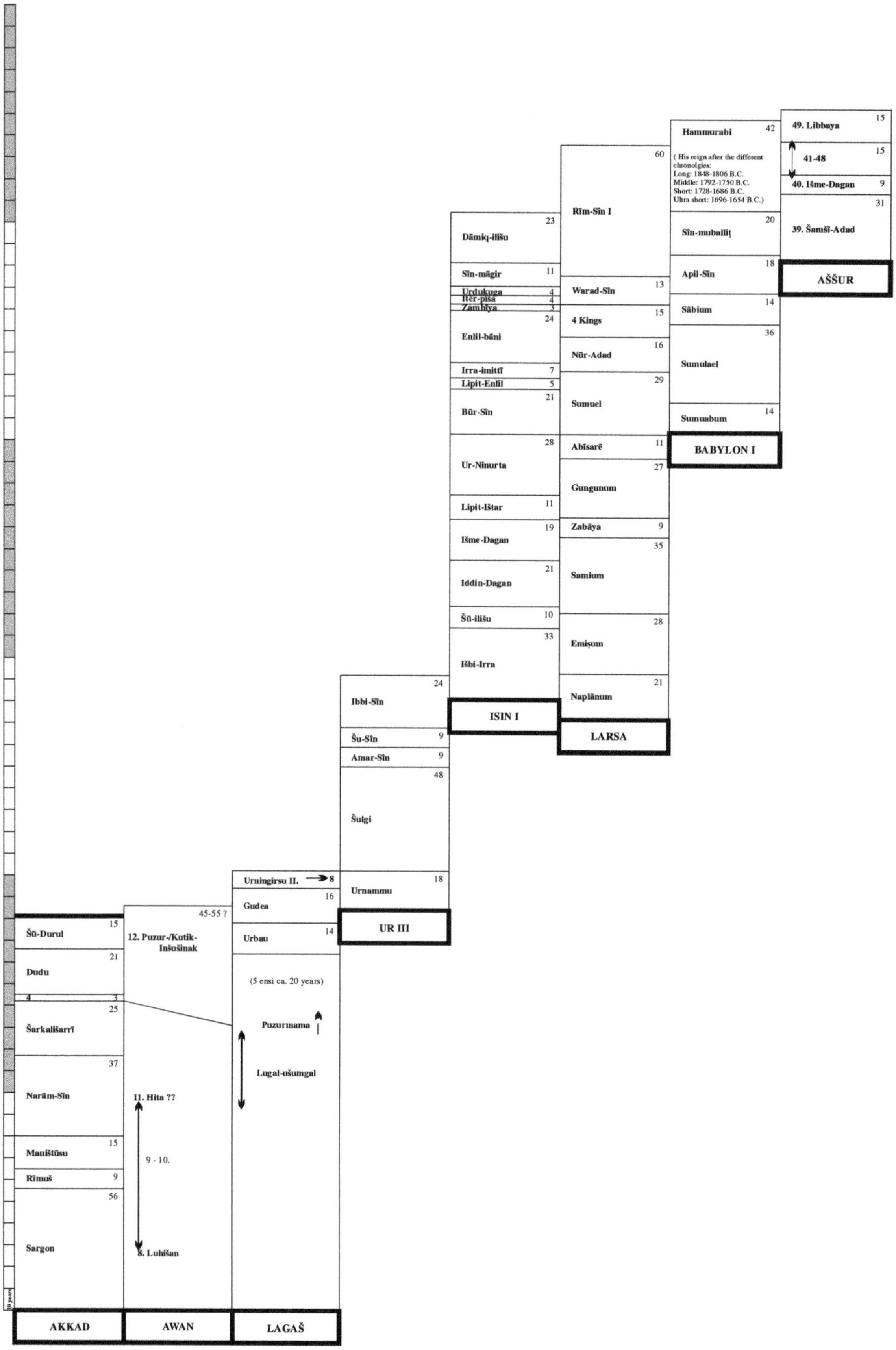

Relative chronology of Mesopotamian dynasties from the Akkadian period to the reign of Hammurabi of Babylon (synchronism from the Akkad- to UrIII dynasties according to Dittmann 1994, 98 Tab. 7, synchronism from the UrIII dynasty to the reign of Hammurabi according to Gasche et al. 1998, Supplement Table)

Plates

Plate 4

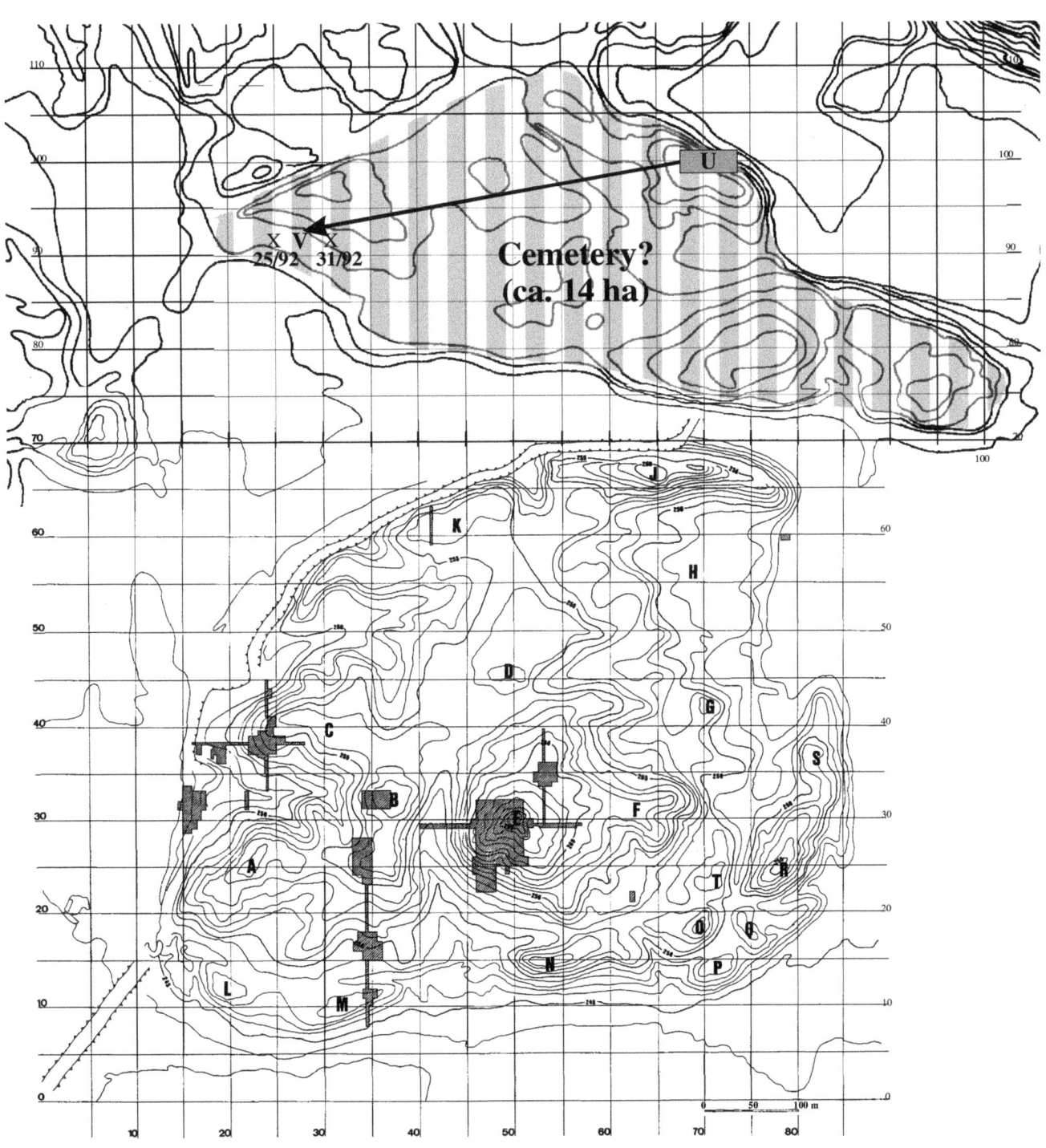

Plan of Tell Bi´a (according to Strommenger - Kohlmeyer 1998, Pl. 6 and Pl. 136)

Plate 5

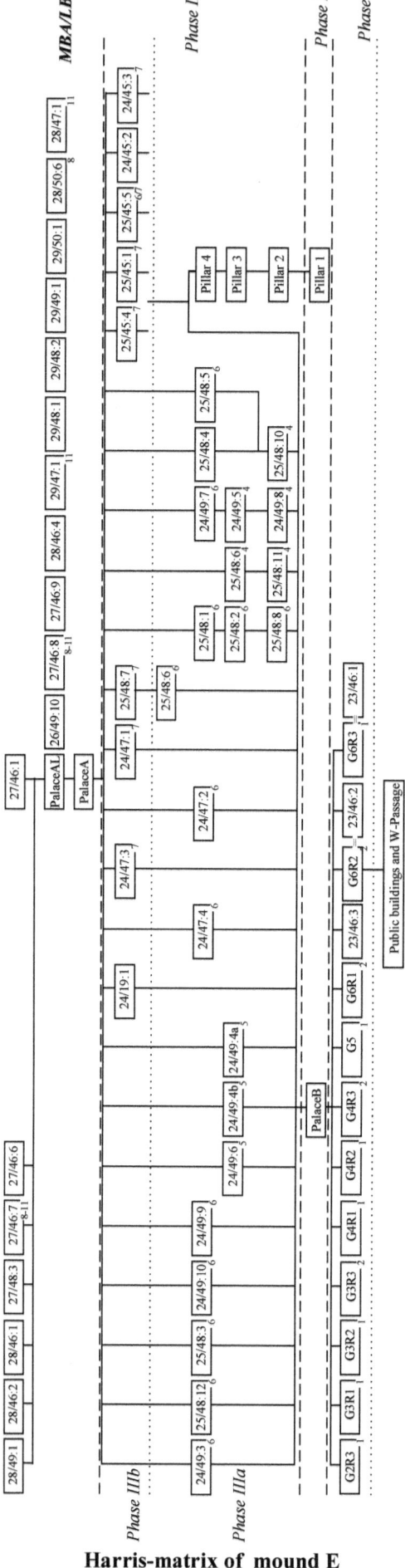

Harris-matrix of mound E

Plate 6

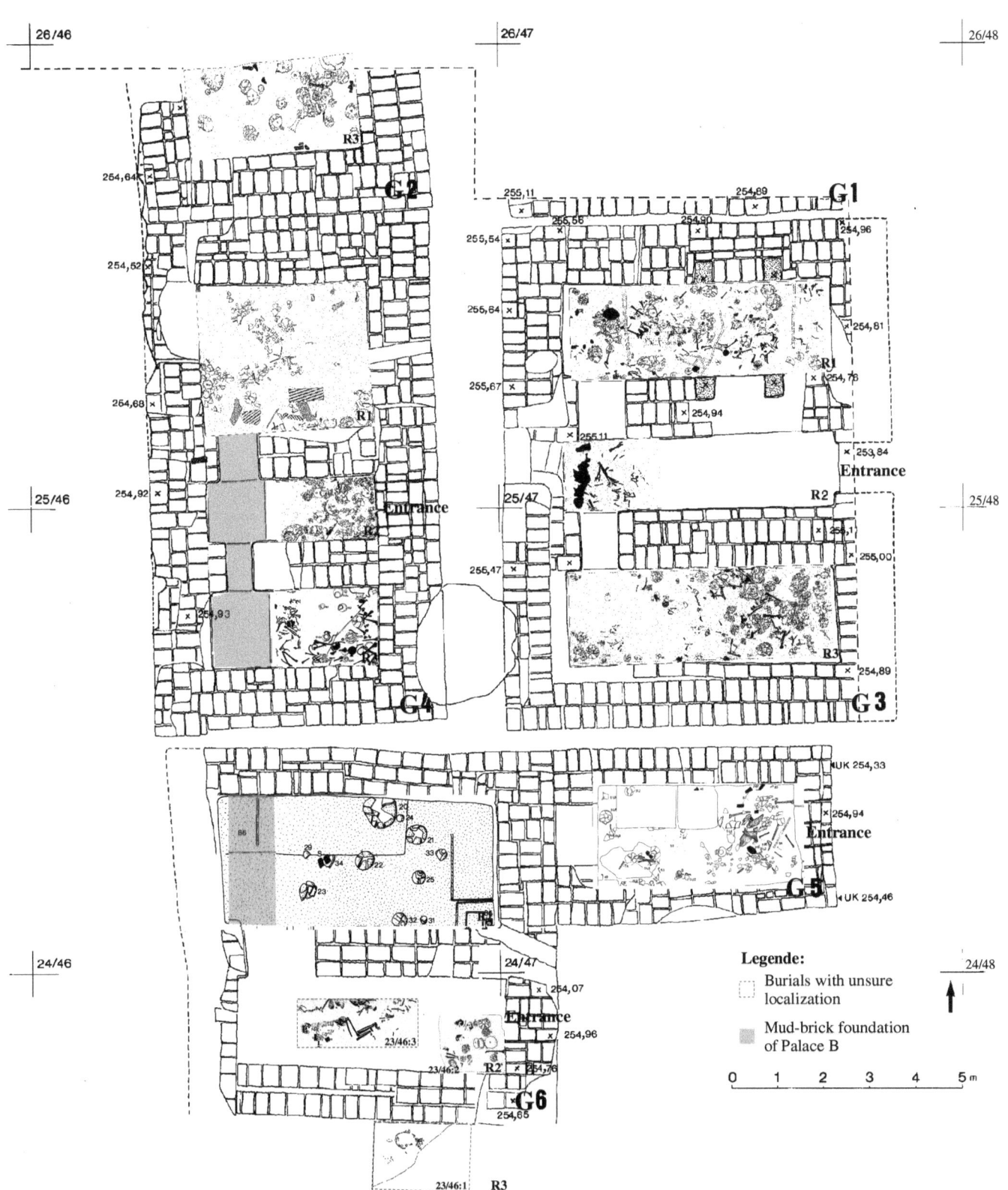

The mausolea and their inventories (after Strommenger - Kohlmeyer 1998, Pl. 56-98)

Plate 7

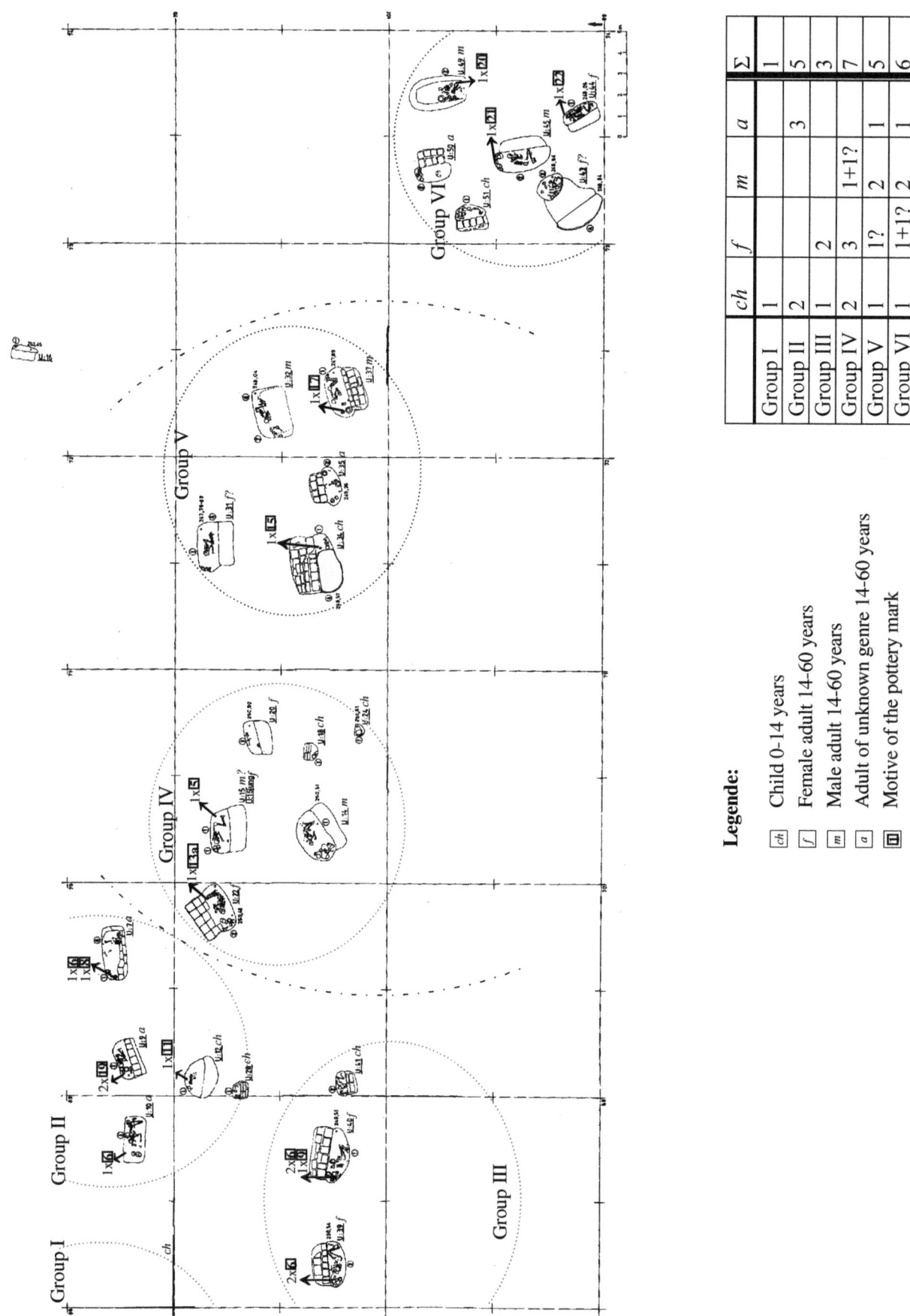

Burials in cemetery U during phase I (after Strommenger-Kohlmeyer 1998, App. 3)

Plate 8

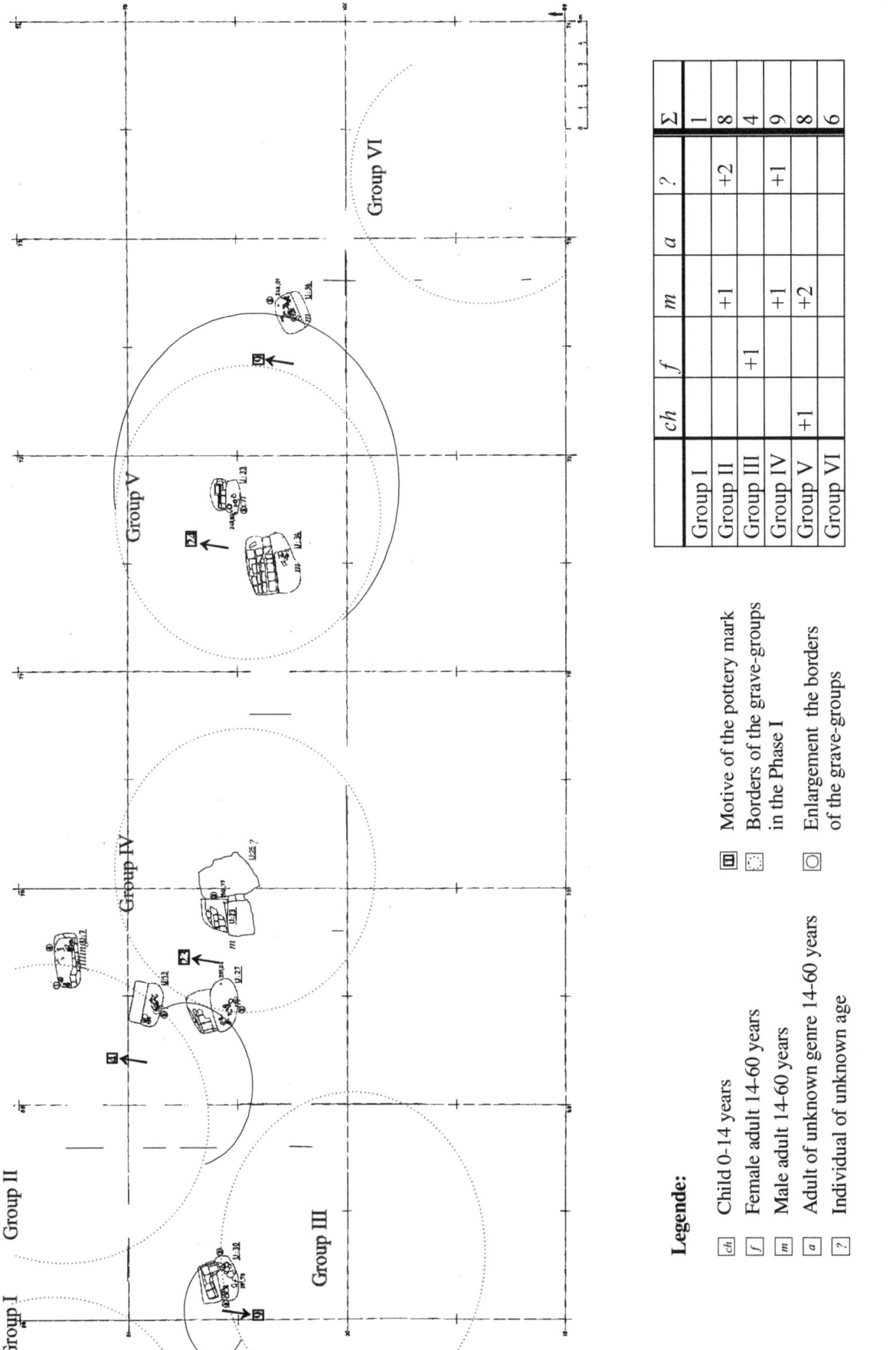

Burials in cemetery U during phase II (after Strommenger - Kohlmeyer 1998, App. 03)

Plate 9

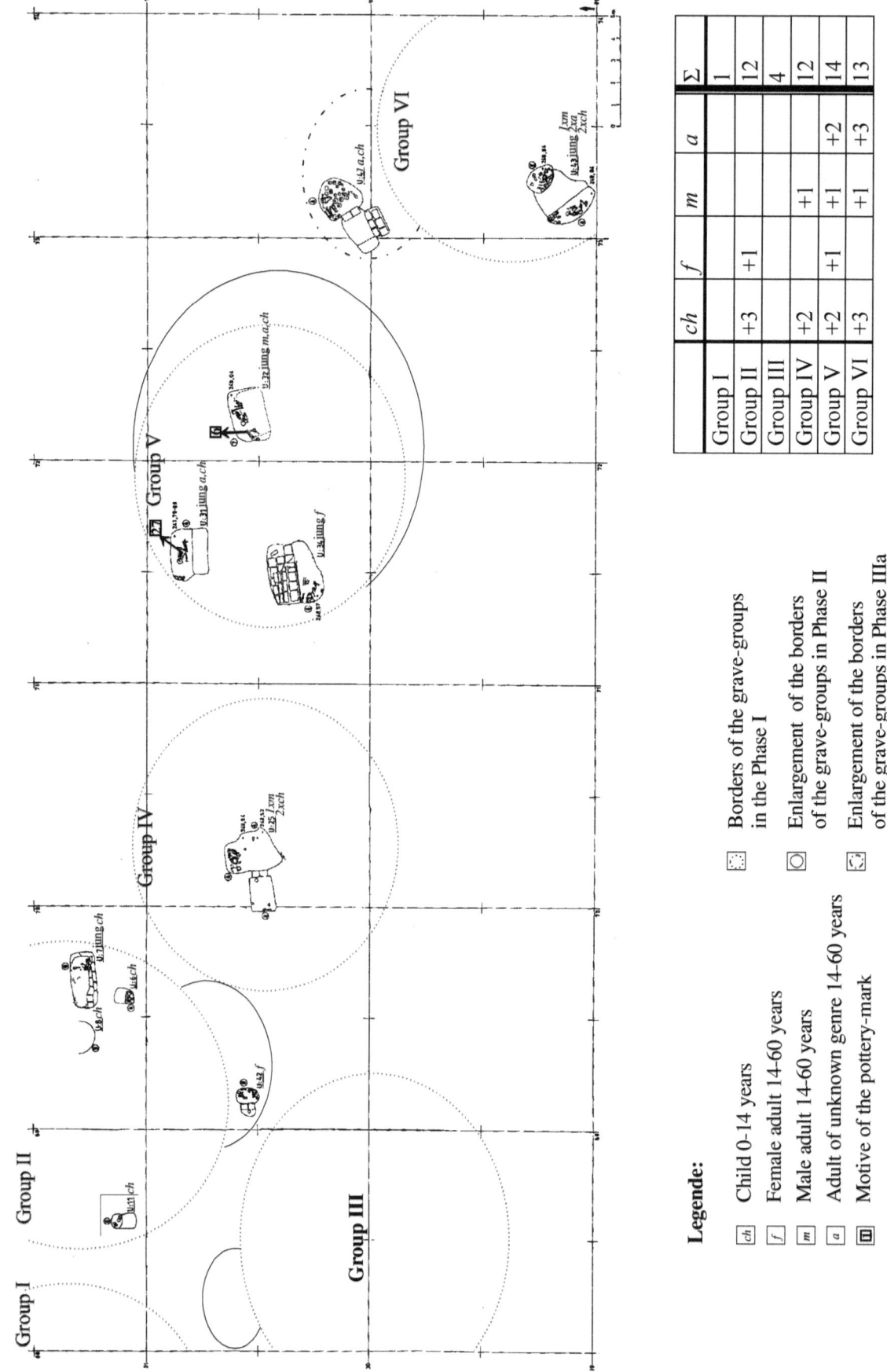

Burials in cemetery U during phase IIIa (after Strommenger - Kohlmeyer 1998, App. 03)

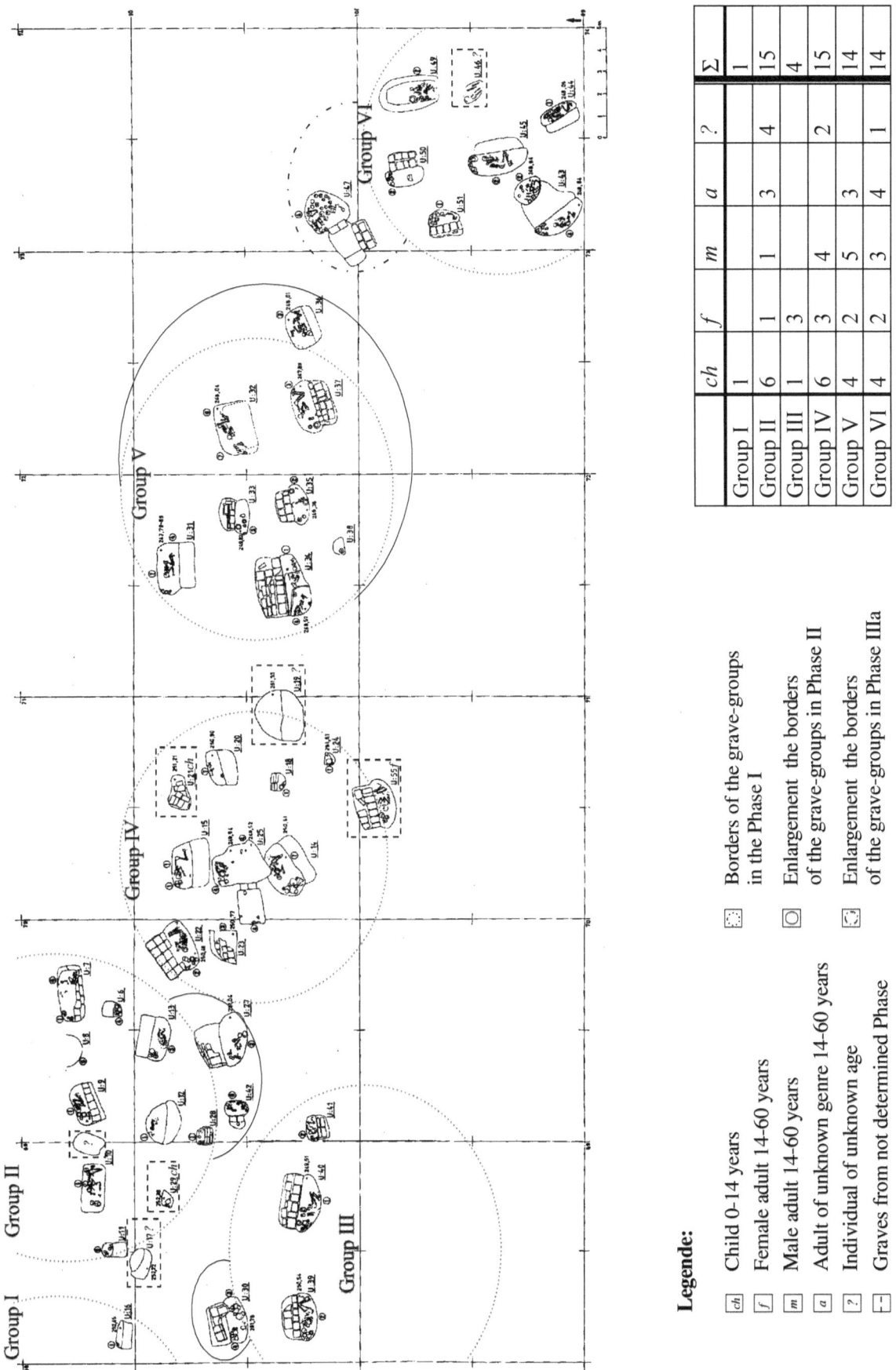

Burials in cemetery U during phases I to IIIa (after Strommenger - Kohlmeyer 1998, App. 03)

Plate 11

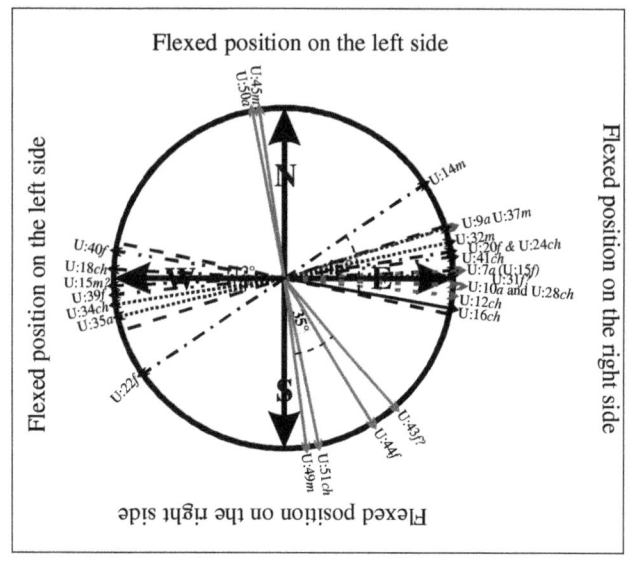

1. Phase I

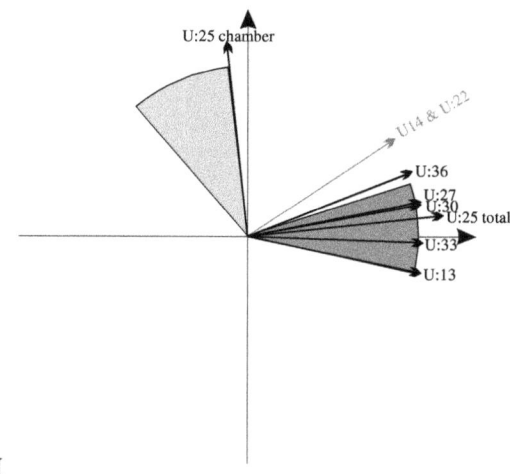

2. Phase II

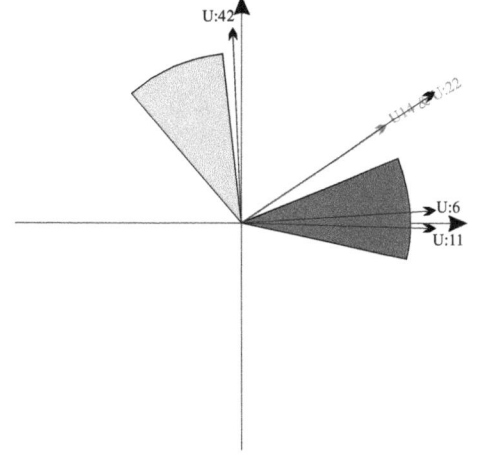

3. Phase IIIa

Orientation of graves in cemetery U

Plate 12

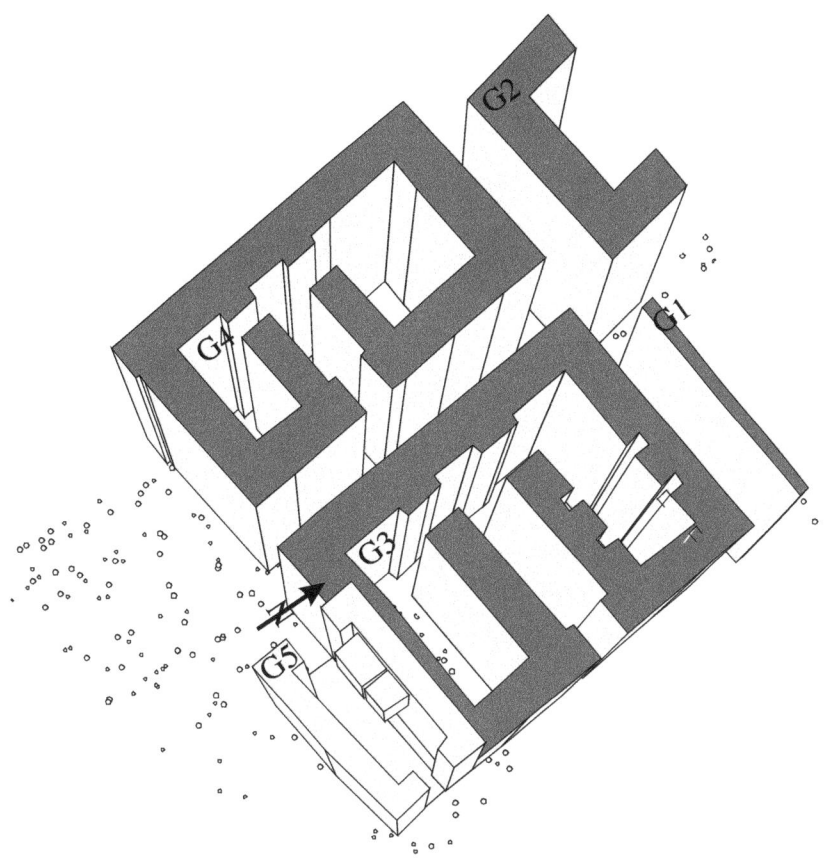

1. Isometric reconstruction of the mausolea before the erection of G6

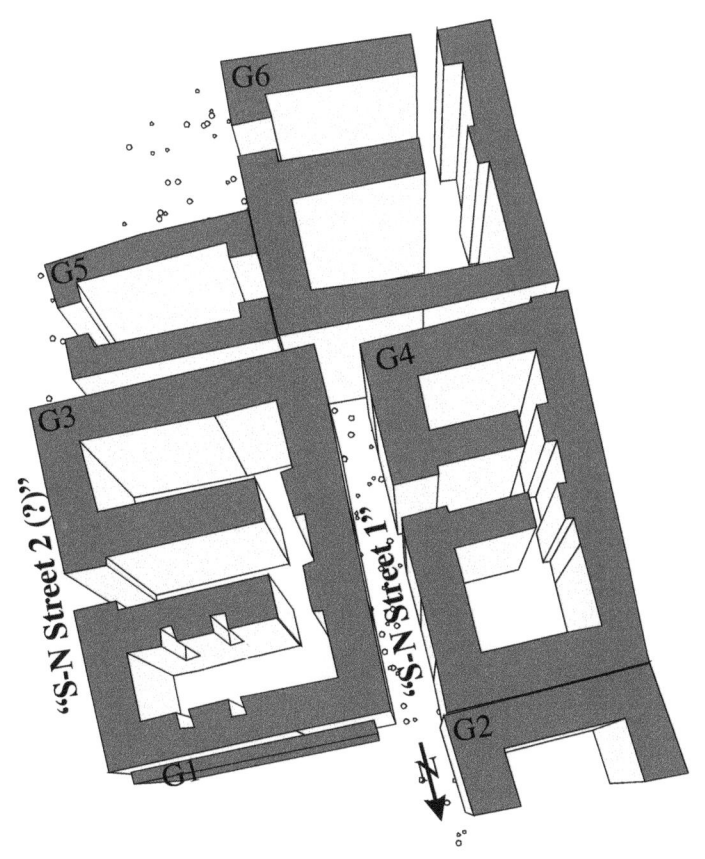

2. Isometric reconstruction of the mausolea at the end of phase I

Plate 13

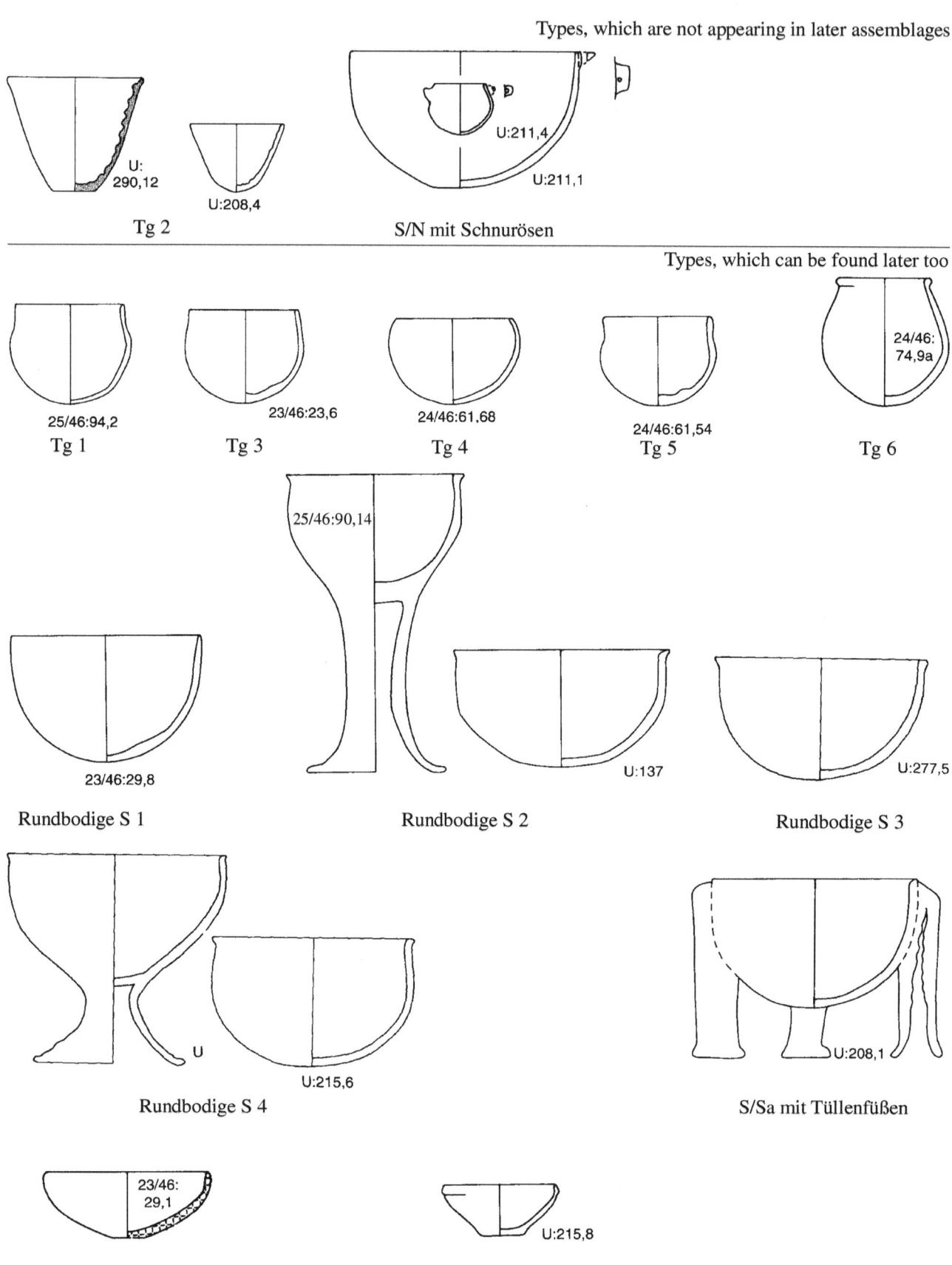

Phase I - drinking vessels (Tg) and different bowl types (S, N and Sa)

Plates

Plate 14

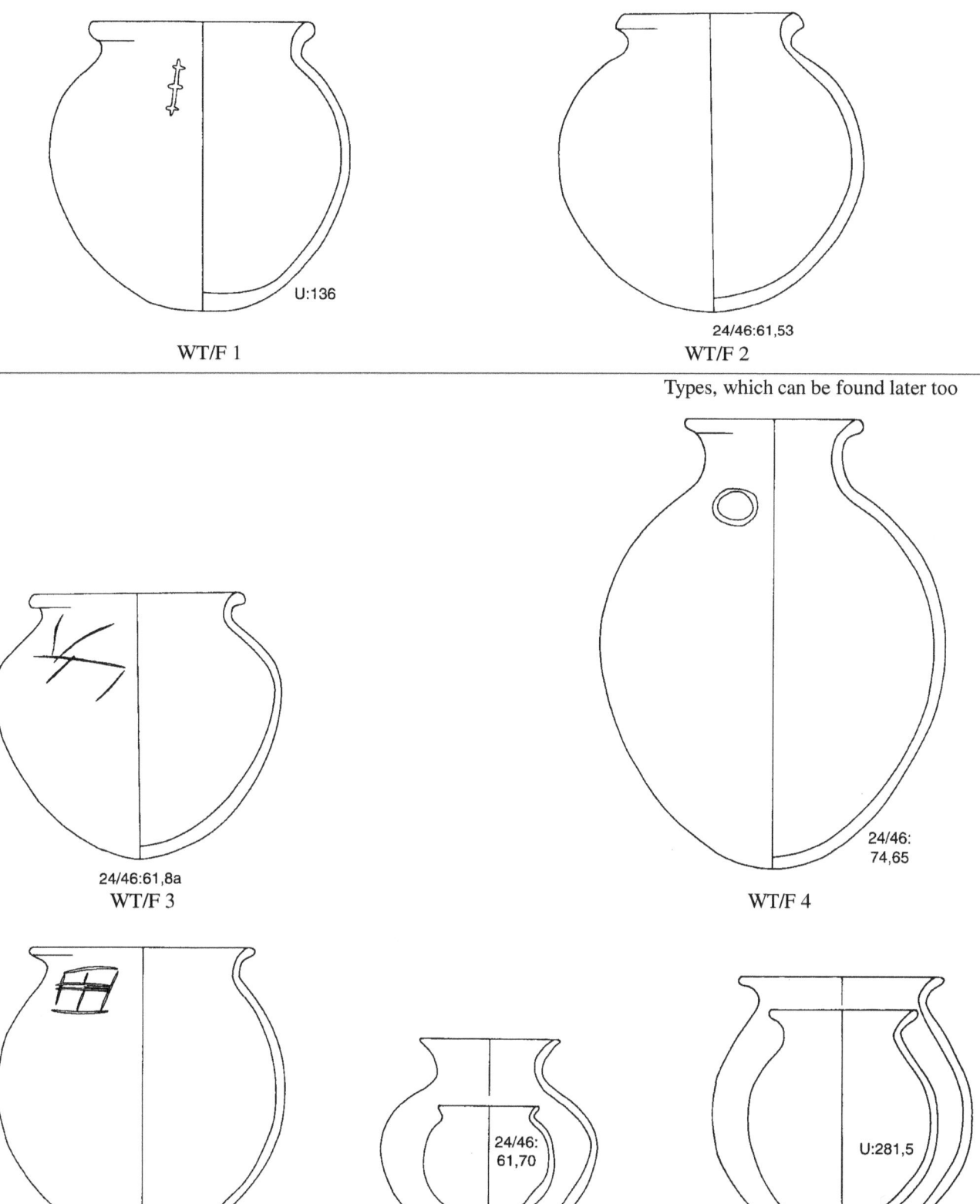

Phase I - open mouth pots (WT) and jars (F)

Plate 15

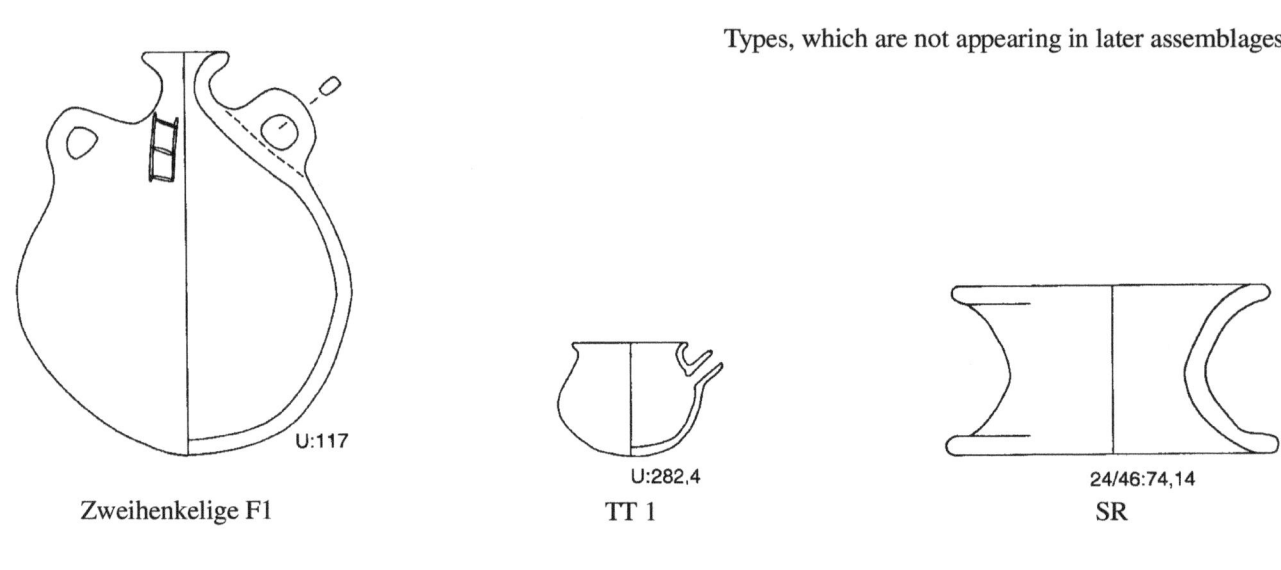

Types, which are not appearing in later assemblages

Zweihenkelige F1 — U:117
TT 1 — U:282,4
SR — 24/46:74,14

Types, which can be found later too

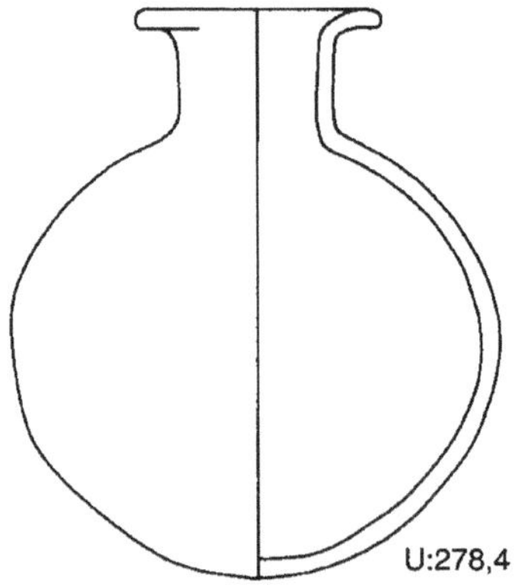

F1 — U:278,4
Zweihenkelige F 2 — Ra 84-0-32 b2
KT mit Tülle — U:215,7

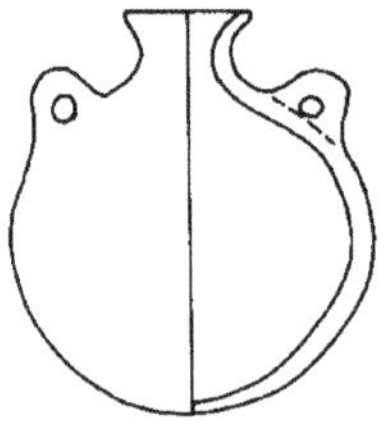

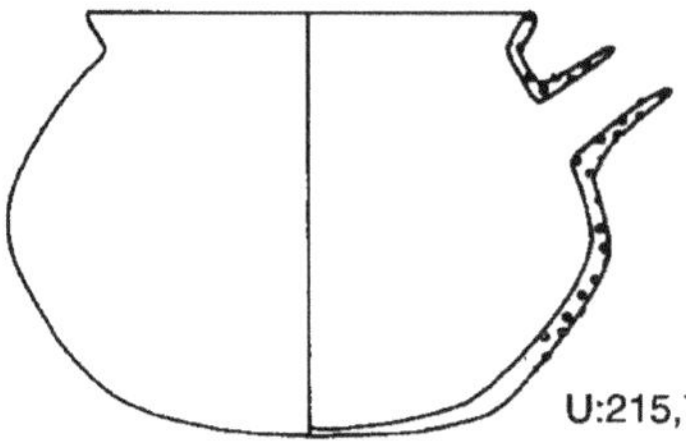

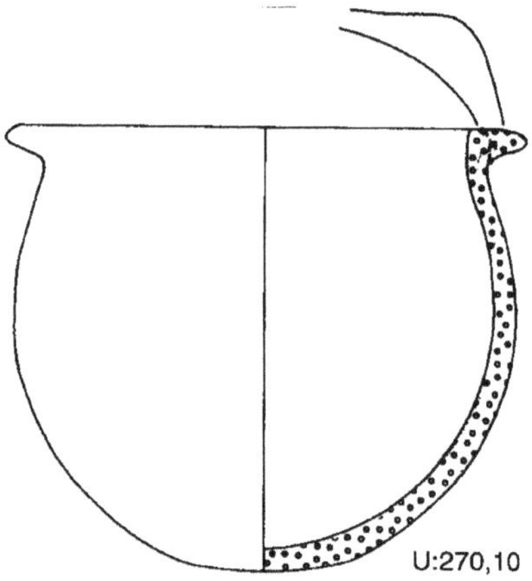

KT mit Griffleisten — U:270,10
M1 — 24/47:140,17
Si — 25/46:94,7

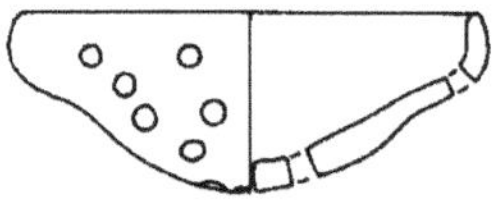

Phase I - jars (F), spouted pots (TT), cooking pots (KT), miniatur vessels (M), stands (SR) and sieves (Si)

Plates

Plate 16

Types, which are not appearing in later assemblages

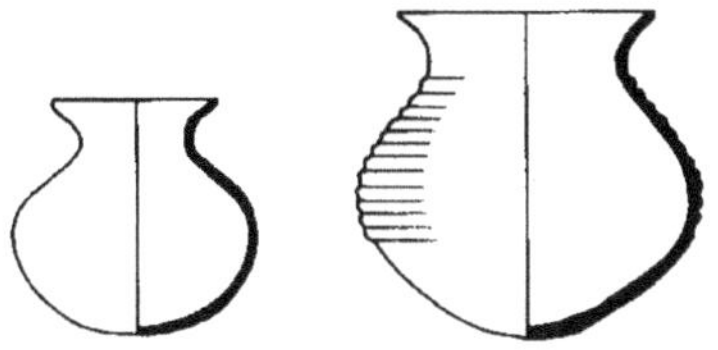

Ra 84-0-32 e   24/47:140,5
Lu 1

Types, which can be found later too

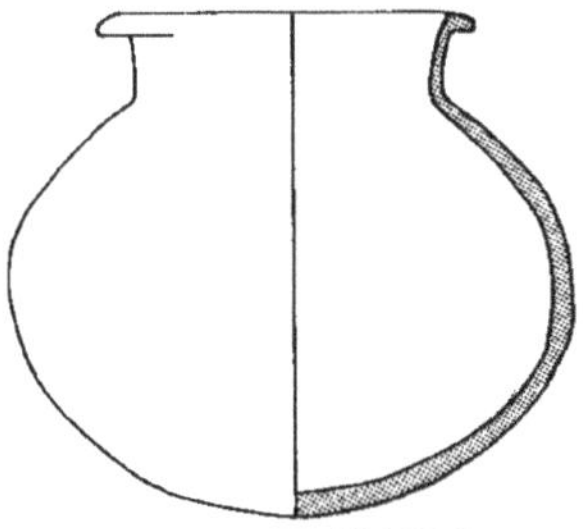

U:302,8
Lu 2a

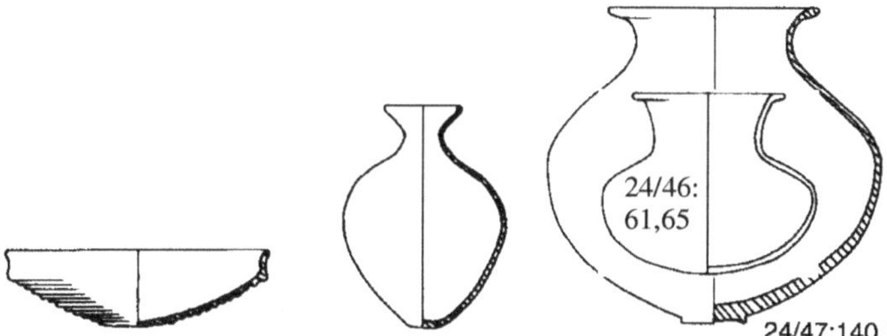

Ra 84-0-32 b3   Ra 84-0-32 b1   24/46:61,65   24/47:140,11
Lu 3

23/46:31,1

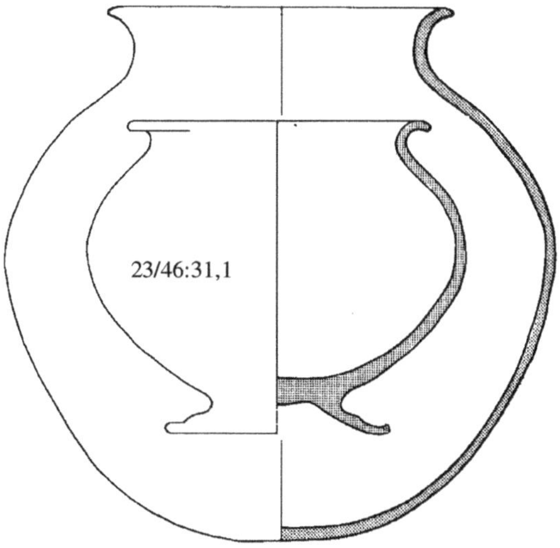

25/47:133,29
Lu 4

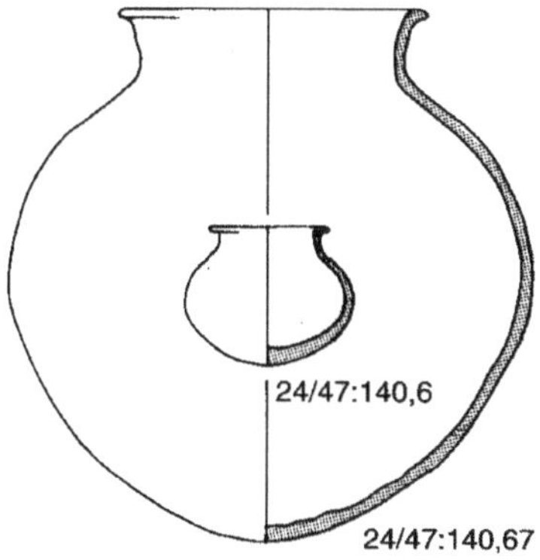

24/47:140,6
24/47:140,67
Lu 5a

Phase I - "luxury vessels" (Lu)

Plate 17

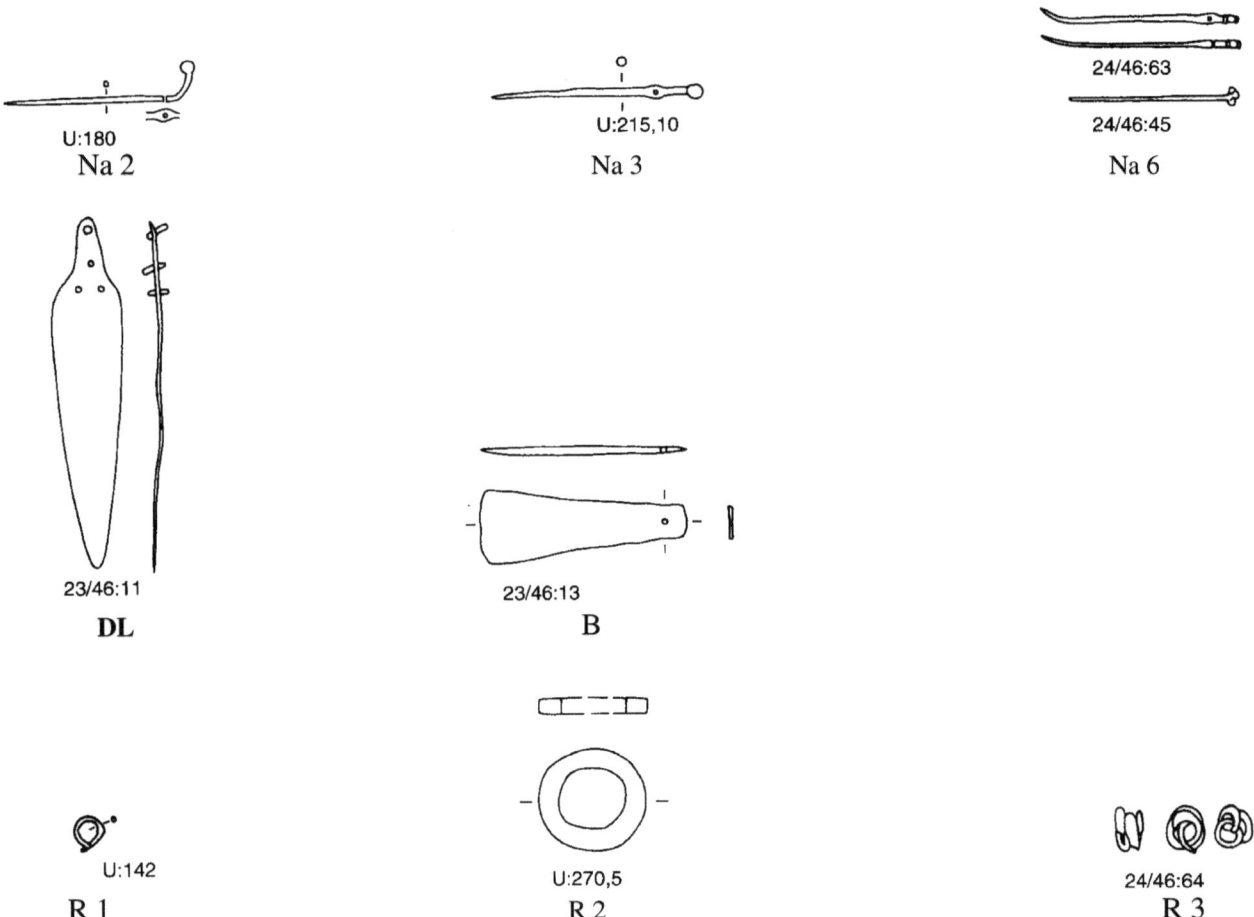

Phase I - metal objects: pins (Na), daggers or spears (DL), axes (B) and rings (R)

Plates

Plate 18

New types

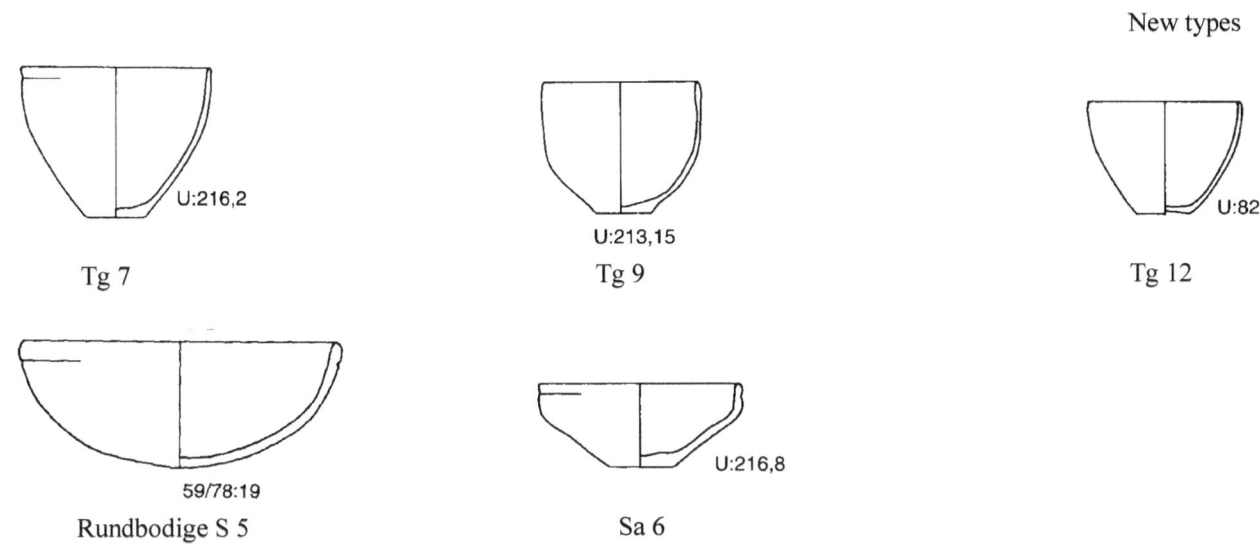

Types, which are not appearing in later assemblages

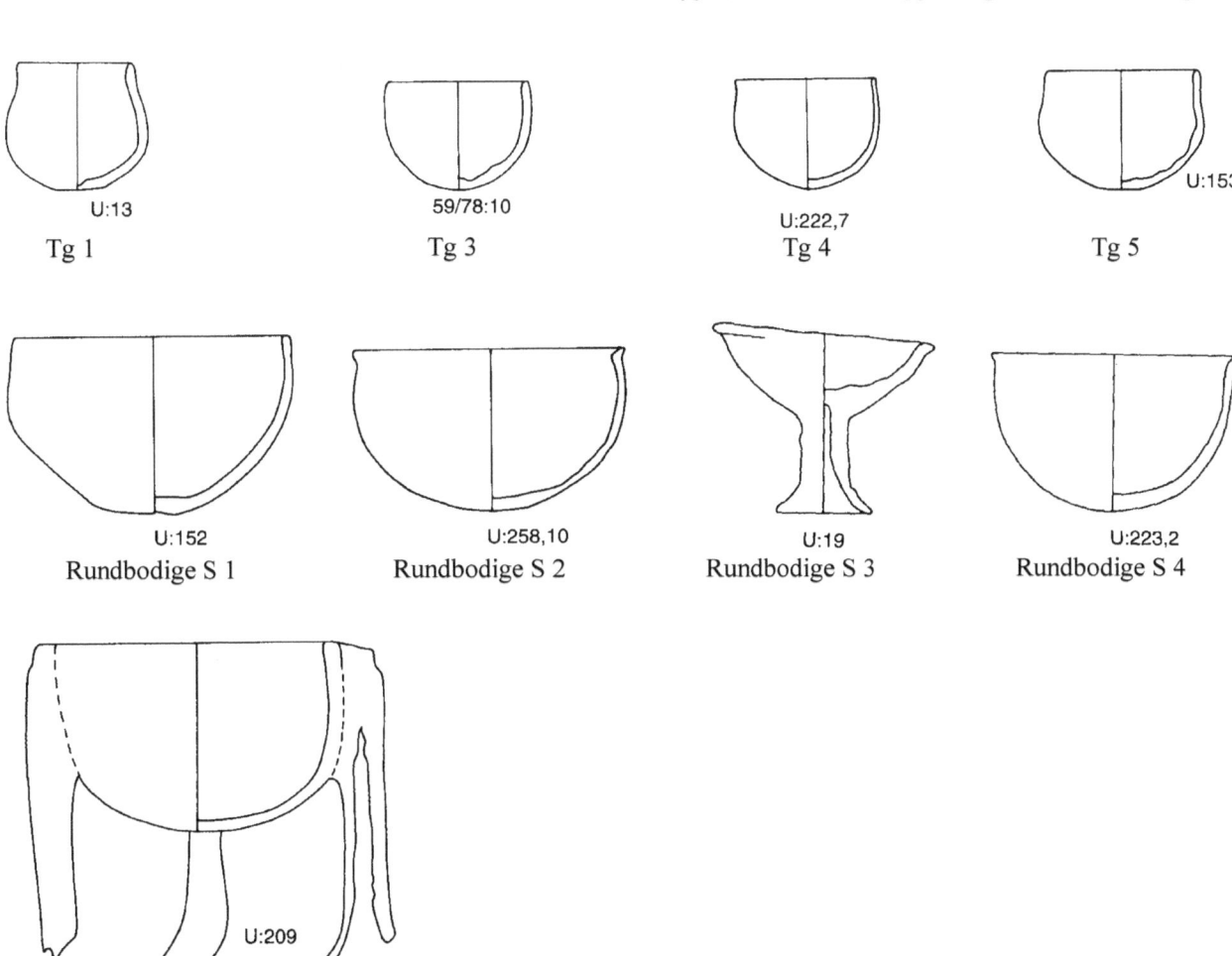

Phase II - drinking vessels (Tg) and different bowl types (S and Sa)

Plate 19

New types

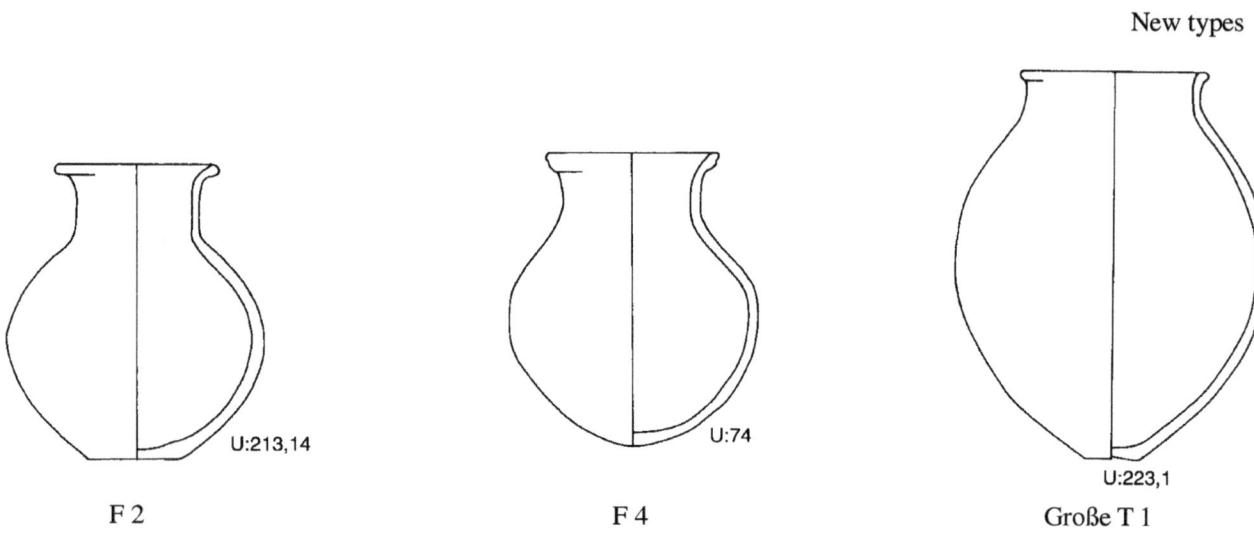

F 2   F 4   Große T 1

Types, which are not appearing in later assemblages

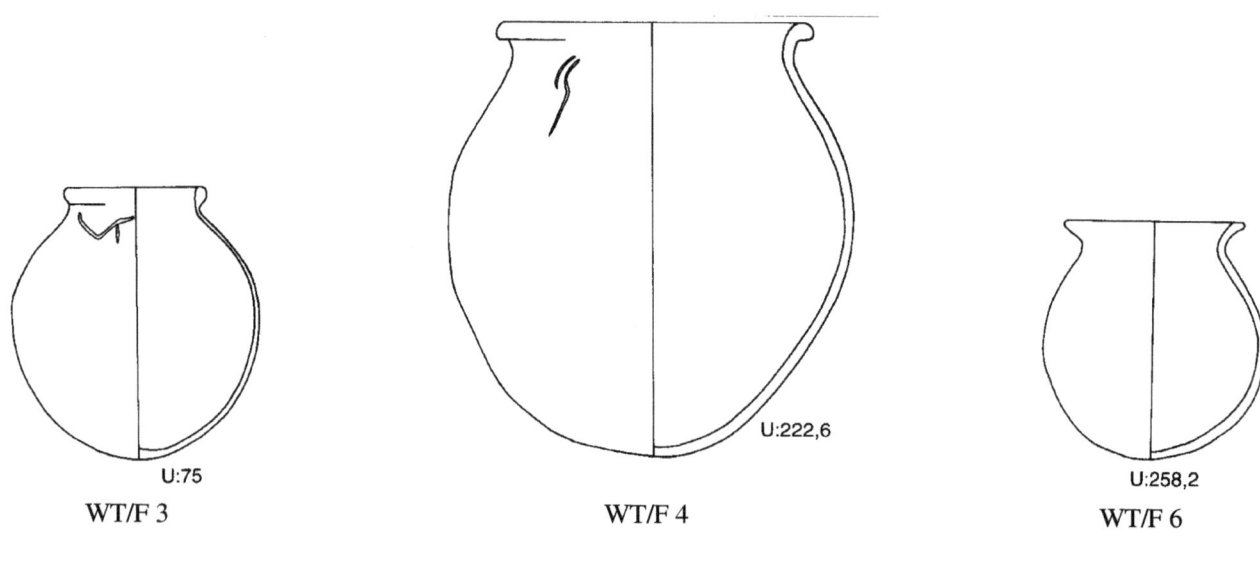

WT/F 3   WT/F 4   WT/F 6

Continuous types

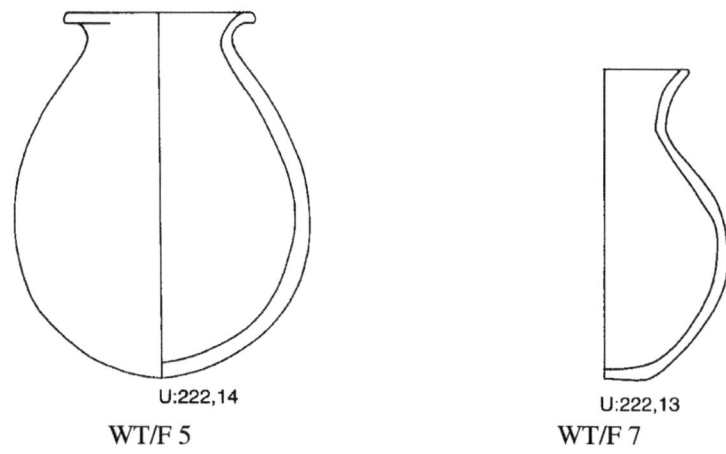

WT/F 5   WT/F 7

Phase II - open mouth pots (W T) and jars (F)

Plates

Plate 20

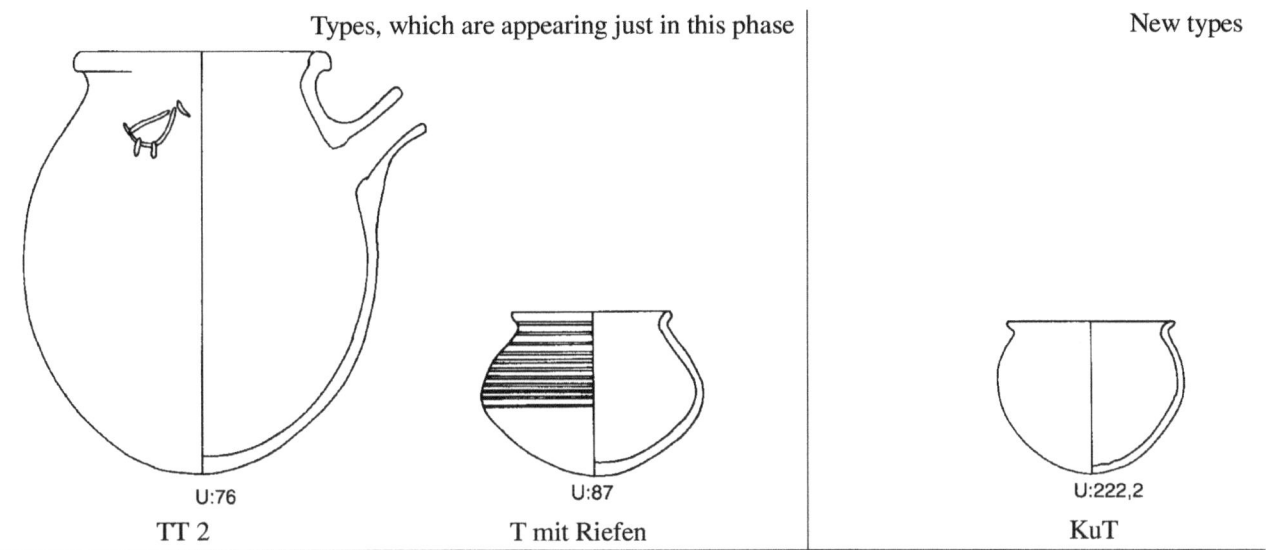

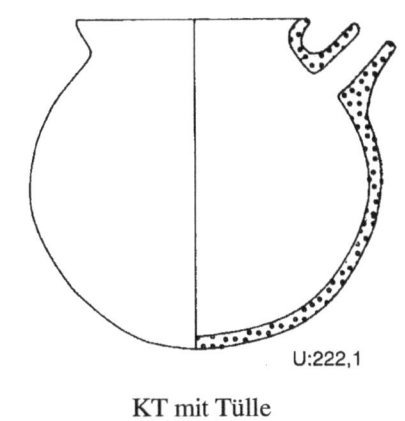

Phase II - spouted pots (TT), cooking pots (KT), globular pots (KuT), miniatur vessels (M) and sieves (Si)

Plate 21

New types

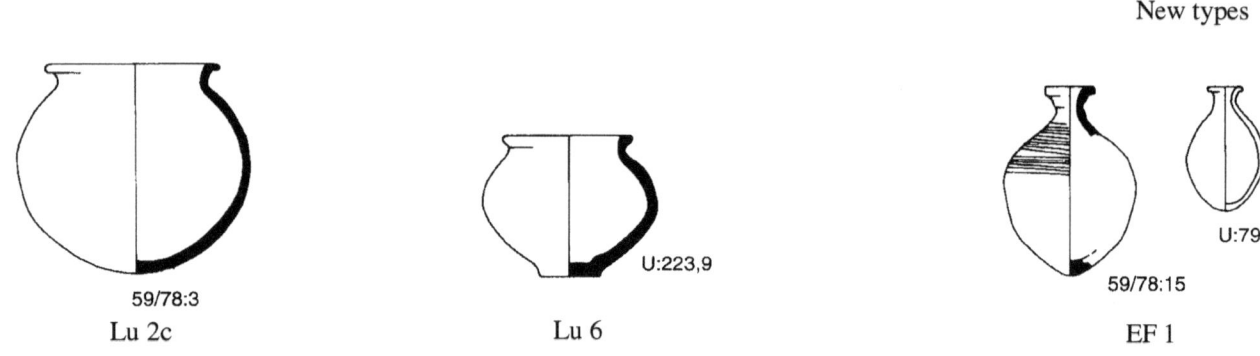

59/78:3
Lu 2c

U:223,9
Lu 6

59/78:15 U:79
EF 1

Types, which are not appearing in later assemblages

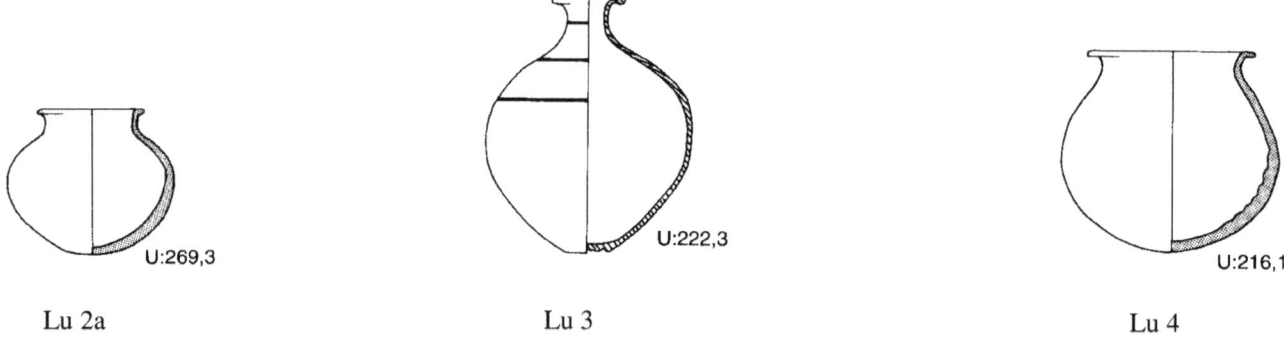

U:269,3
Lu 2a

U:222,3
Lu 3

U:216,1
Lu 4

Phase II - "luxury vessels" (L) and bottles with narrow necks (EF)

Plates

Plate 22

Types, which are not appearing in later assemblages

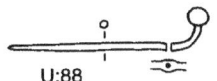

Na 2

Continuous types

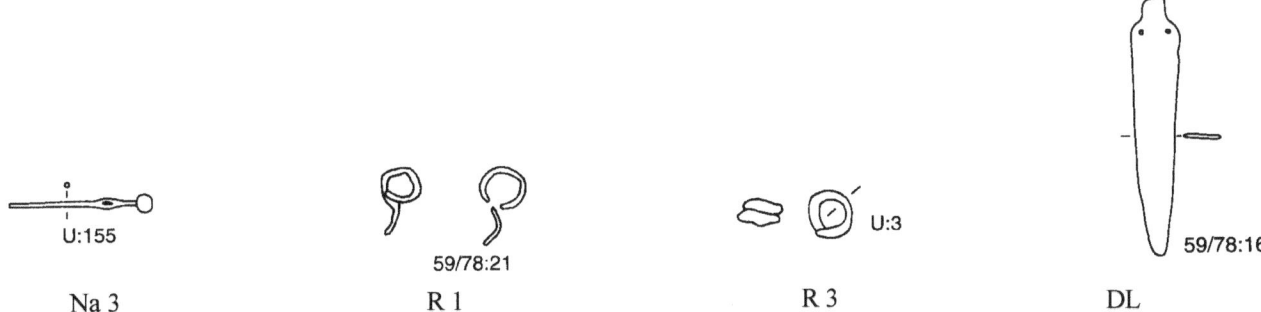

| Na 3 | R 1 | R 3 | DL |

Phase II - metall objects: pins (Na), daggers or spears (DL), axes (B) and rings (R)

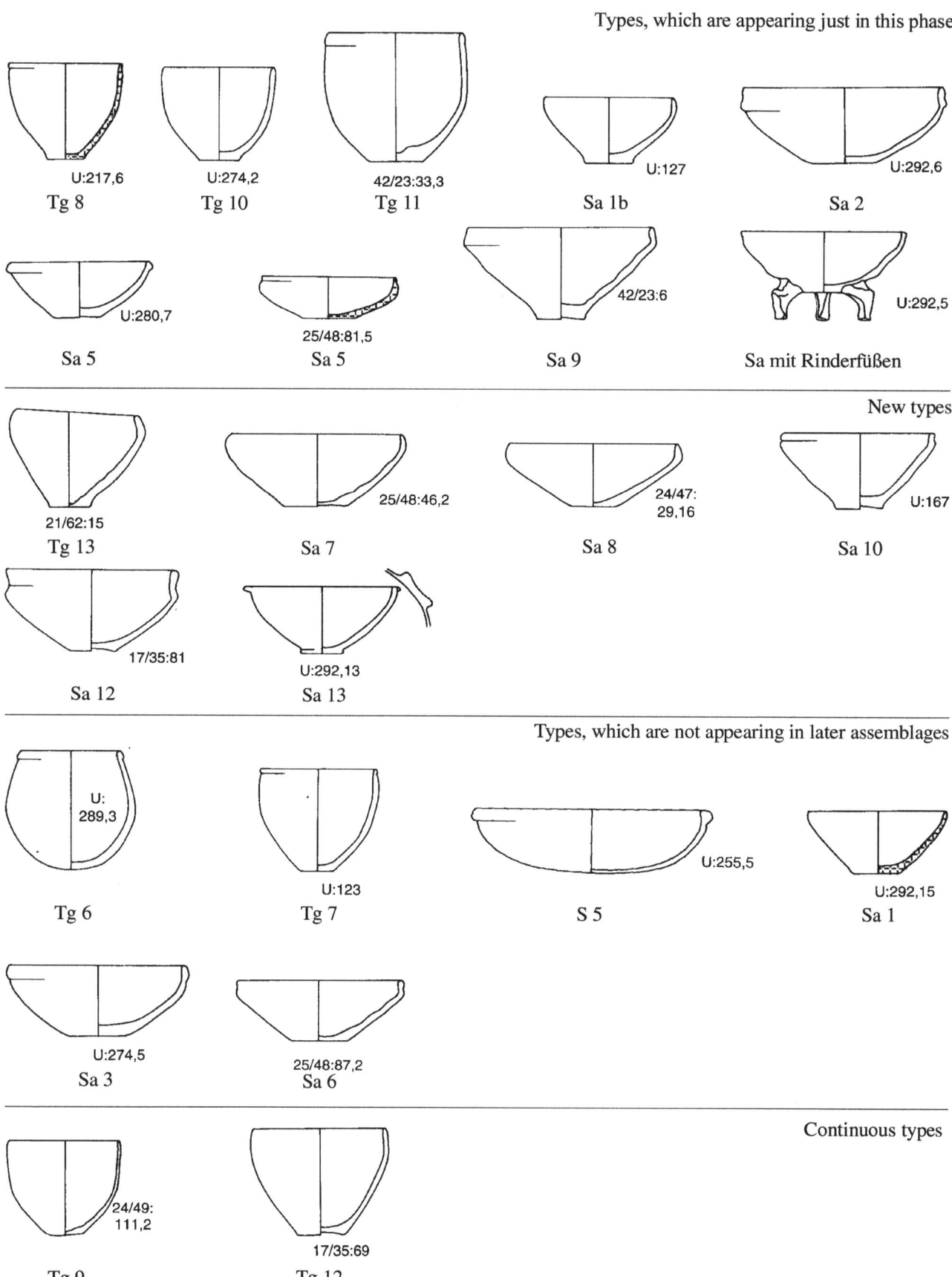

Phase IIIa - drinking vessels (Tg) and different bowl types (S and Sa)

Plates

Plate 24

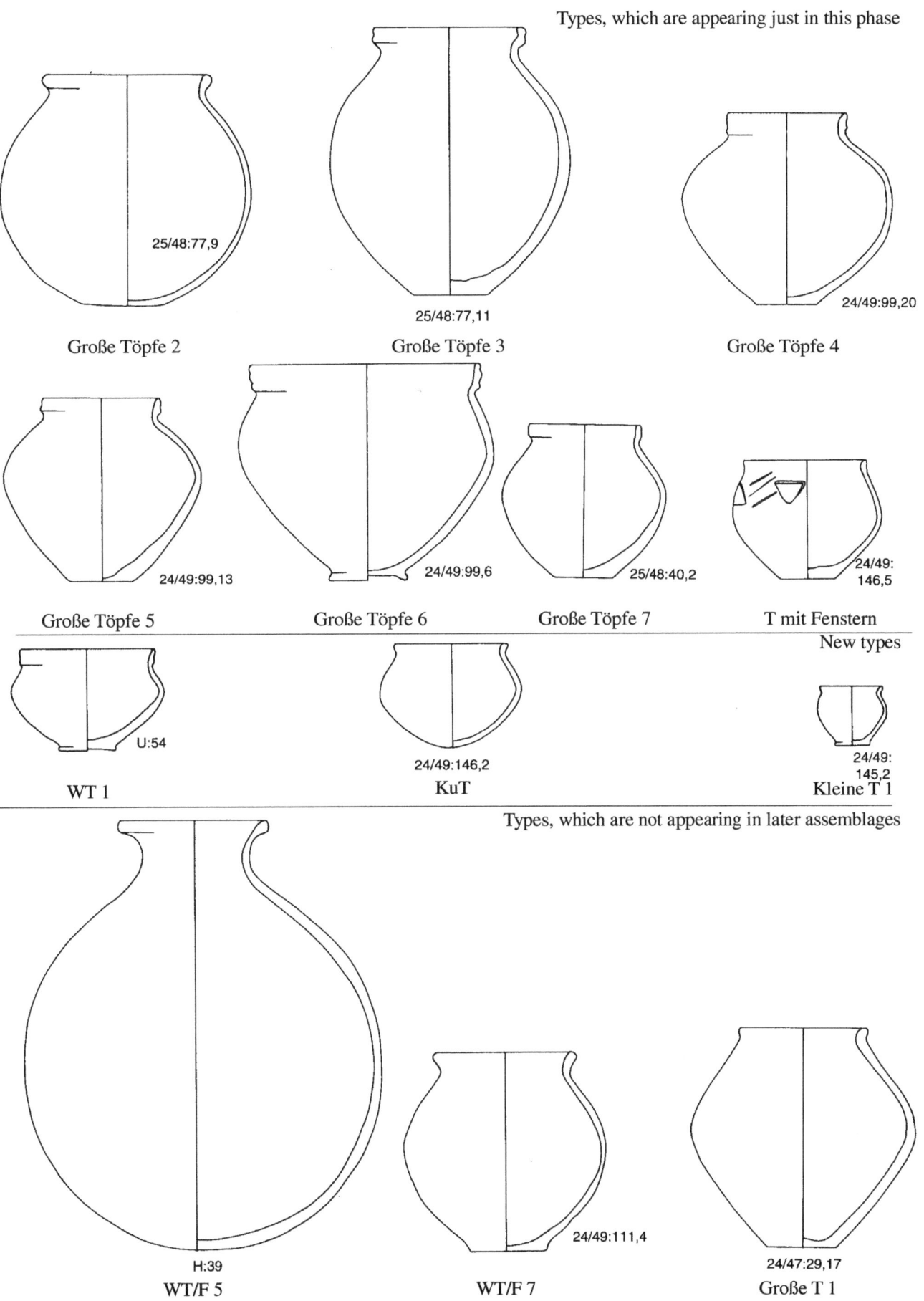

Phase IIIa - open mouth pots (WT), globular pots (KuT) and jars (F)

Plate 25

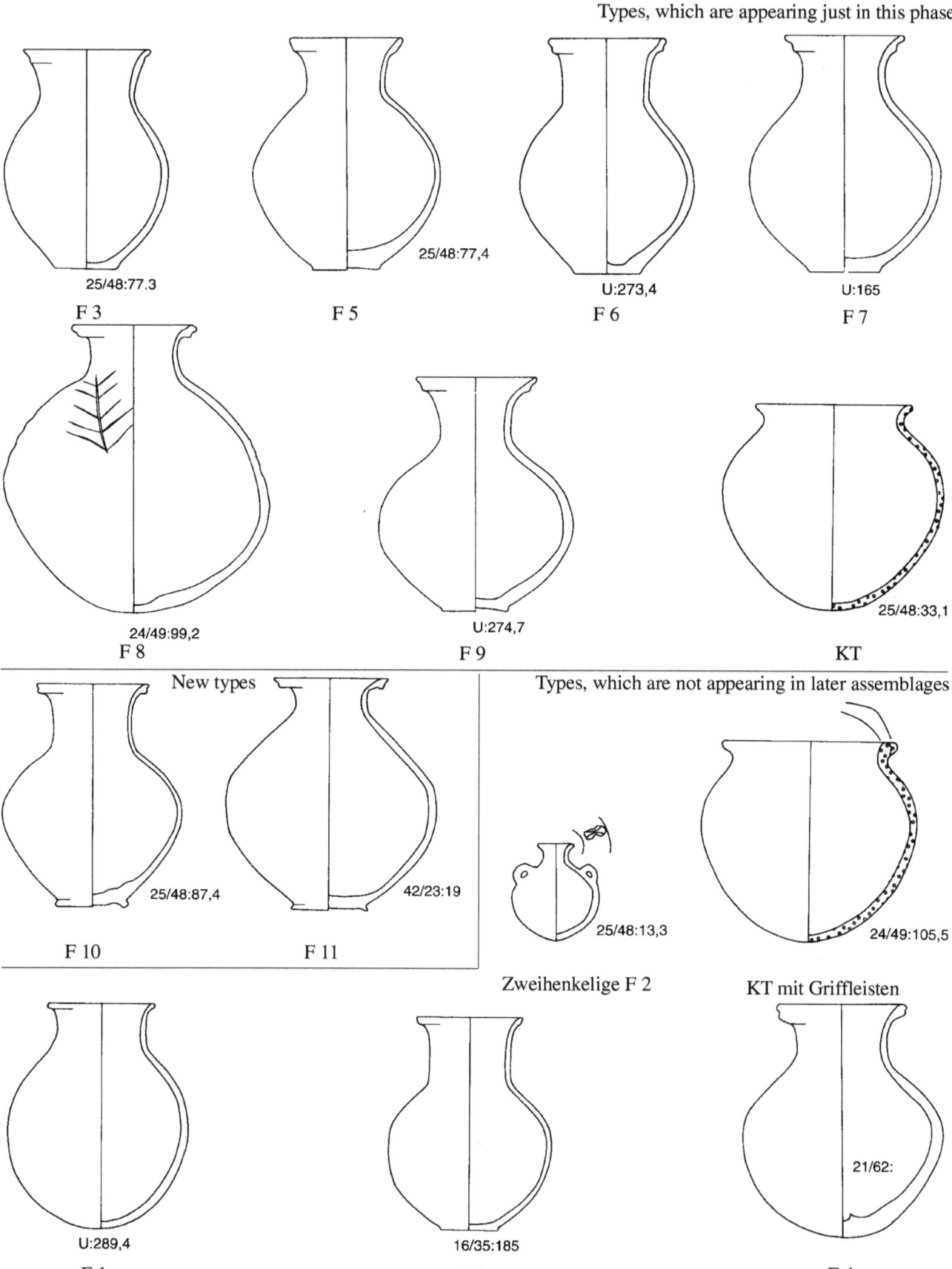

Phase IIIa - jars (F) and cooking pots (KT)

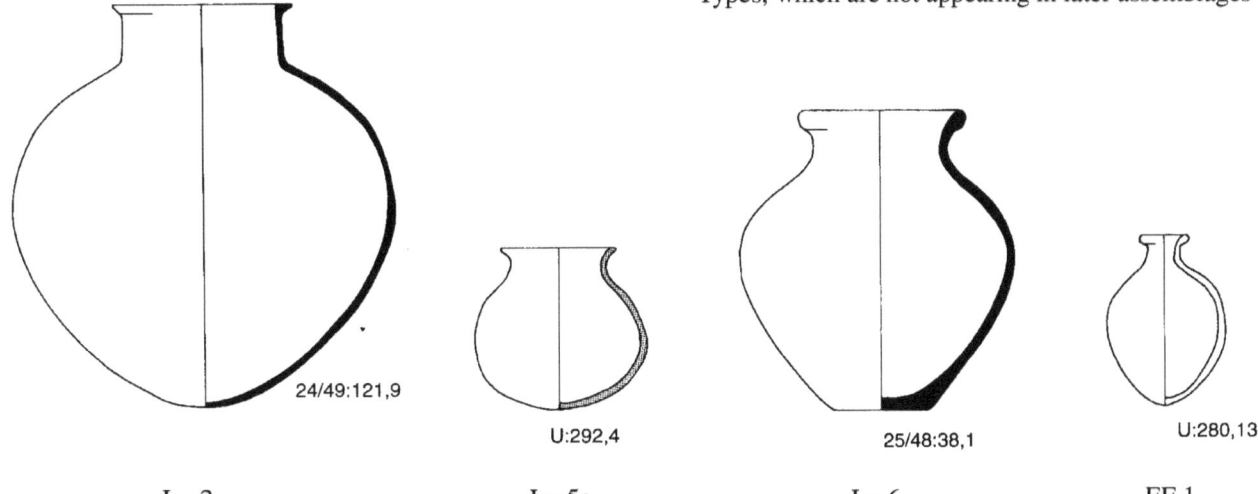

Phase IIIa - "Luxury vessels" (Lu), bottles with narrow necks (EF)

Plate 27

Types, which are appearing just in this phase

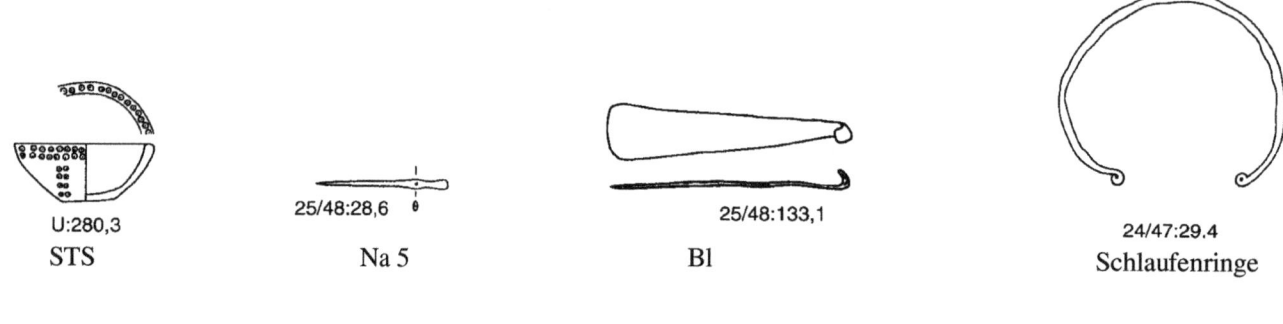

| U:280,3 | 25/48:28,6 | 25/48:133,1 | 24/47:29.4 |
| STS | Na 5 | Bl | Schlaufenringe |

New types

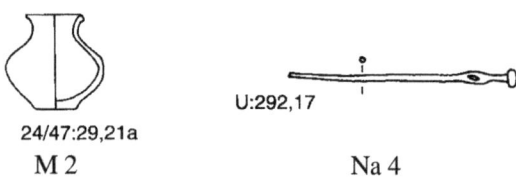

| 24/47:29,21a | U:292,17 |
| M 2 | Na 4 |

Types, which are not appearing in later assemblages

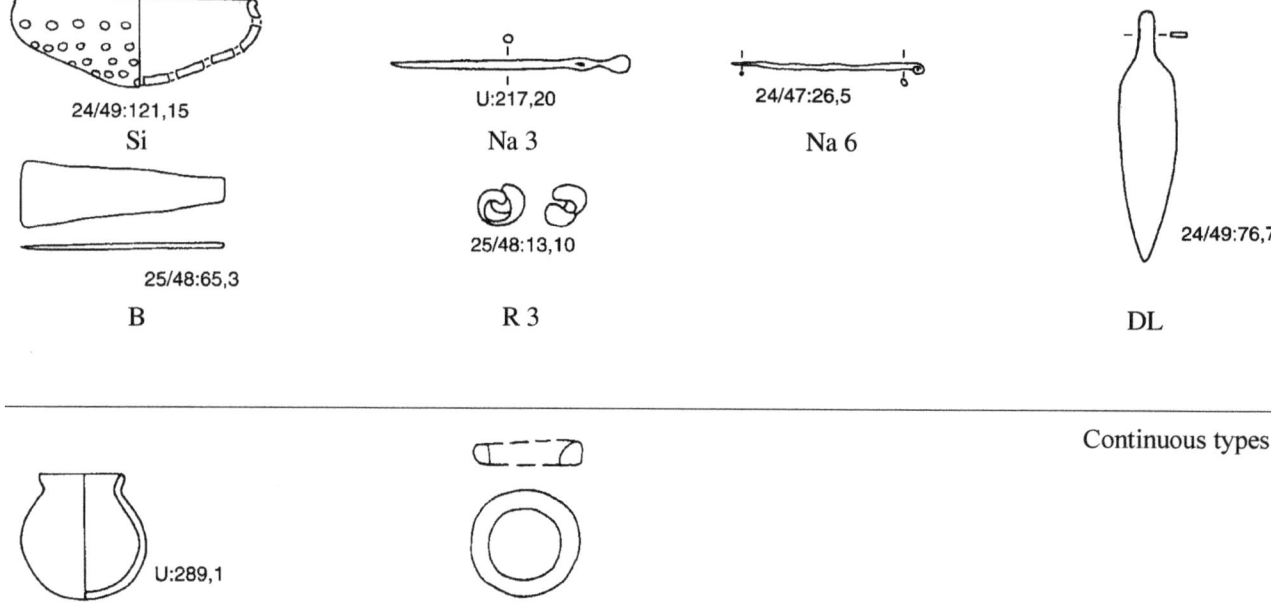

Continuous types

Phase IIIa - miniature vessels (M), sieves (Si), stone vessels (StS), pins (Na), daggers or spears (DL), axes (B), sheets of metal or hooks (Bl), rings (R)

Plates

Plate 28

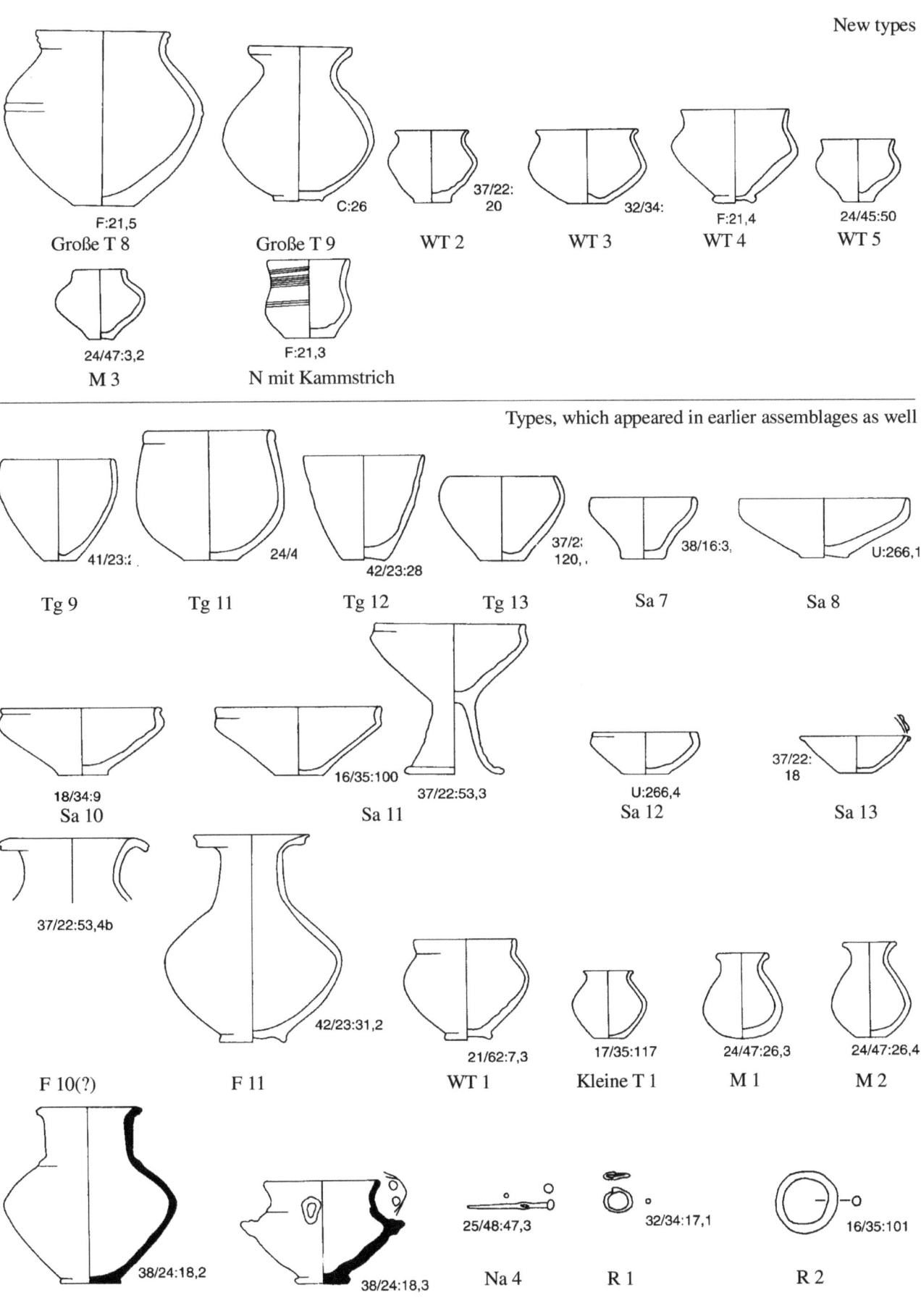

Artefacts of phase IIIb

Plate 29

		G1R3	G2R3	G3			G4			G5	G6				Σ:
				R1	R2	R3	R1	R2	R3		R1	R2		R3	
			partly excavated									23/46:2	23/46:3	23/46:1	
WTF (simple-ware)	max. H		35,3	35,0		34,5	36,0	41,2	33,4	24,3	43,0				
	min. H		15	21,6		4,7	36,0	18,0	8,0	17	19,8				
	average		25,6	28,9		24,3	36,0	27,7	18,9	20,8	34,7				
	quantity		10+(9)	12+(6)	[(2)]	28+(5)	1+(8)	41+(8)	12+(3)	3+(4)	3+(6)	(1)		0	110+(52) 50,2%
Lu3 (Euphrates-ware)	max. H					15,0		8,1							
	min. H					15,0		8,5							
	average					15,0		8,3							
	quantity					1+(1)		2+(1)						(3)	3+(5) 2,5%
Lu2a, 4 and 5a (stone-ware)	max. H			40,0		25,8			10			28,4	10,2	10	
	min. H			5,9		5,7			10			12,8	10,2	10	
	average			21,6		12,0			10			18,5	10,2	10	
	quantity			4		13			1			3	1	1+(1)	23+(1) 7,4%
pot/jar (black-ware)	max. H					10									
	min. H					10									
	average					10									
	quantity					1									1 0,3%
pot/jar (fine ware)	max. H					16									
	min. H					10									
	average					12,1									
	quantity					3									3 0,9%
pot (cooking-pot-ware)	max. H								18						
	min. H								18						
	average								18						
	quantity			(1)		(2)			1	(1)		(1)			1+(5) 1,8%
Zweihenkewlige F1	max. H			51,9											
	min. H			51,9											
	average			51,9											
	quantity			1											1 0,3%
Σ pot/jar	average		25,6	27,1		19,5	36	27,7	18,3	20,8	34,7	18,5	10,2	10	
	quantity		10+(9) 67,9%	17+(7) 40%	[(2) 66,7%]	46+(7) 69,2%	1+(8) 69,2%	41+(8) 76,6%	16+(4) 58,8%	3+(5) 66,7%	3+(6) 75%	3+(1) 33,3%	1 100%	1+(4) 83,3%	142+(63)=205 63,3%

Distribution of pots and jars in the mausolea

Plate 30

Cups table:

	G1R3	G2R3	R1	G3 R2	R3	R1	G4 R2	R3	G5	R1	G6 R2 23/46:2	G6 R2 23/46:3	R3 23/46:1	Σ:
cup (simple-ware) max. H		7,5	11,4		7,5	8,3	13,2	7,8	6,1		7,4		7,8	
min. H		7	4,4		5	7,6	6,6	5,6	6,1		7,0		7,8	
average		7,16	7,3		6,6	7,8	8,8	6,7	6,1		7,2		7,8	
quantity		5	16		12	2	10	10			2		1	59 *18,3%*
cup (another wares) max. H				6,8	7		7,1							
min. H				6,8	7		6,7							
average				6,8	7		6,9							
quantity				[1]	1		2							4 *1,2%*
cup with loop max. H					5									
min. H					5									
average					5									
quantity					1+(1)									1+(1) *0,6%*
cups Σ average		7,16	7,3	6,8	6,6	7,8	8,6	6,7	6,1		7,2		7,8	
quantity		5 *17,9%*	16 *26,7%*	[1] *33,3%*	14+(1) *19,2%*	2 *15,4%*	12 *18,8%*	10 *29,4%*	1 *8,3%*		2 *16,7%*		1 *16,7%*	64+(1) *20,1%*

Bowls table:

	G1R3	G2R3	R1	G3 R2	R3	R1	G4 R2	R3	G5	R1	G6 R2 23/46:2	G6 R2 23/46:3	R3 23/46:1	Σ:
bowls (S) max. H			11,4		9			4,8		7	10,4			
min. H			7,3		5,2			4,8		6,6	9,5			
average			9,35		6,5			4,8		6,7	10			
quantity			2		4+(2)	1 sieve		1		3	2			13+(2) *4,6%*
bowls with pedestal max. H		24,6												
min. H		24,6												
average		24,6												
quantity		1				(1)								1+(1) *0,6%*
bowls Σ average quantity		1 *3,6%*	2 *3,3%*		4+(2) *7,7%*	1+(1) *15,4%*		1 *2,9%*		3 *25%*	2 *16,7%*			14+(3) *5,2%*

Distribution of drinking vessels and bowls in the mausolea

Plate 31

	G1R3	G2R3	G3 R1	G3 R2	G3 R3	G4 R1	G4 R2	G4 R3	G5	G6 R1	G6 R2 23/46:2	G6 R2 23/46:3	G6 R3 23/46:1	Σ:
pedestal max. H		13,0	12,3		13,4		14,5	15	12,2		12,9			
pedestal min. H		12,3	6,4		13,2		10,4	13,6	11,6		7			
pedestal average		12,6	10,4		13,3		12,4	14,4	12		10			
pedestal quantity		3	13+(1)		2		3	3	3		2			29+(1) 9,3%
pedestal with "windows" max. H			9,8		8,8						9,5			
pedestal with "windows" min. H			9		8,8						9,5			
pedestal with "windows" average			9,5		8,8						9,5			
pedestal with "windows" quantity			4		1						1			6 1,8%
Σ average		12,6	10,2		11,8		12,4	14,4	12		9,8			
Σ quantity		3 10,7%	17+(1) 30%		3 3,8%		3 4,7%	3 8,8%	3 25%		3 25%			35+(1) 11,1%

	G1R3	G2R3	R1	G3 R2	G3 R3	G4 R1	G4 R2	G4 R3	G5	G6 R1	G6 R2 23/46:2	G6 R2 23/46:3	G6 R3 23/46:1	Σ:
Σ all vessels	19+(9) 100%		52+(8) 100%	[1+(2) 100%]	67+(11) 100%	4+(9) 100%	56+(8) 100%	30+(4) 100%	7+(5) 100%	6+(6) 100%	10+(2) 100%	1 100%	2+(4) 100%	255+(68) =323 100%

Distribution of pedestals and all vessels in the mausolea

Plates

Plate 32

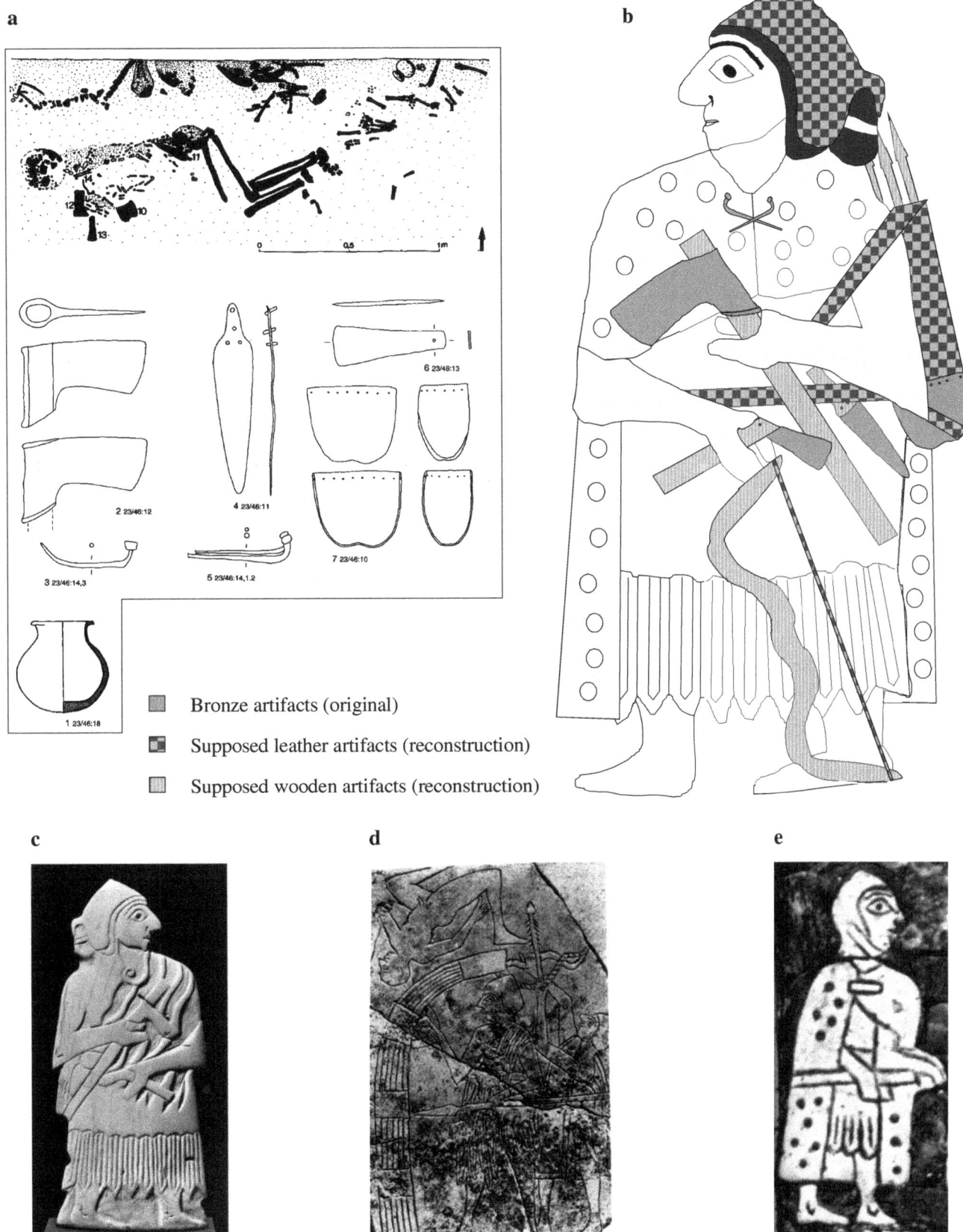

Reconstruction (b) of the equipment of a warrior according to Burial 23/46:3 (a) and to the representations in Mari (c, d) and Ur (e)

91

Plate 33

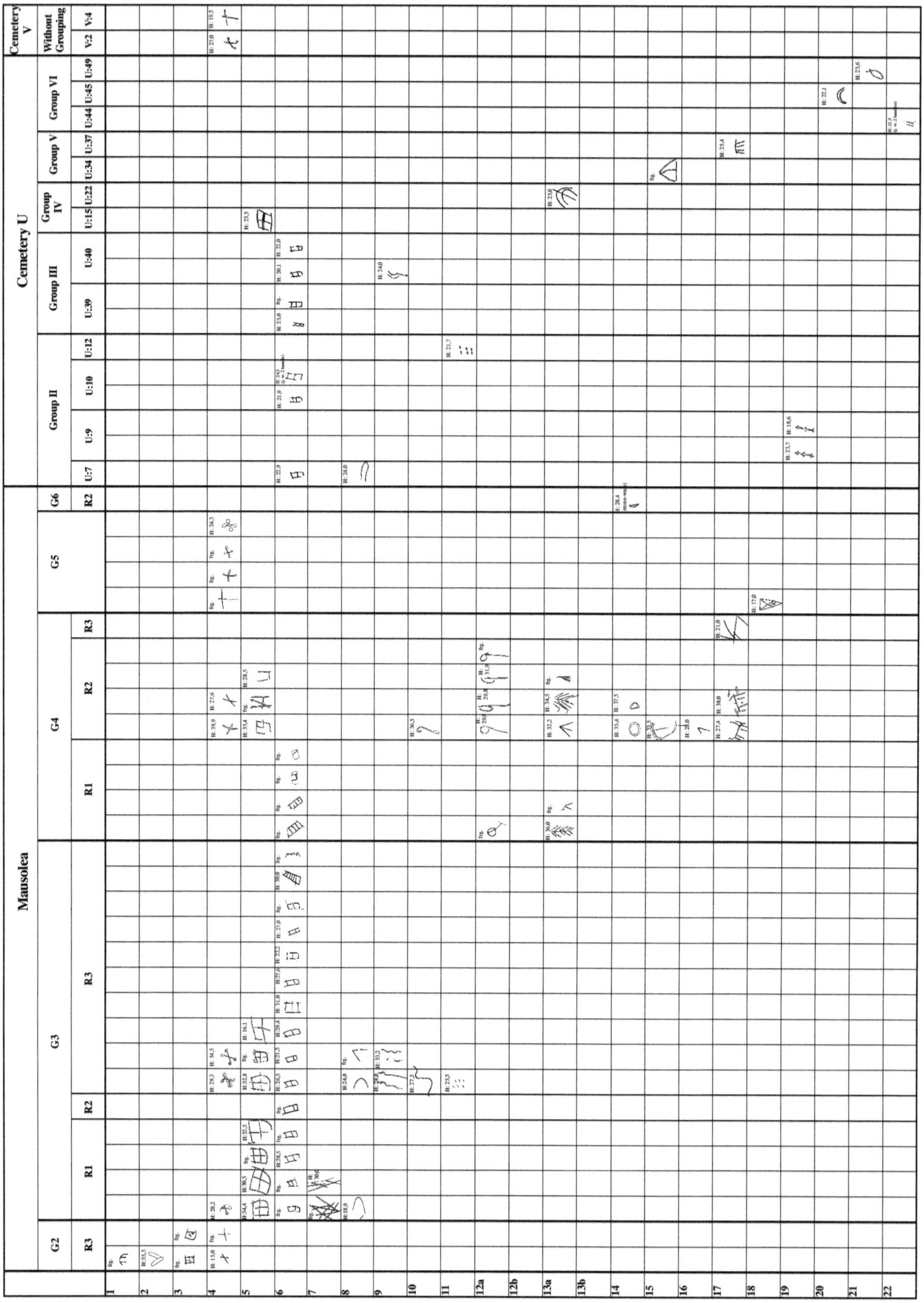

Pottery marks in phase I

Plate 34

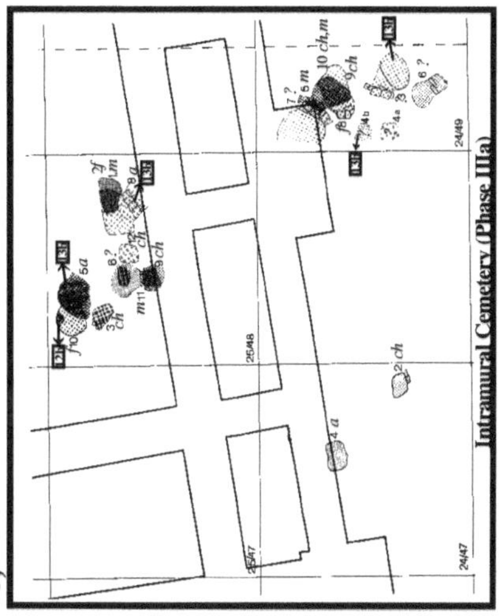

Pottery marks in phase II (a) and IIIa (b) and the map of the intramural cemetery (c)

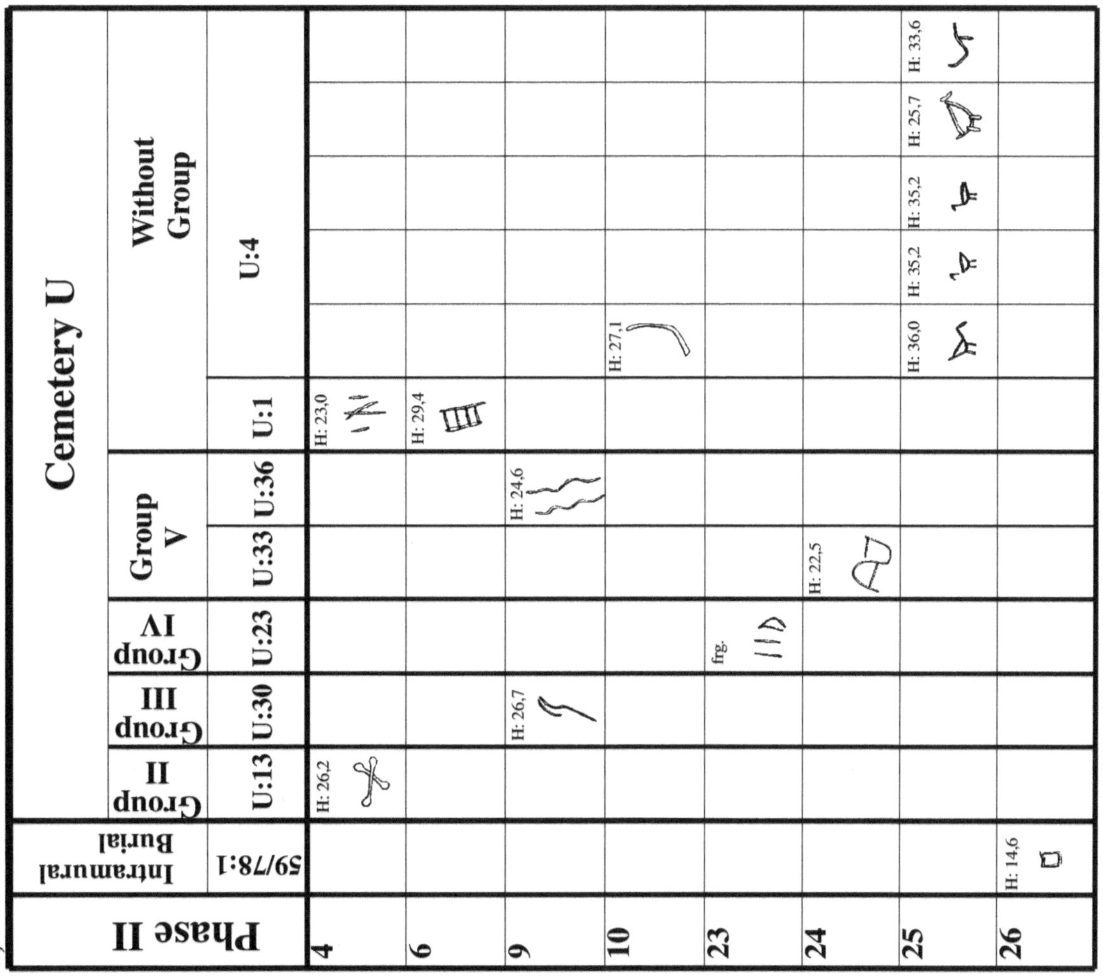

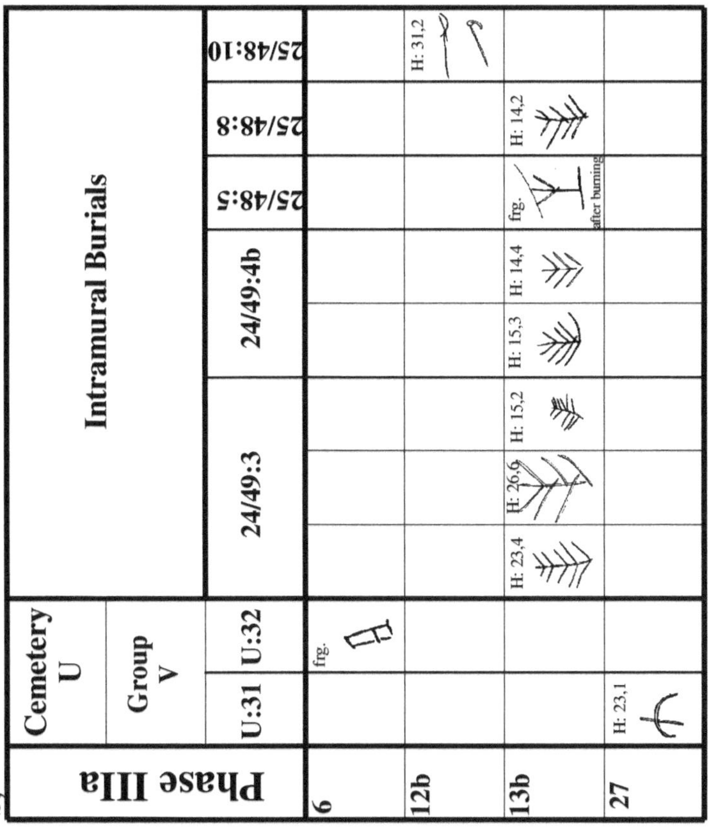

Plate 35

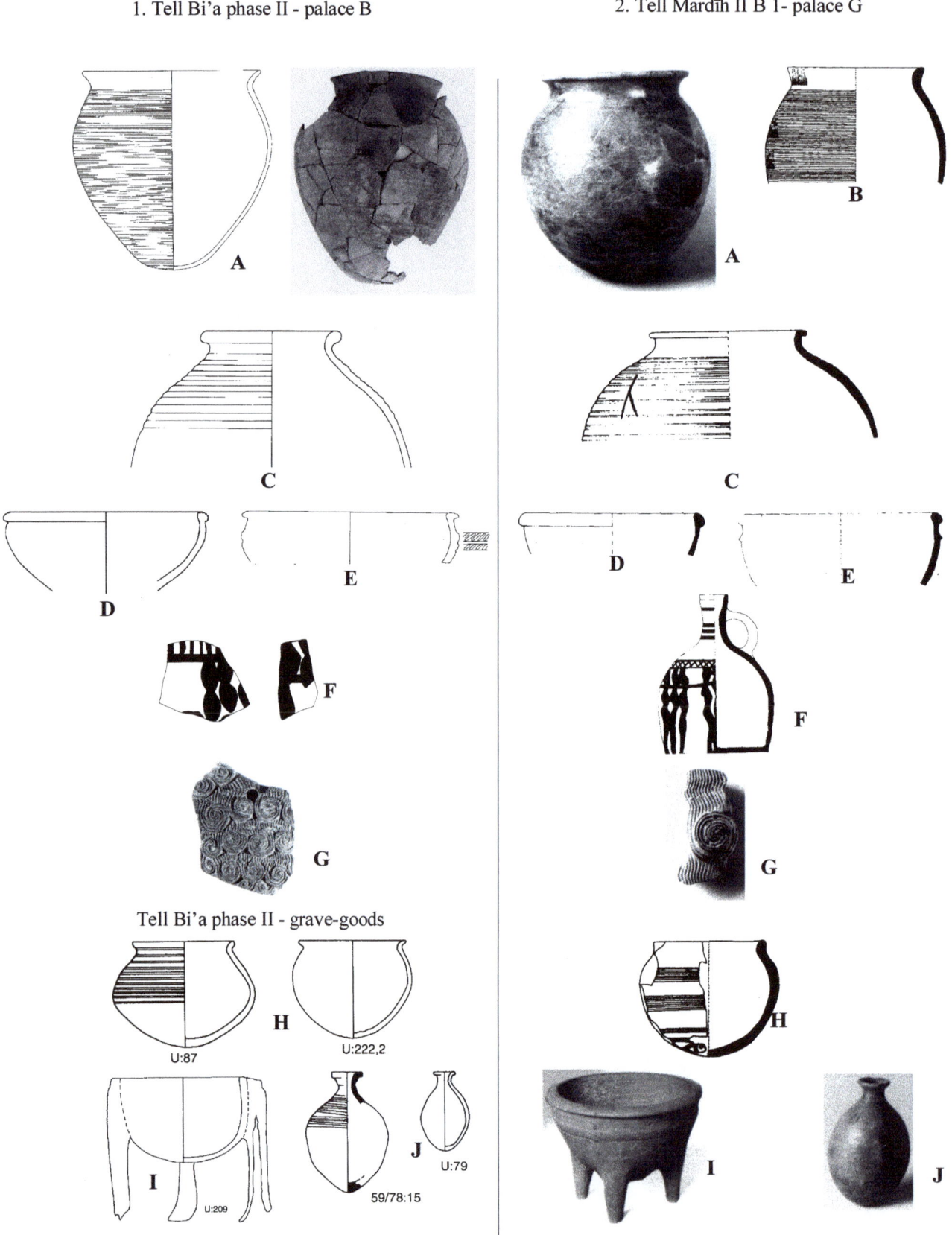

Comparison of selected types from Tuttul and Ebla

Plate 36

Bi'a Motivs	Halawa A (Settlement) Hempelmann 2002	Wreide (Cemetery) Orth-mann - Rova 1991	Sams ed-Din (Cemetery) Meyer 1991	Tawi (Cemetery) Kampschulte - Orthmann 1984	Tell Banat (Tomb I) Porter 1995	Abu Hamed (Cemetery) Falb 1999	Ebla (Palace G) Mazzoni 1988	Sweyhat (Settlement) Holland 1977	Habuba Kabira (Settlement - ceramic production) Strommenger 1976
1									
2									
3									
4	Motiv 6 (+7)	Abb.15/W54A:55; Abb.18/W54A:75; Abb.20/W54C:45; Abb.21/W54C:58	Abb.39/3	Tafel 4/19; Tafel 7/53,56; Tafel 10/93; Tafel 15/34; Tafel 26/209	37/P24,P26; 42/P64	Tafel 35/6-9	97 Fig.5/7	54 Fig. 6/17	
5									
6	Motiv 16							56 Fig. 7/21	
7				?Tafel 32/1				56 Fig. 7/20	
8	Motiv 19					Tafel 36/2		58 Fig. 9/2-3	
9									
10									
11									
12a	Motiv 27						105 Fig. 9/4	54 Fig. 6/8	MDOG 103, 35 Abb. 19/8-11
12b									
13a		Abb.10/W11A:15; Abb. 25/W66:14					101 Fig.7/3		
13b								44 Fig. 2/16; 56 Fig. 7/16	
14			Abb.39/1				99 Fig.6/4		
15									
16									
17	Motiv 47-49								
18								?56 Fig.7/13	
19									
20									
21									
22	Motiv 3	Abb.23/W54C:71				Tafel 35/1-3	97 Fig.5/5		MDOG 103, 35 Abb. 19/6
23									
24									
25			Abb.32 (Boese)						
26			Abb.39/14				97 Fig.5/6		
27									

Comparison of pottery marks in Tell Bi'a and at the Euphrates region

Plate 37

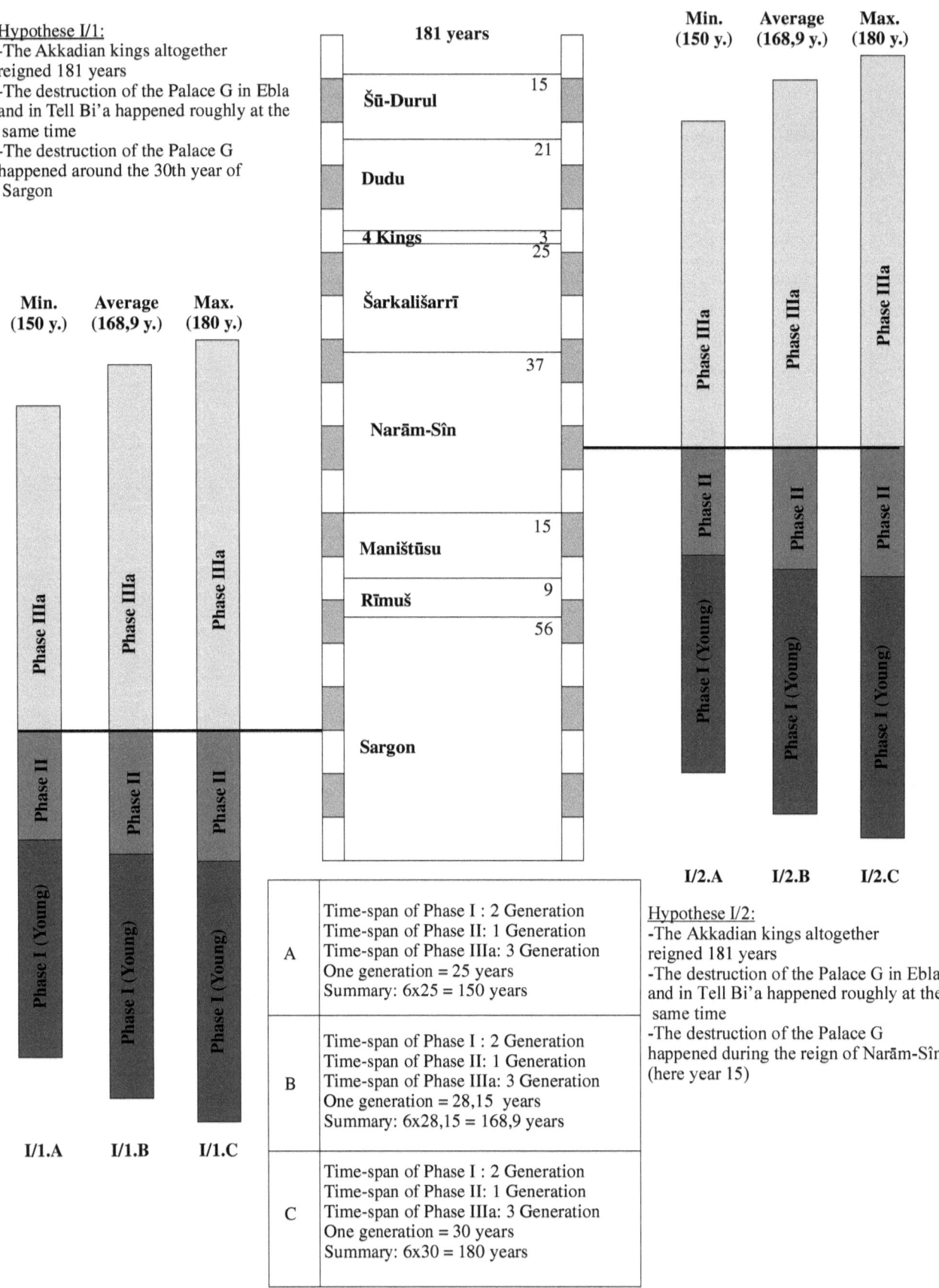

Correlation of the relative chronology of the kings of Akkad and the archaeological results in Tuttul (Hypotheses I/1.A-C and I/2.A-C)

Plate 38

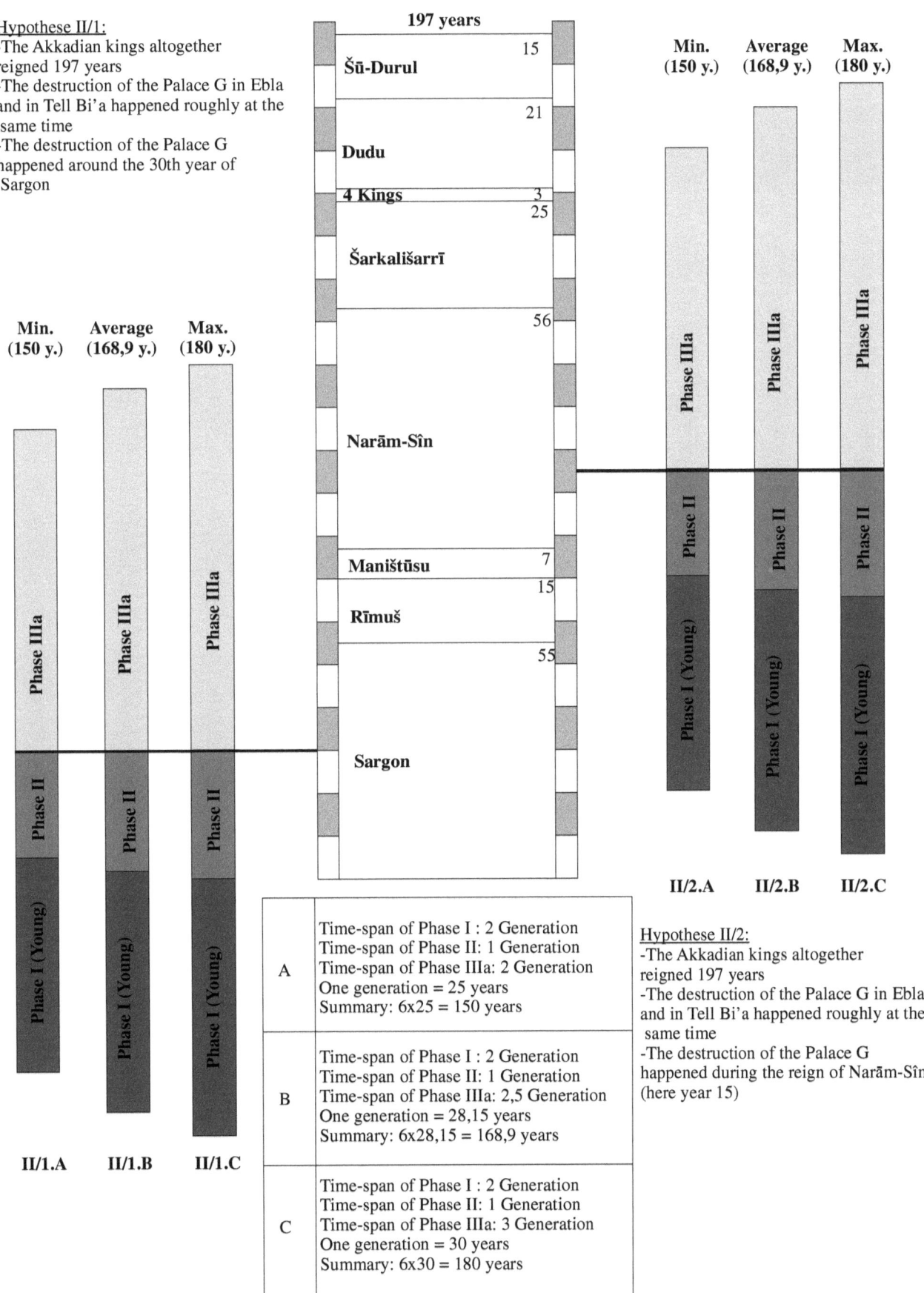

Correlation of the relative chronology of the kings of Akkad and the archaeological results in Tuttul (Hypotheses II/1.A-C and II/2.A-C)

www.ingramcontent.com/pod-product-compliance
Lightning Source LLC
Chambersburg PA
CBHW061544010526
44113CB00023B/2790